A SHORT GUIDE TO POLICY DEBATE

Alexander Hiland

NEW YORK AND LONDON

First published 2025
by Routledge
605 Third Avenue, New York, NY 10158

and by Routledge
4 Park Square, Milton Park, Abingdon, Oxon, OX14 4RN

Routledge is an imprint of the Taylor & Francis Group, an informa business

© 2025 Alexander Hiland

The right of Alexander Hiland to be identified as author of this work has been asserted in accordance with sections 77 and 78 of the Copyright, Designs and Patents Act 1988.

All rights reserved. No part of this book may be reprinted or reproduced or utilised in any form or by any electronic, mechanical, or other means, now known or hereafter invented, including photocopying and recording, or in any information storage or retrieval system, without permission in writing from the publishers.

Trademark notice: Product or corporate names may be trademarks or registered trademarks, and are used only for identification and explanation without intent to infringe.

ISBN: 9781032613116 (hbk)
ISBN: 9781032613123 (pbk)
ISBN: 9781003463078 (ebk)

DOI: 10.4324/9781003463078

Typeset in Times New Roman
by KnowledgeWorks Global Ltd.

CONTENTS

Preface vii
Introduction ix

1 Analyzing Debate Topics   1

2 Performing Debate Research   12

3 Affirmative Cases   34

4 Negative Cases   59

5 Cross-Examination   83

6 Answering Cases   92

7 Rebuttal Speeches   116

8 Judging Policy Debate   127

9 Practice and Tournament Preparation   140

   Conclusion   150

Bibliography 156
Appendix A Sample Affirmative Case 158
Appendix B Sample Negative Case 164
Index 171

PREFACE

When I began competing in collegiate policy debate in 2007, I was immediately overwhelmed by the complexity, nuance, and educational value of the activity. Although I knew I was learning more than I could in any one class, I also knew that I was missing much of the nuance in what other speakers were saying and not meeting my competitive goals because there was simply too much happening for me to parse on my own. What I needed was a guide so that I better prepare for debates and have some context for what other debaters were saying. After 15 years of experience as a competitor and coach, experimenting with many texts along the way, I decided to put a guide together to help new students get ready for collegiate competition.

This guide is designed to help students with little or no background in interscholastic debate get ready for competition. It is designed to provide a step-by-step process which at the same time prepares students for competition, while also giving enough context that students know what is happening when they debate against more experienced peers. This guide differs from many similar argumentation and debate textbooks in that it emphasizes competition and preparation, and works to avoid overburdening the reader with deep explanations of argumentation theory that are a valuable part of an argumentation curriculum but can be too tedious for quick and handy use in preparing for competitive debates.

Another feature of this guide is that it acknowledges the way that history, culture, and custom have shaped intercollegiate debate as an activity. Many debate textbooks balk at doing this because they work with the assumption that good argumentation is universal, so attention to the specific norms and conventions of a particular debate organization or format seems to be unnecessary. Years of competition and coaching have convinced me that this is not the case. Primarily because the debate is no different than any other realm of human communication, where our speech practices and expectations of our interlocutors are shaped communally rather than in adherence to some idealized norm. What you will find in this text is a balanced approach that melds more traditional approaches to argumentation theory with specific application to the norms and conventions which are generally common in contemporary collegiate policy debate.

Although this text is primarily focused on new to debate (what will henceforth be called "novice") students, others who have more experience will still have much to learn from this guide. Policy debate is a complicated activity that most students learn in a very piecemeal manner under the supervision of a coach. Unfortunately, coaches are a scarce commodity, and a coach's time is even more scarce. This guide allows students to have a backstop to help them prepare on their own time and maximize the utility of the coaching that they can receive. Some of the more rudimentary elements of this guide may be redundant, but the depth and specificity of the information will help fill out gaps in the training that even very experienced students have.

In putting together this guide, I am very much aware of all that the debate community has given me over the last 15 years. It is a remarkable activity that functions only because of the extremely hard work and dedication of a remarkable collection of people. I am permanently indebted to the coaches, debaters, and administrators who have sustained the activity. My goal in writing this guide is to pay forward all of the education, growth, and joy that this activity has given me to the next generation of debaters.

INTRODUCTION

In the fall of 2007 the author began his journey as a collegiate debater and coach at the University of Northern Iowa. He had debated in high school, and although he knew essentially nothing about collegiate debate was looking for the same sort of educational and competitive opportunities that had enriched his high school experience. After four years of debating, he entered a post-graduate education that included coaching debate for six years and then spent the subsequent four years assisting and directing collegiate programs at two major universities. After 15 years of debate involvement, he is still learning new things about how the elegant art of argumentation may be practiced, and this guide is not the final word on that matter.

What frustrated the author, and continues to frustrate many students beginning a debate career, is the steep learning curve that must be surmounted before the practices of debating begin to make sense. The problem with this learning curve is aptly captured in the adage, "too soon old, too late smart." Students only have so much time in their debate careers, and struggling to make sense of what they are doing early on hinders the ability to get the most out of this activity. This guide is intended to solve this problem by providing a thorough explanation of debate that paired with practice and coaching can amplify the learning opportunities available to students in debate.

To get the most out of this guide, the author suggests coaches and students use it as a reference to specific elements of debate preparation. Certainly reading it cover to cover has value, but most will find it more helpful to provide a basic explanation of what they observe taking place in particular debates. In this way, the guide can provide context for what is taking place in a debate and why, giving students more informed perspectives on debates and how to improve their own performance.

Nonetheless, the guide seeks to be thorough. The team the author competed on in college was at one point as small as three members with one coach and faced schools that might have as many as twenty members on a team with a half dozen or more coaches. Under those circumstances, it is hard to remain competitive because the time available to coaches and students is sparse. This experience has informed how this guide is structured, which is intended to offer a comprehensive approach to preparing for, participating in, and learning from the debate experience.

The rest of the book is structured in such a way that if a student works through the chapters in order, they will have a systematic approach to preparation. This introductory chapter will offer some history of policy debating and a basic walk-through of what a policy debate competition entails. From this point on, the book is structured to follow the same steps that a debate team would take in preparing for competition. Chapter 1 discusses the debate topics used in policy debate and how to use the wording of the topic in preparing for debate competition. Chapter 2 focuses on how to perform research necessary for competitive success. This chapter is especially focused on strategies for researching smarter, not harder. Chapter 3 describes how to put the research techniques discussed in Chapter 2 to work preparing affirmative cases, explaining what types of affirmative cases are commonly read, and the strategic considerations in developing an affirmative case. Chapter 4 offers the same sort of insights for the negative side, with an emphasis on how to select the most strategic positions to address various types of affirmative cases. These first four chapters make up the bulk of the preparation for debate discussion.

Subsequent chapters will focus more on debate performance. Chapter 5 discusses cross-examination as a particularly important feature of debating and offers guidance on how to take advantage of this often undervalued speaking time. Chapter 6 focuses on the middle portion of the debate and how those speeches are used to refute the cases which have been presented by the affirmative and negative sides. Chapter 7 focuses on rebuttal speeches and how to go about the process of distilling a large number of complex issues into a persuasive appeal for the judge. Chapter 8 focuses on how debate judges render decision. Although it is written more as a guide for rendering decisions, for competitors it is a glimpse inside what often seems to be the enigmatic mind of debate judges. Chapter 9 provides a guide to practicing in preparation for debate tournaments, offering drills, activities, and strategies for preparing arguments beyond the rudimentary aspects of case preparation.

The concluding chapter is less a guide to debate than a guide to how to enjoy debate. As an activity, debate is incredibly educational, intellectually invigorating, and fun. It is also at times challenging, frustrating, and stressful. Like any activity, it is not uncommon to see newcomers burnout because in their excitement they overwork themselves or look for shortcuts to success, which undermines sustainable growth. The conclusion is intended to offer some guidance on setting reasonable goals for a debate career, healthy limits for debate competition, and offer advice on how to use debate to advance personal development academically and professionally.

This summary of the text may make debate sound intimidating. That is not the author's intention. Instead, it is to offer some reassurance that if the reader has a question or is struggling with an idea in debate, this text will offer guidance for how to work your way toward a solution. At the time of writing this text, policy debating as a nationally competitive enterprise has been going on in the United States for over 77 years, and in that time has contributed to the growth of innumerable students. This activity may be challenging, but it is equally rewarding for those willing to dedicate themselves to proficiency.

Origins of Policy Debating

In 1947 the United States Military Academy at West Point (USMA) hosted the first National Debate Tournament (NDT) which would become the longest-running collegiate policy debate championship. Policy debating as we understand it today is the result of an evolutionary process that began with that tournament. Understanding this evolutionary process provides helpful context for understanding what norms and expectations persist in policy debate today.

Prior to the advent of the NDT much of the debating that took place between Universities in the United States was in the form of match debating, where students from two schools would debate a single proposition for a public audience. There were some debate tournaments, featuring multiple schools competing in multiple rounds of competition, but they tended to be regional events and did not produce a national standard for debate formats. This should not be taken to mean that there were no national debating organizations at the collegiate level, but they tended to be organized as fraternities, such as Delta Sigma Rho, Tau Kappa Alpha[1], and Pi Kappa Delta. There were myriad others that were smaller and shorter lived, but impressively the fraternities named above persist today. Though there was some tournament debating taking place within these fraternities, there was not a national championship for those fraternities.

What made the NDT remarkable is that it operated entirely independently of these fraternities and was deliberately intended to transcend boundaries that defined them such as school size and geography. The aim was to create a tournament that featured the best teams from across the country selected through a rigorous qualifying process, and a legacy of that trend is the continued perception in the policy debate community that the National Debate Tournament is the most prestigious, competitive, and exclusive tournament in the United States. USMA would continue to host the tournament until 1967, when the American Forensics Association (AFA) would take over responsibility for hosting the tournament and begin rotating hosting responsibilities between different campuses based on a bidding process.

A general arc over the course of this early period of the NDT was a trend toward increasing specialization among many debate programs toward qualifying for and competing in the national tournament causing a parallel trend toward specialization and standardization in debate practice. Most notably, match debating declined in importance for many debate programs and was replaced by tournament models that emphasized a large number of debates to better demonstrate the competitive prowess of debate teams. Overtime these tournaments adopted more standardized formats and an increasing degree of specialization that changed the way debate was practiced. One notable change was the trend toward more specialized judging by debate coaches and former debaters rather than judging by members of the host school faculty or the general public. This tended to result in a degree of insularity that influenced argument development by standardizing case formats, producing more consistent perspectives on argumentation theory, and creating an impetus toward more stylized performances. This has led forensics historians Bartanen and Littlefield to characterize the early years of the NDT as a part of a transition toward what they describe as "technical debating."[2]

In part because of these trends, the exclusivity of the NDT created by its qualifying process, and a desire to offer an alternative to focusing on policy-driven debate topics another organization was created by debate coaches that would operate independently of the NDT. Originally referred to as the Southwest Cross-Examination Debate Association today it is known as the Cross-Examination Debate Association (CEDA). It began in 1971 as a regional debate format that was a complement to policy debate which grew rapidly and in some parts of the country began to supplant it. As a part of this growth, it developed its own features that would contribute to the evolutionary process which led to the development of debate as it is practiced today.[3]

A defining feature of CEDA as an organization is that contra the qualifying process required to attend the NDT, CEDA created an open national championship that had no qualification process and included sweepstakes awards that expanded recognition to include season-long and teamwide successes. This legacy of being more open and rewarding more aspects of competition has led to the CEDA National Championship tournament colloquially being referred to by some debaters and coaches as "the people's tournament."

The most substantial contribution of the Cross-Examination Debate Association to policy debating is in the name of the organization. Cross-examination, a period when a debater from one side is allowed to ask a debater from the other side a question, had not been a feature of debate at the National Debate

Tournament, but eventually became a common practice. This contribution persists today, where following constructive speeches a debater from the side opposite the one who just spoke is able to ask the debater who just finished delivering a speech questions about their position. This practice began to cross over from CEDA into tournaments happening in the National Debate Tournament circuit informally, but would eventually become standard practice.

One of the interesting aspects of CEDA history was that it debated two topics in a year announced in September and December, much closer to the start of competition. The impetus for this choice was to curb some of the perceived excesses produced by the NDT-style debating. By limiting research time the coaches with teams competing in CEDA hoped to limit over-preparation and make debate more accessible to students with limited time commitments. Another feature of the early CEDA topics was a focus on debating "value" propositions on the presumption that evidence would be somewhat less important for debating those propositions.

Why the discussion of value debating in a topic about policy debate? As will be discussed in Chapter 1, there is a difference between value propositions and policy propositions, but in some ways, all policy propositions have a basis in discussions of value and vice versa. Overtime the value-oriented argumentation in CEDA would evolve into a specific argumentative form which will be discussed in Chapter 4 called a "kritik". This argument is not always necessarily reliant on value-oriented claims, but has embedded within it an echo of value argumentation that has renewed currency today.

Over time CEDA style debating began to become less of an antagonistic alternative to NDT, and instead became a parallel activity with many schools supporting both formats. By the late 1990s, many of the defining features of CEDA had disappeared, the topics were selected for a yearlong duration and were more policy focused, and there was an effective merger when the NDT decided to adopt the CEDA debate topic and the differentiation between divisions and tournaments were no longer perceived to be valuable outside of the national tournaments.

There is a third organization that practices policy debate, the American Debate Association (ADA), and its history has influenced contemporary debate practices as well. The ADA was formed in 1985 and had a regional focus as well, essentially in the Mid-Atlantic and Southeastern regions of the United States. It was created to satisfy a number of functions, including offering a national championship in policy-style debating that did not include the qualification process of the NDT.

One of the features of the American Debate Association was that it worked to insure a focus on the policy debating style associated with the NDT. As CEDA and the traditional NDT competitions became closer the ADA worked to provide tournaments that limited some of the CEDA influence. This led to some rules created to specifically limit arguments common to CEDA from being argued at ADA nationals. The most prominent example of this is the "kritik" which for many years was explicitly against the rules for competition at ADA nationals. Overtime some students ignored the rule and eventually it became a practice that is not altogether uncommon at the tournament, but it is comparatively less popular at that specific tournament than it is at other tournaments over the course of the year.

Today the differentiation between these organizations is much reduced. Many of the tournaments hosted over the course of the year count toward sweepstakes awards for both debate formats, and the practices found in debates are essentially the same. There does persist some differentiation in style, but the differences are now more of degree than kind, and this book is written to be of equal value regardless of the particular organizations a debater or their team competes under.

Policy Debate Tournament Procedures

Across the three primary organizations for policy debate in the United States there is not a standardized travel schedule, although teams looking to qualify for the NDT (a process that will be discussed in Chapter 8) will attend particularly large and long-running tournaments which are generally hosted on the same weekends every year. In general, schools that wish to host will select a weekend, frequently coordinating with other schools in their region, and publish an invitation for schools to attend the tournament. Currently, most of the invitations are publicly hosted on a web platform which will be discussed at length later titled Tabroom. Although sanctioning by the national organizations does constrain some of the tournament rules, the ad hoc nature of the travel schedule does create some variance in tournament rules. Below the most common procedures are briefly sketched out, but it is always a good idea to read tournament invitations to be clear of the tournament rules.

Schools that attend a tournament have their competitors broken up into teams of two debaters. Henceforth for the duration of this text, if you see the term "team" used, it refers to a pair of debaters from a school who compete together, which is often referred to as a "partnership." Various schools will determine which competitors are teamed up in various ways, but the general trend is to focus on teams consisting of students that have relatively comparable experience commensurate with the divisions of competition at a tournament. Very roughly this amounts to having the most experienced students paired together to compete in a "varsity" or "open" division, students with more than one year of experience compete in teams in the "junior varsity" division, and students with less than one year of experience compete in the "novice" division.

The typical policy debate tournament proceeds in two phases. The first phase is a series of debates in which each school attending has every team it has entered debating simultaneously called "rounds". These rounds function as preliminary debates or "prelims" that are used to determine which teams are eligible to compete for the tournament championship. Each debate in these rounds features two teams from different schools with a single judge from a third school who determines a winner and loser and assigns speaker points[4]. The teams competing in each individual debate in a round are typically paired either at random or based on a pretournament ranking for the first several debates, and subsequently debate against teams with roughly the same win/loss record. Different tournaments have different procedures, but frequently speaker points are used to refine the pairings to help ensure specifically desirable competitive balance in the debates, for instance having teams with higher speaker points compete against teams with lower speaker points that have a similar win/loss record to help produce more clear divisions between stronger and weaker teams. Most policy tournaments consist of either six or eight rounds of preliminary competition and notably have students defending both sides of the topic in an equal number of rounds.

Following the preliminary rounds teams are ranked based first on their win/loss record, then on speaker points with a number of potential adjustments including dropping high/low speaker point scores, variance in the scores assigned, by a judge, etc. Based on these rankings the better performing teams will "break" meaning they will continue debating to be named the tournament champion. How many teams will continue depends on the time available, size of the tournament, and sanctioning rules, but in general, it will be the teams finishing in the top half of the rankings following the preliminary debates. Then begins a second phase of debating variously called "out-rounds", "elimination rounds", or "elims" which will determine the eventual tournament champion. The procedure for this second phase can vary, but generally, the rankings are used to seed teams into a bracket following a high/low process similar to the way the NCAA basketball tournaments operate. Each round is a single elimination with the winner advancing through the bracket. The last team standing is the tournament champion.

The elimination rounds differ from the preliminary rounds in that speaker points are not awarded, and the judging is performed by a panel of 3 or more judges (always an odd number), who are not affiliated with either of the competing schools. Also, unlike preliminary debates, there is no guarantee that teams will debate on the same side an equal number of times. Typically sides are determined by a coin toss, but if two teams are debating for the second time at the tournament they will have their sides flipped from the previous debate to ensure that no team benefits twice from being on a better side of a topic.

One particularly important feature of tournament procedure is the selection of judges. The strategic considerations associated with judging will be discussed in Chapter 9, but a brief discussion here is helpful. At most policy tournaments there are two procedures for selecting judges. The older and far less common procedure has judges randomly assigned from a pool. Most tournaments that follow this procedure offer the attending schools the opportunity to "strike" or eliminate from the list of potential judges those who they think are less desirable. Most tournaments use a more sophisticated system called "mutually preferred judging" where attending schools or teams rank judges and for each debate, they receive a judge that they have ranked comparably to the team they are competing against. In both cases, the goal is to ensure that students receive judging that they believe to be fair and reasonable, with all the caveats to what that means in the context of a competitive intellectual enterprise.

Both procedures have raised important questions about the nature of judging in collegiate debate. Such decisions are obviously important for competitive reasons but also call into question judging as an educational, social, and even political endeavor. This book will not take a stance on such a question, other than to say that such questions are legitimate ones, and the ongoing debates about best practices for determining judging are producing some changes even as this guide is being written. Again, carefully reading and understanding tournament invitations is an important step in preparation.

Policy Debate Format

Policy debating under the auspices of CEDA/NDT/ADA generally follows a consistent format. Debaters from one school compete in teams of two against students from other schools who are similarly in teams of two. Occasionally students from more than one school will be paired together as a team referred to as a "hybrid team" or "hybrid partnership". Not all tournaments permit such pairings, and where permitted they do not always accrue benefits to the schools participating in the partnership. Occasionally, typically due to unforeseen circumstances such as illness, a student may compete as an individual for a single round or extremely occasionally an entire tournament, such debaters are colloquially known as "mavericks". An alternative approach that used to be somewhat popular but is typically not seen today is a team of three students where the competitors are rotated from one debate to the next, colloquially known as a "three-headed monster". Both maverick debating and three-person debating arrangements are generally viewed negatively for their ability to create competitive imbalances, but do occasionally happen.

When the pairings are announced competitors move to the assigned competition room with about 30 minutes to prepare before the debate starts. At this point, a somewhat controversial practice begins, which is called "disclosure." Disclosure entails the teams assigned to be affirmative and negative exchanging information about their arguments. There are some coaches and debaters who oppose the practice on the grounds that it can create competitive imbalances or overemphasizes the role of preparation to the detriment of students being able to "think on their feet." This perspective is increasingly a minority perspective, but not one entirely without merit. The majority opinion tends to hold that given the wide variety of issues that could be raised in a debate exchanging information helps students ensure that they have enough preparation to have a meaningful debate. Without passing judgment on the desirability of disclosure, suffice to say that this is generally an informal expectation (with some tournaments mandating it) that most students will perform in most debates.

The general procedure for disclosure begins with the affirmative team deciding whether they will in their first speech defend a case that they have read in previous debates. If they choose not to do so, and read an entirely new case, rather than one which has only minor revisions from previous debates, they are not generally expected to disclose new information. If they are reading a case that is essentially the same as what has been read in previous debates they are expected to disclose the main arguments which will be made in that case. In exchange, the negative will disclose arguments that they commonly read against such cases in their first speech. Some teams will only engage in disclosure when they are affirmative, but in general, a principle of reciprocity governs the practice.

After the 30 minutes of preparation the debate will begin under the observation and direction of the judge. The first speech is termed the First Affirmative Constructive (1AC) and the speaker who delivers it is generally described as the "First Affirmative" or "1A". This constructive and all of the subsequent constructive speeches will be 9-minute long. This speech will present what is typically described as the "affirmative case" and include the essential arguments for why the affirmative side of the proposition is desirable. Following this speech, there is a 3-minute cross-examination period (all cross-examination periods are 3 minutes) where the debater on the negative side will deliver the Second Negative Constructive (2NC) which is generally described as the "Second Negative" or "2N", will ask the affirmative speaker questions about their case. Following this period the "First Negative" (or "1N") speaker will deliver the First Negative Constructive (1NC) which outlines reasons to reject the case presented by the affirmative. Following this speech, there will be a cross-examination period where the First Affirmative will ask the First Negative questions about their arguments. This cross-examination period will be followed by the Second Affirmative Constructive (2AC), delivered by the "Second Affirmative" speaker (or "2A"). This speech is typically used to both expand on the reasons for accepting the affirmative case delivered in the 1AC and address the reasons for rejecting the case offered in the 1NC. Following this speech is a cross-examination period where the First Negative speaker will ask the Second Affirmative speaker questions about the arguments presented in their speech or the previous speeches.

To this point the debate has followed a simple and predictable course. A team speaks, is asked questions, and then another team speaks. What happens next is a defining feature of policy debating known as the "Negative Block" where the negative team gives two speeches in a row. This change in speaking order seems a bit odd but exists for good reason. In earlier eras, when research and preparation were far more difficult owing to the inefficiencies of research in a pre-computer and pre-internet era the affirmative had a massive advantage in being able to set the terms of the debate in their constructive. The negative was given the large block of speaking time in the middle of the debate to afford a maximum of preparation time in the debate to improve the quality of arguments which were typically made in very general terms that were not especially responsive into much more clearly applicable and relevant arguments. Although technology has worked to mitigate this imbalance, the structure of the speeches has remained the same to offer the negative the ability to make more in-depth and sophisticated arguments that better test the affirmative case.

The next speech in the debate is the Second Negative Constructive (2NC) and is delivered by the Second Negative Speaker (2N). This speech typically will focus on the most important negative arguments that need more explanation and evidentiary support to justify rejecting the affirmative case. After this speech, the Second Affirmative Speaker will conduct a cross-examination of the Second Negative Speaker. Following this cross-examination, the First Negative Speaker will deliver the First Negative Rebuttal (1NR). This rebuttal speech is of 6 minutes and will address important issues in the debate that were not raised by their teammate in the Second Negative Constructive. There is a great deal of strategy in determining which of the negative speakers discuss which issues in the negative block which will be addressed in depth in Chapter 6.

After this speech the sides will resume alternating speeches, beginning with the First Affirmative Rebuttal (1AR), a 6-minute speech (all rebuttals are 6 minutes in length) which is intended to address the most important issues raised in the negative block and previous affirmative speeches. Because it is a 6-minute speech that responds to 15 minutes of speaking by the negative side, many new debaters find it to be an intimidating speech. It need not be, and strategies for dealing with this time imbalance will be discussed in Chapter 7. That said, this has led to the misconception among some practitioners that it is the most difficult speech in a debate round.

In reality the most difficult speech belongs to the next speech, the Second Negative Rebuttal (2NR). This penultimate speech requires the speaker to address all of the issues raised in the first affirmative rebuttal, outline reasons why the judge should vote for the negative, predict what the arguments made in the last affirmative speech will be, and attempt to discredit those arguments. Predicting what the other side will argue is a major challenge, and students who become adept at that skill are considered to be superlatively talented.

The last speech is the Second Affirmative Rebuttal (2AR). This speech should address the issues raised in the second negative rebuttal, and outline the reasons why the judge should prefer the affirmative side of the topic. This speech often consists of summary as much as it does argumentation and tests the rhetorical skills of the speaker. Because there are no further rebuttals by the negative this speech offers the speaker a relatively free hand in making arguments, so long as they are an extension of claims already made in the debate.

After the second affirmative rebuttal the judge will take some time to reflect on the arguments that have been made, then render a decision on who won the debate, assigning rankings and points to the speakers on what today is usually an online form. After completing this task, the judge addresses the debaters to explain their "Reason For Decision" (RFD), articulating who they have decided won the debate and what the reasons for that decision are, and provides feedback to the debaters on ways that future performance can be improved. These results are tabulated to create the "pairings" for the next debate.

Conclusion

This brief introduction to policy debating is simply a taste of the more complicated issues that will be discussed in the following chapters. If this seems overwhelming it is because policy debate offers one of the most rich educational opportunities available to collegiate students. While the complexity can be intimidating, with patience and experience it quickly falls into place. The aim of this guide is to accelerate this falling into place by giving the reader a sense of the norms and expectations that influence policy debating.

The reader will note that this is not the most academic approach to debating, which is intentional. The goal of this guide is to provide practical instruction that is more sensitive to the current trends and nuances of policy debate. One of the aspects of policy debating which is most interesting is that while sound argument practices are of course central to the activity, it is equally a product of the debater's creativity. Where creativity abounds, strict adherence to rules can make it challenging to account for what is happening in a debate.

> **GLOSSARY**
>
> **Resolution** The resolution is the wording of the topic which will be debated by the major policy debate organizations for an academic year.
>
> **National Debate Tournament** The National Debate Tournament is the longest running and most competitive national championship for collegiate policy debate.
>
> **Cross-Examination Debate Association** The Cross-Examination Debate Association is the primary governing body for collegiate debate, responsible for selecting the topic for a year's worth of competition.
>
> **American Debate Association** The American Debate Association is another governing body of collegiate policy debate. This organization emphasizes more traditional approaches to policy debating and has an open national championship which does not require qualification.

Notes

1 Delta Sigma Rho and Tau Kappa Alpha merged in the 1960s into a single organization.
2 Michael Bartanen & Robert Littlefield, *Forensics in America*, (Lanham, MD: Rowman & Littlefield, 2014), 64–67.
3 Ibid 74–76.
4 Speaker points are generally awarded to individual debaters by the judge of the debate based on the quality of the speeches delivered. More detail on how these points are awarded is provided in Chapter 9.

1
ANALYZING DEBATE TOPICS

One of the harder to grasp aspects of policy debate is the unique way that the topic functions. To help make sense of how policy debate topics are discussed and how they proceed requires simultaneously an understanding of the history behind debate topics, the topic selection process, and grammar. It also requires an understanding of some rather unique aspects of argumentation theory that are somewhat proprietary to policy debating. This chapter covers all of those topics and provides a demonstration of how the 2023–2024 debate topic can be analyzed.

Policy Debate Topics

The selection of topics in policy debate has varied considerably since the advent of the National Debate Tournament (NDT), and the nature of topics has changed significantly as well. The consistent through line is that the topics are designed to be timely and avoid a biased wording that favors the affirmative or negative side of the proposition. They also are controversial, sometimes to a degree that invites questions about the nature of the debate itself.

Historically, the most famous example of this controversy comes from the 1954 to 1955 topic "Resolved: That the United States should extend diplomatic recognition to the communist government of China." This topic was protested by the United States Military Academies and other schools on the basis that defending the affirmative side would require arguing against established United States foreign policy and could make students susceptible to communist propaganda. Additionally, for students at the military academies, the ongoing hearings about communist infiltration of the armed forces raised a concern that the debater could not be separated from the uniform that they were wearing.[1]

Similar concerns have presented themselves on more recent topics. One example was the 2013–2014 topic, "Resolved: The United States Federal Government should substantially increase statutory and/or judicial restrictions on the war powers authority of the President of the United States in one or more of the following areas: targeted killing; indefinite detention; offensive cyber operations; or introducing United States Armed Forces into hostilities." The affirmative side of this topic would ostensibly have forced a student at one of the Academies to criticize the President, who in their capacity as Commander-in-Chief could be argued to be a commanding officer, which would place the debater in violation of the Uniform Code of Military Justice.

Topics are of course not only controversial for students in the military academies; many of the topics address issues that directly impact the lives of students. One such example was the 2010–2011 topic, "Resolved: The United States Federal Government should substantially increase the number of and/or substantially expand beneficiary eligibility for its visas for one or more of the following: employment-based immigrant visas, nonimmigrant temporary worker visas, family-based visas, human trafficking-based visas." For some of the students debating, this topic was a challenge because their status in the United States could have been directly impacted by some of the policy changes possible under the auspices of this topic. The question of what issues were appropriate for debate under this topic was an open one, a feature that is not infrequent in policy topics.

There are also some topics that are controversial because they tend to produce a degree of bias favoring one side or the other. An example that many long-serving directors will point to is the 2001–2002 topic, "RESOLVED: That the United States Federal Government should substantially increase federal control throughout Indian Country in one or more of the following areas: child welfare, criminal justice, employment, environmental protection, gaming, resource management, taxation." This is of course an important policy question that deals with fundamental questions of justice. Unfortunately (in some respects), at the time (and still today) there was relatively little support for giving the Federal Government a greater degree of control in the administration of indigenous affairs in the United States among most scholars studying the matter, and as a result, debaters had a difficult time crafting compelling arguments on the affirmative side of the topic.

Timeliness has also been an issue on a number of occasions. One particularly stark example was the 2011–2012 topic, "Resolved: The United States Federal Government should substantially increase its democracy assistance for one or more of the following: Bahrain, Egypt, Libya, Syria, Tunisia, Yemen." On this topic, which was debated during a period of substantial change in United States policies toward the countries listed thanks to the series of revolutions that came to be called the Arab Spring, many teams could find that their cases could be invalidated by policy changes from one week to the next. Given the effort required to produce new cases, this presented a number of challenges for many debate teams.

These examples demonstrate the difficulties inherent in crafting a debate topic, which must be: Controversial but not so personal as to be threatening, timely but relatively stable for an entire year, and unbiased but still of great importance. It may be fairly argued that threading these needles is an impossible task, at least to the satisfaction of all debaters and coaches. Nonetheless, the Cross-Examination Debate Association (CEDA) has developed a sophisticated process that works to accomplish these goals. Understanding this process is important for understanding just how to interpret debate topics.

How Topics Are Crafted

To give a fuller picture of this process requires a brief historical digression. The current topic selection process evolved out of the decision in 1996 for the NDT to adopt the CEDA topic, effectively merging the two debate organizations. Prior to that decision, there were different topics used by CEDA and the NDT that had different processes. The current model is designed to give the collegiate debate community a topic that is capable of sustaining relatively balanced debates for the entirety of the debate season. This is a challenging task, as the innovativeness of debaters combined with the shifting trends in current events can easily bias the topics selected in favor of one side or the other. The tension between these goals may not be altogether perfectly resolvable, but the rigor in the process speaks to an impressive level of commitment by the debaters and coaches to create the best topics possible for a season of debating.

The selection of a debate topic begins in the spring prior to the debate season and consists of five stages. In the first stage, coaches, debaters, and alumni of collegiate debate submit "topic papers" proposing topics for the following year. The topics proposed have to fit within a four-year rotation for general area, cycling through legal, foreign, and domestic policy with the fourth year being open to any potential topic. Historically, topic papers were written in essentially an essay format intended to argue for the desirability of a topic. In recent years, they look much more like briefs of collected evidence indicating a substantial literature base and relatively equal division of desirable arguments for both sides of the topic. In the second stage, these submissions are initially reviewed by a "topic committee" which has nine members including two members of the executive leadership of CEDA (President, First Vice President, and/or Second Vice President), undergraduate and graduate member representatives, three at-large members elected by the general membership, a representative from the NDT, and a representative from the American Debate

Association. This committee must by May 8 submit at least three topic papers to be voted on by the general membership of CEDA.

This third stage of the selection process has each school provide a ranking of the topics desired constituting their vote, with the winning topic determined by a proportional system. Essentially, if a single topic receives a majority of the first-place rankings, it is selected. If no topic achieves a majority, the topic with the fewest first-choice rankings is removed with the subsequent rank assuming first on the teams ballots where the first rank is no longer eliminated. The impetus for this system is to ensure that the topic selected reflects a majority view of what a good topic would be rather than giving a large minority complete control over the selection of the topic. A byproduct of this system is that the topic selected is often ranked second or third on many ballots.

In the fourth stage, the topic committee meets[2] to develop at least three different wordings for the topic. The term given to these specific wordings is "resolution" to emphasize the difference between the resolution that designates what arguments each side must defend to present a complete case from the topic area that speaks to the relevant issues that may arise in a debate. If this distinction seems slippery, that's because it frequently is, but will be clarified in the section below. In the fifth stage, the general membership will vote on the wording options provided by the committee using the same procedure as was used earlier in the topic selection process. The winning resolution is announced on the third Friday in July, at which point teams begin preparing for their debate season.

This process is complicated, and necessarily so, but is not without its critics. There is currently a reform effort geared toward expanding participation and engagement with the topic drafting process, which could result in reforms to the process outlined above. As it stands, part of the criticism is that the topic writing process makes engagement from diverse audiences challenging given the short time between the end of the debate season and the beginning of the next topic selection process.[3] Until such time as a reform comes to pass, it is incumbent on debaters and coaches to stay abreast of the topic selection process that begins as soon as the NDT and CEDA National Tournament are concluded.

As any reader would surmise from the preceding explanation, the construction of a policy debate topic involves an extended process that is by various turns extremely democratic and somewhat insular that balances an extremely large number of concerns. A cynic might liken the result to what you get when you form a committee to put together a horse: a camel. A more charitable approach would suggest that the process of constructing policy debate topics produces broad topics encompassing a diverse set of policy issues that make it possible for a season of debating to be sustained.

For the duration of this guide, the topic that will be the primary focus of the discussion and examples provided will be the 2023–2024 CEDA policy debate topic.

Resolved: The United States Federal Government should restrict its nuclear forces in one or more of the following ways:

- adopting a nuclear no-first-use policy;
- eliminating one or more legs of the nuclear triad;
- disarming its nuclear forces.[4]

A simple reading will illustrate some of the features described above. First, this topic is broad in that although it is limited to nuclear forces policy, there is a list of changes that are available to the affirmative. These changes are also able to be combined (the affirmative is not limited to one option), and within each of the changes mandated in the list, there are multiple approaches that are available. Any of those changes would implicate domestic policy (if for no other reason than a change in nuclear policy would have political ramifications for the sitting president), military policy, and geopolitics between not only the United States and potential adversaries and allies but also the other countries, whose foreign relations are mediated through the United States nuclear umbrella.[5]

Making Sense of Debate Topics

In preparing for policy debates, topic analysis serves three essential functions. The first is to develop a tentative understanding of what specific issues will be argued by both sides of the topic. The second is to develop a strategy for how to research the topic, to maximize the likelihood of being adequately prepared to be competitively successful. The third is to determine what the affirmative must demonstrate to be true in order to justify the judge voting for them, and by extension what the negative side will have to disprove.

To satisfy the first function, a debater would be well served to consider two things. The first is what area of policy is the focus of the resolution. The easiest way to make this early determination is to identify the relevant "terms of art" within the resolution. These terms are typically nouns or verbs that, either singly or frequently in combination, denote something greater than what is found within the dictionary for the terms used individually. These terms of art typically are used by the topic committee to ensure that the resolution reflects debates taking place outside the narrow confines of the debate community.

To identify terms of art, there are a couple of productive steps that one should follow. First, consider punctuation, the inclusion of hyphens or quotation marks are good indicators that a term of art is in use. Second, look for terms that only seem to make sense in conjunction with each other. Below, we will look at one example from the 2023–2024 debate season. One more strategy would be to review the controversy paper submitted for the topic, which often has research compiled about the terms of art relevant to the controversy.

Using the 2023–2024 debate topic, one example would be the phrase "nuclear triad." A search of the term from Merriam-Webster would return no results, but a search that entailed looking for "nuclear" and "triad" separately would produce results that provide definitions of both words. The result would be:

Nuclear: 2c(1)
: being a weapon whose destructive power derives from an uncontrolled nuclear reaction[6]
Triad: 1
: a union or group of three: TRINITY[7]

This combination of definitions provided without context might allow someone familiar with the term to deduce the correct interpretation, but for those who are less familiar with the term of art, it is not an especially helpful pair of definitions because it doesn't really provide much specificity for how those words are used in conjunction.

By contrast, recognizing the term "nuclear triad" as a term of art allows rather rudimentary searches (for more detail on how to perform searches, see Chapter 3) to produce much more helpful definitions contextualized to ongoing debates in the field of nuclear weapons policy. For example, the Center for Arms Control and Non-Proliferation, a non-partisan non-profit that advocates for the reduction of nuclear arsenals,[8] defines the "nuclear triad" in the following way,

> The U.S. nuclear arsenal comprises thousands of nuclear weapons and three methods of delivery, sometimes called "legs." Warheads can be launched from the air via strategic bombers carrying gravity bombs or cruise missiles, from the sea by submarines holding ballistic missiles, or from underground silos housing intercontinental ballistic missiles. Collectively, these delivery methods are referred to as "the Triad." Currently all three legs of the Triad are being modernized at a cost of $494 billion, or about $50 billion every year from 2019 to 2028.[9]

This definition, although it carries a suggestion of bias given the interests of the organization offering the definition and the emphasis placed on the cost of modernizing the legs of the triad, is much more helpful because it is contextualized to ongoing debates about what to do with the triad. To help ensure the validity of the definitions provided for a term of art, it's always a good idea to find two or three definitions that are essentially similar to help control for bias.

After identifying terms of art within the resolution to help clarify the topic students would be well served to grammatically interpret the topic in order to validate their interpretation of how the topic will be debated. Although many debaters and their coaches ignore this step because they assume the wording of the topic is secondary to the norms for how collegiate debate typically functions, those assumptions can be risky, especially where certain terms might carry a substantial meaning for the topic depending on their usage. More importantly, for those looking to get started debating, this step can be remarkably productive in understanding how debates tend to play out.

In the resolution which we will be using, the object of the sentence is identified as the "United States Federal Government," which is significant because in standard English grammar, the object of the sentence has agency to affect the subject of the sentence; hence, the United States Federal Government is referred to as an agent. The verb in the sentence is "should restrict," indicating that the agent of the resolution will be obligated to curtail the subject of the sentence which is indicated by the determiner "its." The subject of the sentence is "nuclear forces." The sentence is modified after the subject by the phrase "one or more" meaning that the affirmative might choose between multiple options, with a list indicated by "following ways" and the subsequent colon.

In each of the listed items we have a gerund form of the verb indicating that where the interpretation of the verb is not clear from the definition of the word it will be interpreted as a form of the initial verb in the sentence (restrict). This illustrates why reading the topic grammatically is helpful because it clarifies that the gerund form of the verb beginning each sentence subject to the term restrict, meaning the affirmative cannot defend an expansion of nuclear forces.[10] Subsequently, each line has a subject noun that sets the parameters for what the United States Federal Government can do under the auspices of the resolution by constraining the number of subjects which can be acted upon.

By combining inquiry into the terms of art in the topic as well as close grammatical reading, the coordinates of the topic begin to come into view. The next step is to develop an interpretation of the topic, which can then be used as a basis for research. To do this, a debater will write out an interpretation that incorporates the definitions of the terms which they are using to define the topic to prevent mystification created by terms of art. An example is provided below.

> The national government of the United States will change its policy for nuclear weapons in a manner that is a limit or reduction from the way things are currently. There are three actions which are possible independently or in conjunction with each other. Other actions not covered in the list of possible actions will not be part of the topic. The first is a change in policy that prevents the United States from using nuclear weapons first in a conflict. The second would be to eliminate land based, air based, or sea based nuclear weapons from the United States nuclear arsenal. This could entail eliminating more than one of the weapons listed above. The third action would be to eliminate all of the nuclear weapons that the United States has.

The interpretation provides a plain language approach to the topic. Like many activities in this guide, the point of performing them is to make them obsolete. This sounds counterintuitive, but the idea is that by performing the activity, a debater gains clarity such that they don't need to reference the work again. In this case, writing out an interpretation forces the debater to develop a rich understanding of the meaning of the resolution such that they can remember it without having to persistently check the wording as they perform research and write arguments.

Issue Identification

The last step in analyzing a topic is taking the interpretation that a debater or the team has developed and using it to identify the likely issues which will be argued in the topic. This process is typically performed concurrently with creating a research agenda, which is discussed in Chapter 2. The aim of this process is to begin organizing the more abstract ideas that a debater has about the resolution into more concrete arguments. The challenge in this process can perhaps be most easily explained in terms of what is called the Menos paradox. Described in Plato's dialogue *Meno,* this paradox posits that to learn something new, a person must know that they do not know something. But to know that they do not know something, then they must already know the same thing.[11]

Unfortunately for debaters, Plato's answer that this problem is solved by people having gained knowledge in their past life, which is remembered through experiences in this life, is not especially helpful. More helpful is to think of issue identification as a way to invite exposure to new knowledge by using the limited understanding of an issue the debater already has. In the context of a resolution what this means taking the terms in the resolution and using them as starting points to imagine the conflict taking place.

This could be done in one of two ways, depending on how a debater or team would like to proceed. One approach which is very broad, and by definition more time-consuming, is to identify a list of the issues which pertain to the topic as a general area. This approach works well where the topic is focused on an area that is very unfamiliar, and so anticipating likely issues is challenging. For the resolution which is the focus of this guide, this strategy would entail listing the issues which the debater can imagine relating to the United States nuclear forces.

An alternative approach which is more targeted would instead focus on using the resolution to create a list of possible arguments made by the affirmative and negative sides. This is more efficient but requires a greater degree of knowledge about the resolution. It also carries the risk that research on the topic may be more narrowly targeted (which is more efficient) and ignores issues that might have been recognized in a more general approach. To illustrate the contrast, the left column in Table 1.1 represents a more general approach, while the middle and right columns represent more narrow approaches.

TABLE 1.1 Sample table showing the beginnings of a list of affirmative and negative arguments that are likely to be debated on the topic

Issues	Affirmative arguments	Negative arguments
Foreign relations	United States–China relations	United States–Japan relations
	United States–Russia relations	United States–NATO relations
Deterrence	Deterrence credibility (conventional weapons are better)	Allied proliferation (fear of abandonment causes proliferation)
	Multi-nationalism	United States leadership

Notice that in the general approach, issues are given broad titles, while in the narrow approach, more specific titles are used. The debater in the narrow approach has identified which of the issues handled more generally are likely to favor the affirmative or negative side in the debate. The debater taking the more general approach is in a good position to learn about the topic and will eventually be in a position to produce the more narrow list, but in starting from a more general list they may well identify issues that are ignored in the more narrow list.

Both approaches can be effective. Over the duration of the research process, both approaches tend to arrive at the same place. Perhaps more important is maintaining a self-aware and systematic approach over the course of this process to insure that time is spent effectively and well. As debaters have many demands on their time such as classes, jobs, and maintaining a social life using time efficiently is very important.

There is one further set of issues that need to be identified. As has been discussed in the introduction, one of the important innovations in policy debate has been the development of arguments which do not necessarily affirm the resolution or engage directly in the policymaking aspects of the affirmative case. These arguments which tend to have the adjective "critical" attached to them as a way to signal their inherent critique of more traditionally oriented approaches to debate also deserve attention as a part of the issue identification process, but they are by nature a bit less structured and absent some experience hard to predict (which is part of the appeal for teams who like to pursue this type of argument). To the extent that it is possible, the process might look something like this.

Begin with a focus less on the specific actions suggested in the topic and more on its stem (in this instance the part of the resolution prior to the colon). Consider the more philosophical issues to which that stem (reduction in nuclear forces) pertains. Obviously, international relations theory would be relevant, especially as it pertains to militarism as a feature of United States foreign relations. Identifying the relevant different theories as issues would be a good place to start. The next step would entail considering what issues that topic elides or hides. For example, a pressing issue in United States politics and culture at this moment is racism. A team seeking to argue in a manner that is at a degree of removal from the topic would likely find this to be an attractive issue to argue, even if disconnected from the topic.

Issue identification is a challenging task, and doing it without the resolution as a guide can feel like an impossible guessing game. It's important to remember that this is equally true for all debaters. The ones who do better don't do better because they are necessarily smarter, or know more, but because they are organized and systematic. They take their time to think and plan so that they get the most out of the knowledge and talent that they have. Sometimes this still doesn't produce the desired result, but that is after all what usually happens in competitions.

Conclusion

Analyzing a topic is a task which is often given too little attention by many debaters. The desire to begin researching and producing arguments causes debaters to skip this process. When they do, often a great deal of time is spent unproductively researching issues that are not germane to the topic. In the context of this resolution, a debater who is not careful in their analysis of the topic might spend a great deal of time preparing for arguments which never come to fruition. When the authors debated a similar resolution, they spent an immense amount of time researching the industry that supports the United States' nuclear forces. The author eagerly began researching the topic (without really reading the resolution) and pursued their own research without consulting their teammates and coaches. Much to the author's chagrin, not only did they discover that this was only tangentially related to the topic, but the arguments derived from this research were never presented during the debates that season.

This illustrates two important lessons. First, analyzing the resolution is vitally important to using time to prepare for debates effectively. Second, analyzing a resolution is best done with peers and coaches. Analyzing a resolution in isolation leaves a debater susceptible to their own biases, interests, and knowledge. Working with other debaters and coaches helps make sure that a debater's time is not wasted because of their own idiosyncrasies. There is an added benefit to this approach because policy debate is done in teams analyzing a resolution together provides a team with a shared understanding and language to pursue collaborative argumentation. It also makes policy debate much more fun. While there is always work that debaters should do individually to improve their abilities and knowledge, performing the more exacting and tedious tasks collectively provides a shared learning experience that contributes to the bonds and friendships that make team activities enjoyable.

> **GLOSSARY**
>
> **Topic Committee** The committee operating under the auspices of CEDA responsible for evaluating the topic papers for viability and subsequent to public voting producing a slate of specific wordings from which the resolution will be selected.
> **Topic Papers** Packages of evidence used to make the case for a specific topic area.
> **Topic** The general issue which is going to be debated.
> **Resolution** The specific wording of the topic which sets the parameters for the debates.
> **Term of Art** Terminology specific to an area of expertise which is used to formulate a debate topic.

Notes

1 Ronald Walter Greene and Darrin Hicks, "Lost Convictions: Debating Both Sides and the Ethical Self-Fashioning of Liberal Citizens," *Cultural Studies 19*, no. 1 (2005): 100–126.
2 In recent years, these meetings have been livestreamed so that they are available to the public, and frequently non-committee members provide research and input to support the committee members. For students who want to better understand debate topics watching these meetings can be very instructive.
3 Ned Gidley et al., "Topic Selection Process Reform," in *Reimagining the Future of Intercollegiate Debate: Pedagogy, Practice, and Sustainability*, eds. Kelly Young and David Cram Helwich (Chestnut Hill, MA: American Forensic Association, 2023), 143–45.
4 Cross Examination Debate Association. "2023–2024 Resolution," 2024. Accessed 1st March. https://cedadebate.org/2023-2024-resolution/.
5 Nuclear umbrella referring to countries which the United States has offered a security guarantee. See David Vergun, "U.S. Nuclear Umbrella Extends to Allies, Partners, Defense Official Says," U.S. Department of Defense, 2019. Accessed 24th April. https://www.defense.gov/News/News-Stories/Article/Article/1822953/us-nuclear-umbrella-extends-to-allies-partners-defense-official-says/.
6 Merriam-Webster.com Dictionary. s.v. "nuclear," 2024. Accessed 1st March. https://www.merriam-webster.com/dictionary/nuclear
7 Merriam-Webster.com Dictionary. s.v. "triad," 2024. Accessed 1st March. https://www.merriam-webster.com/dictionary/triad.
8 Center For Arms Control and Non-Proliferation. "About the Center for Arms Control and Non-Proliferation," 2024. Accessed 1st March. https://armscontrolcenter.org/about/.
9 Center For Arms Control and Non-Proliferation. "Fact Sheet: The Nuclear Triad," 2021. 21st January. https://armscontrolcenter.org/factsheet-the-nuclear-triad/.
10 As will be discussed several times in this guide, officially the United States has a policy of strategic ambiguity regarding nuclear weapons. Thus, absent subjugating the verb in each item in the list to the verb in the stem (restrict) ostensibly the affirmative could argue in favor of expanding nuclear forces by, for example, adopting a nuclear no-first-use policy.
11 Plato, *Meno*, trans. Benjamin Jowett (Champaign, IL: Project Gutenberg, 1999), 31.

2
PERFORMING DEBATE RESEARCH

One of the defining features of policy debate is the emphasis placed on research. Students who are new to policy debate all too frequently use the same techniques that they might use when they are writing a paper for a class that they have left until the last minute. They write the argument, then attempt to perform the research that would support the argument, only to discover that their argument does not reflect the positions adopted by the most credible sources on the topic. As a result, they produce arguments that sound persuasive but consistently lose because there is no good evidence to support the argument. That is one reason why this text discusses good research practices before discussing sound argumentation.

The other is that the unique value in policy debate relative to other formats is the emphasis placed on research. Most other formats require a certain amount of research, but the focus placed on debating diverse resolutions or limited preparation in other formats means that the research produced in preparation for those debates is less comprehensive, and frequently eschews sources that are not public-facing or journalistic in nature. In incentivizing research into these somewhat less accessible but more expert sources, policy debate offers advanced research skills that tend to serve students especially well in legal and academic careers. Some students even find, as the author himself did, that arguments that students begin as undergraduates go on to have second lives as dissertations or even books.[1]

From a practical perspective, the goal of research in policy debate is to produce what are called files, which contain all of the arguments that a team would make on a topic. For example, the affirmative file will contain the affirmative case (the arguments made in the first affirmative constructive) as well as the arguments that are prepared for the subsequent affirmative speech. When producing their speeches, debaters will combine arguments pulled from many different files to produce speeches, which makes organization as essential as thoroughness in producing research.

This chapter is designed around preparing students for the broad and comprehensive research that is typically done at the beginning of the year. As the year advances, some more nuanced approaches are necessary. These will be covered at the end of this chapter, but some strategies will also be found in Chapter 8, where tournament preparation is discussed.

Developing a Research Strategy

Research is a time-consuming activity that can be extremely frustrating because time invested does not always produce fruitful results. So much so that some debate teams will exclude their novice students from participating in research and will instead have them focus their time on other forms of debate preparation.[2] Without commenting on the desirability of this particular strategy, suffice to say that when performing research maximum efficiency optimizes the educational benefits and competitive possibilities for both individual debaters and debate teams. Developing a research strategy before setting out to research helps teams avoid inefficiencies and ensure time is spent productively.

In developing a strategy, it is important for debaters to begin by considering the resources available to them. This begins by understanding what the structure of their own debate team allows them to accomplish. Debate teams that are older and more well established will have research from past topics, which may be sufficiently current that only minimal updating is required for large parts of the topic. Debate teams that are larger can pool their time and energy with divided responsibilities to ensure that each individual debater is better prepared through collective effort. Debate teams that are housed in University systems with better research resources and tools can take advantage of those resources by finding higher quality sources not available to other teams.

Of course the inverse can be true as well. It may be that a debater finds themselves on a newer team, with few members, and limited resources. Given these disadvantages, it would seem that for some debaters the ability to compete at a high level is severely constrained and perhaps impossible. Some debate coaches lament that such disadvantages are insurmountable and undermine the future possibilities for debate competition. As will be discussed below, it is apt to be the case that in an era when performing research was done using almost exclusively print sources, which may take several days or even weeks to be delivered, when database access was limited, less effective, and less comprehensive, that structural limitations really were insurmountable for top-level competition. In the last 15 years, the modernization of research tools available at the University and the shift toward open-sourcing research (this will be discussed at length later) have minimized these challenges.

For a team, the relevant considerations for developing a research strategy are: Time available to perform the research, resources available at the school, number of researchers available, compiled research from past topics, and expertise among team members and coaches. The goal in formulating the strategy is to take advantage of the strengths available to the team and find ways to either avoid or address the weaknesses to make sure that the team has the best opportunity for success.

In an ideal scenario, research can begin as soon as the resolution is announced.[3] Given that this typically predates the start of the competitive season by at least 6 weeks, it is possible to produce an impressive amount of research and pursue a breadth-oriented strategy, exploring as much of the topic as possible. In cases where less time is available, a more depth-oriented strategy focusing on a smaller number of issues might allow debaters to make better use of their time but does sacrifice some degree of competitiveness.

Most schools and universities have access to a library system that is underutilized by undergraduate students. The trend toward digitization of library holdings has served to level the playing field for many teams and students, increasingly widespread adoption of e-books, combined with more universal investment in databases means that students have access to a much wider array of resources than at any point in debate history. That said, identifying weaknesses in the library (for example, some polytechnic universities have limited holdings on topics like political science) can help identify places where research will take longer or be less efficient. An outstanding resource for the debate team to help in quickly and accurately making these evaluations is a librarian. In practice, these highly specialized and underused experts in the storing and organization of knowledge are frank about navigating the resource process and making up for the limitations that might exist at any University. An additional underrated resource is the faculty on campus who themselves research many of these issues and can direct students to sources of evidence that they may not find otherwise.

Those important considerations aside, the most important resource for a team is its people. It is no coincidence that the most competitive teams in the country are the teams that have made a longstanding commitment to research excellence. By fostering research skills in each generation of students over time, teams develop institutional knowledge in the form of research, which is stored from one year to the next. This allows them to complete research for parts of a topic quickly by updating already existing files rather than starting from scratch, a time- and labor-intensive process. These same schools also rely on the interests of students and coaches to develop areas of expertise that allow information to be shared more efficiently than requiring each debater to learn all of the relevant aspects of a topic independently. Finally, numbers do make a difference. Teams with more competitors can perform more research, have more diverse expertise and knowledge, and can work collaboratively to maximize their abilities.

So, what does a strategy look like? First, it is setting objectives for the research priorities outlined in the previous chapter. Those objectives have to be defined by a combination of the strengths and limitations outlined above, mediated through the demands of sound argumentation, with an eye toward curiosity and interest on the part of the debaters. Second, it entails dividing responsibilities for which people are going to research which issues. Third, it requires deadlines for when those objectives have to be satisfied. For a team, this is typically a collaborative process designed to best prepare the team as a whole for competition.

Consider the following hypothetical as a guide. A relatively small team of four debaters with a single coach who has only been around for a relatively short period of time is preparing for a tournament at the start of the season. Such a team might set objectives that are deliberately modest in response to the topic. Rather than trying to research the entirety of the topic, they might focus more narrowly, starting with the issue identification process described in the previous chapter. Their goal would be to put together lists of issues for each of the affirmative areas on the topic, focus only on those issues which occur with the highest frequency, and then proceed to less frequent issues. Their aim would be to produce an affirmative case built around the issues most commonly argued knowing that they will then have adequate research for most debates. This might mean that one debater prepares the affirmative case, while the other debaters and coach prepare the negative positions necessary to rebut that case. While this team may be behind in some debates, they are able to be competitive, and over the course of a season, they can make up the difference.

By contrast, a team that is very large, perhaps 20 debaters with five coaches will use issue identification as a way to research the entirety of the topic. This allows them to be prepared for essentially every debate, but to take advantage of this requires great attention to detail in sharing information between debaters because they will research very different issues. For this team, the problem of researching might be simpler, but the task of using this research effectively becomes much harder.

For individual debaters, a similar process follows from the team's decision but operates slightly differently. The individual process entails making decisions about what to look for, where to look, and how much looking to do. For example, if a debater is tasked with researching an affirmative case, they might look ahead to the next chapter and make determinations about what is necessary to produce an affirmative case. They will identify ahead of time where to look for the necessary sources so that they do not have to invest time in searching randomly. While researching they will budget time for researching each argument they believe they will need to make, and if initial efforts are not fruitful move on to other issues. Over time, debaters that consistently pursue this process develop strong instincts for when they are using time well and become exponentially more efficient.

Starting the Research Process

The research process for debate is colloquially referred to as "card cutting." The origins of this term are historically interesting and instructive for understanding contemporary research practices. The oldest approach to research in debate had students consulting print sources and copying down a sentence or two from those sources along with a citation onto notecards. As copier technology developed, debaters shifted from copying text by hand onto notecards toward photocopying larger pieces of text then using scissors to cut out the relevant sections and taping them onto printer paper with a citation to allow them to use larger pieces of text in the debates. Individual pieces of evidence were still referred to as "cards," and because the process of creating cards required them to be cut out, the process of evidence production came to be known as "card cutting."

In modern debate practice, most teams have shifted toward "paperless debating" where the evidence is copied into Word documents, which facilitates information sharing and avoids some of the logistical problems created by paper debating. For example, a well-prepared team prior to the advent of paperless debating might store their evidence in a collection of plastic or rubber tubs, which would be heavy, bulky, and expensive to travel, especially if tournaments were far enough away to justify flying. The shift toward paperless debate around 2010 solved this problem, but important aspects of the evidence production remained essentially the same.

The research tools available to students competing in modern debate formats are dramatically more powerful than those of a previous era, which dramatically accelerates the early stages of the research process. For debaters competing in the modern era, the process usually begins by throwing a series of search terms into their preferred search engine and selecting links that seem relevant to their research topic. This first search might return a quantity and quality of sources that for previous generations of students would have taken a week to compile. In the near future, it may be the case that this step is itself unnecessary, perhaps using some iteration of "artificial intelligence" students will be able to simply ask an automated program to research the topic for them. The problem with the current common practice, and potential future research practices, is that it is not especially systematic, and can leave the researcher with an incomplete picture of their topic.

A better approach emphasizes planning before and during the research process to make sure that the best tools are used. Rather than randomly using search terms in a generic browser, a better approach would begin by creating a list of places to perform those searches, and then a list of search terms to be used in each of those places. A good starting point for this is the issues list that was suggested at the end of Chapter 1. Alternatively, a debater could develop a list of search terms by perusing the topic paper that was presented to advocate for the resolution (for notes on this process, see Chapter 1) to help them recognize the key terms used for the search.

Where to Perform Research

After the list is created, decisions need to be made about where to begin looking. Depending on the type of information that the debater needs for their argument, certain places are going to be more helpful than others. In making their decisions about where to look, students should consider three important questions. First, how timely does my source have to be? Some current events that are debated change rapidly, sometimes even over the course of a few hours. Looking for a book will not help a debater if the argument is about one of those rapidly changing issues because books take a long time to publish. Second, how expert does the source have to be? If an issue is controversial having sources with a high degree of expertise can be very valuable, but most of those sources are unlikely to be journalists who are commenting on current events, so a debater will have to look for places where such an expert is more likely to publish. Third, how objective should a source be? This question is dealt with in a later section of this chapter about evaluating evidence quality, but for now, consider a debate about what the likely outcome of a change in U.S. nuclear weapons policy would be. A paper from a military officer defending the current policy might have a high degree of expertise, but that source is likely to be biased in favor of keeping current policies in place because a change might cost them their position.

There is unlikely to be a single source that is perfect for all of these issues. Instead, a debater should make priorities based on the nature of the argument they are making. If their argument is premised on something that might change rapidly, say the perceived popularity of the President, their best source might be a news article referencing a poll. The journalist who wrote that article might have limited expertise, and their writing might veer toward more of an opinion piece, but the timeliness of the article might be a more important consideration. By making decisions about what priorities a debater has, they can make better decisions about where and when to spend their debate preparation time.

The Internet

More than any other technological innovation in the history of policy debating, the development of the Internet has elevated the quality of argumentation. The ability to access more data, of higher qualities, than could ever be housed in a single university building has made policy debate as a practice infinitely more accurate in reflecting reality. Consider the kinds of intellectual maneuvers required to discuss nuclear weapons policy when the only sources available might be a book written during the Cold War available in the University library. This is the kind of problem that faced debaters prior to the Internet.

The Internet has also in specific debates had the opposite effect. For example, a debater plumbing the depths of the weirder parts of the Internet might, absent a discerning eye, find conspiracy theories applicable to their topic. As far-fetched as this phenomenon sounds, it has happened many times, and not just to debaters. When the author was teaching a public speaking course, they had to have a very serious discussion with a student who argued in their speech that the attacks on September 11, 2001, simply had not happened.[4] For debaters, this illustrates the duality of the Internet as a resource. It is both extremely valuable and risky unless the person performing the research is willing to be discerning.

Researching on the Internet using web browsers provides access to two types of sources that are extremely valuable, and a host of others that vary much more widely in quality. The first of those is journalism. If a debater wants the most up-to-date version of current events on an issue, the Internet provides the widest survey possible of writing on the topic. The ability provided with most browsers to filter results based on recency of publication makes this particularly potent. In recent years, the tendency of news outlets to place their articles behind paywalls has limited the utility of Internet searches somewhat, but clever debaters have found various workarounds for those paywalls including finding them using a browser search and then using databases accessed through their library to read them.[5] These journalistic sources are extremely valuable because they provide the most up-to-date information on the topic, but the authors may not be the most expert or objective on the topic.

The second great source available to students on the Internet are publications by the government or private entities, such as think tanks, intended to provide information to the public. These publications are likely to have elements of bias but can be extremely timely. More importantly, they tend to have information that is not available in other places. For example, documents produced by the Congressional Research Service[6] might not be reported on by journalists and so provide data that simply cannot be accessed in any other way. Especially for debaters who are new to researching the wide net afforded by browser-based searches provides the easiest way to locate many of these sources.

Outside of those two examples, there are a number of sources available on the Internet which vary a bit more in their quality but can be valuable. For example, blogs that are published by scholars can be very valuable because they often advocate for policies or positions that debaters will argue for and against. The problem is that blogs often include poorly evidenced ideas, and a lack of editorial oversight means the quality can vary widely. That is not to say that debaters cannot use these sources, but that they must be cautious and diligent in evaluating the quality of the source they are looking at. Additionally, the availability of these sources has generally declined as authors of popular blogs have started to follow the lead of journalistic outlets in putting their commentary behind paywalls.

This raises the question, how does one use the Internet effectively? To answer this question well requires some attention to be paid to the way most people access the Internet, which is through web browsers. Although there are a number of web browsers available, in the end, most of them function effectively the same way but can produce different results. Browsers work by performing their own automated searches of webpages and the links contained therein, which are subsequently indexed by the web browser so that when a user submits a search, they receive a list of websites relevant to their search. On clicking the link, the browser submits a request to that website for that information, which is then translated from a code script into the combination of text and image that the user sees. This process creates ample opportunity for different browsers to produce different results based on their specific index of websites. The ability of a browser to generate revenue from privileging returns from one website over another creates an additional opportunity for distorted results.

As a result, the Internet can be a very uneven place to perform research. This doesn't make it bad, but it requires debaters to be thoughtful about their process. A good practice is to perform searches using multiple different browsers and to use multiple different keywords when performing searches to ensure that the searches for specific issues are thorough and not simply the product of what a single platform has privileged.

Another useful tool is using web browsing tools specialized for academic use. For example, Google Scholar[7] excludes from its results any items that are not published in journals of one sort or another. This generally excludes results that have a strong profit motive and also ensures that the source has undergone some sort of editorial review. As such, it tends to ensure relatively high quality of sourcing. The one limitation for many of these browsing tools is that in order to read many of the articles the University that the debater attends must have access to the journal that houses the article. Where this access is not provided, one strategy is to request the article from the library, which requires a small delay.

No discussion of using Internet-based research would be complete without some discussion of one of the most popular sources for university students writing on a deadline: Wikipedia. As any student who has had to write a paper for any class already knows, if they have a question they can find something about it on Wikipedia. For the purposes of a debater, it is a helpful starting point to gather background information and especially to learn the terminology used in relation to an issue. More developed Wikipedia pages also include citations, which are themselves often great sources to read in a debate. The problem with Wikipedia as a source is twofold. First, the provenance of the information is uneven because the platform can be edited and not all of the editors are of comparable quality. Second, Wikipedia, much like the encyclopedias that it is increasingly replacing, rarely provides the sort of dialectical argumentation that is most useful for debaters. On a separate note, and perhaps more reflective of the perspective of classroom instructors who grade papers that cite Wikipedia, it appears lazy. Arguments that use Wikipedia as their dominant source simply do not appear to be the product of rigorous inquiry to most instructors and debate judges.

As stated at the beginning of this section, the Internet is an incredibly potent tool for debate research. For debate purposes, the ability to cast a very wide net and access sources that are otherwise unlikely to be available makes it extremely valuable. Nonetheless, there is good cause for concern because the quality of sources is a bit uneven. Debaters using the Internet would be well served to pay attention to the evaluating evidence section below.

The Library

If there is an underrated resource for collegiate debaters, it is the library housed on their campus. Although there are some campuses with better library systems than others, there are certain shared characteristics that make them an ideal place for starting research. The most universal of these is the existence of experts trained in finding information and directing others in how to find that information. These experts are known as librarians, and their job is to figuratively (and in some cases literally) know where the bodies are buried. Many students would be well served to start their research by asking a librarian what resources are best suited to researching their topic and where to locate them.

Beyond librarians, the library offers two resources that are otherwise unavailable to most students. The most obvious resource in most libraries is the collections of published works, including books (and their electronic variants) and academic journal publications. In most university libraries, the emphasis on physical collections is on the decline because the cost of purchasing and storing books and academic journals is perceived to be relatively high. This should not deter students from using them, but does change how students should approach them. The other resource is the database access provided by universities that allows access to resources that would otherwise be extremely expensive for students.

Library collections are less important for debate research than they once were because of the availability of journalistic sources that have occupied the role that used to be held by more scholarly sources. Nonetheless, for some issues, books are still an extremely helpful source. For example, on the topic that is the focus of this guide, there are a number of books published by scholars, military officers, politicians, and other researchers on the role of nuclear weapons in United

States foreign and military policy every year. The reason why the research is presented in a book format is because the book format enables a degree of in-depth discussion that is not available in other formats. As a result, debaters who take advantage of these sources are able to provide more specific and detailed insights than their peers. This is especially true for debaters who are more interested in making arguments that are critical of traditional approaches to United States nuclear weapons policy because much of the research following that topic is published by academic presses.

One concern that many students have is that the collection at the library on their campus is not especially well supplied. For example, students who attend polytechnic universities might find that the political science collection at their library is effectively non-existent. At essentially every university library in the United States, there are two solutions. One of those is the e-book collection, usually accessed by searching the catalog at the campus library. The other option is through an inter-library loan system, where the library on campus will procure copies of a book from other libraries to satisfy the needs of their students. As a general rule, if a book exists, using their campus library, any debater will be able to procure a copy.

The other incredibly potent tool available thanks to the libraries on a debater campus is database access. What these databases provide is the ability to access academic journals which provide what is generally speaking considered to be the most reliably high-quality evidence for debaters. The reasoning for this stems from the standard of proof for research to be published in an academic journal.

In order for an article to be published in an academic journal it must first be submitted and the editor of the journal will perform an initial vetting to see if the article is worthy of publication. Assuming the article meets this standard it is then submitted to at least three peer reviewers who will determine if the article is worthy of publication based on its merits. These reviewers do not know who the author is, and the author does not know who the reviewers are, so the article is judged based only on its merits. To proceed to publication the article must receive three affirmative reviews, often requiring multiple revisions and refinements. By the time this process has been completed an article has had an extremely thorough vetting. As a result, concerns about bias are reduced and while they may not be the most timely sources (this process can take months or even years) they tend to age well.

Because the databases that a debater may access vary widely from one institution to the next, an exhaustive list is not especially productive. One example that is very representative and widely available is JSTOR. JSTOR indexes articles very helpfully because while it contains articles from essentially every field from physics to communication studies, it offers the ability to narrow the search to disciplines so that as long as a debater knows the field where the issue they are arguing is discussed they can search more efficiently. This rapidly accelerates the search process and ensures very high quality sources. There are countless other databases, but all of them serve the function of providing access to high-quality sources without the debater being obliged to pay for expensive memberships.

Campus and Community

If there is an underutilized resource for collegiate debaters it is the community of experts available on their own campus. Admittedly, this will be very uneven across campuses, different schools have variations in their programs and research agendas and so the hiring of faculty might not be of universal quality. Nonetheless, most campuses have experts in most debate topics that students would be well suited to search out. Although personal conversations with faculty are typically not used as evidence in the debate (efforts at doing this in the past have generally not proved to be as fruitful as one might imagine), they can quickly help debaters get up to speed on what the various perspectives on an issue are. They also are a productive sounding board for new ideas that otherwise might be difficult to test.

The easiest way to access this community of experts is to search the webpages of departments relevant to the topic being debated. Most departments have pages that list the faculty and direct the user to personalized pages for those faculty. Scanning these pages can generally turn up faculty with relevant expertise that debaters can take advantage of. After identifying potentially helpful faculty the next step is to send an email inquiring about the ability to meet during a period of availability. Given that most faculty have extremely underutilized office hours, making arrangements is typically relatively easy.

A similar underutilized resource is experts from the community or relevant industries. In both cases, the lived experience of these sources gives them insight into issues that otherwise would be overlooked. To give an example, the author's father has sat on the board of a rural electric cooperative, a non-profit entity that provides electricity to a large area (not all of it rural), and is responsible for making a number of decisions including whether or not to install greater electric production capacity. In preparing for a debate topic the author consulted with his father on the merits of solar energy and learned that one of the major problems with increasing solar energy production has to do with zoning issues. Essentially, even when electric companies wish to increase solar energy production local opposition to building solar panels in the sort of large spaces required for efficient energy production is strong enough that a place to install the panels might be impossible to find because nearby residents and businesses will oppose the approval to zone the land for energy production. In much of the public-facing research on solar energy production this dilemma is not discussed in many sources because of the very local nature of the problem, but the author found enough evidence that it proved to be the basis for a number of fruitful arguments.

For students interested in more critical approaches to debate (discussed at greater length in Chapters 3 and 4), this can be a particularly productive avenue. Some teams have been well known for their use of thoughts, commentary, and insights from community members in shaping their arguments.[8] What these teams found was that a lot of issues, especially those that pertain to social issues, are not well reported on, studied, or publicly discussed outside of very local contexts. By seeking out locally situated knowledge to develop their arguments, these teams were able to focus the debate on issues that they understood better because their opponents had not done the challenging work of studying the lives of people in their community and the issues they faced.

These sources are a bit harder to find than university faculty. The best place to start is by identifying how the topic (which is usually more nationally oriented) would impact people in your community. This will give you some good clues as to what local groups or movements might be taking action on the local effects of the topic, and then allow you to start contacting leaders in those movements to see if they would be willing to share their ideas and information. This will likely take time, and it may not produce evidence that gets read in debates, so much as provide a language and personal connection to the topic, which can make you more effective.

To the extent that such sources would be used as evidence, some cautionary notes are in order. First, it helps give provenance to the source if their views are published. Otherwise, concerns about evidence fabrication (the unethical practice of debaters citing non-existent sources) can cause your source to be doubted. If that is not possible, the next best approach is to have a transcript of the conversation, which is available in full and made available to other debaters and judges. Second, it is important to be sensitive about the potential risks that helping you could create for your sources. For example, if the topic is about police reform, having a source in a community watchdog group can be helpful, but using their name might subject them to increased surveillance. When in doubt, a good approach is to use community sources only for background. Alternatively, starting by consulting with the Institutional Review Board of the debater's home institution and even submitting an application can be helpful for ensuring ethical research.

Evaluating Evidence

After a debater locates sources that can be used to provide evidence for their arguments, the next step is to evaluate evidence quality. In some ways, this is done before searching for evidence as debaters set priorities for what they need, but the last step has to happen while debaters are reading evidence to assess its quality. There are a number of variables at play in evaluating evidence quality, and making the determination about what is good and bad evidence is immensely context reliant. In performing their research, most debaters find far more pieces of evidence than they would ever read in a debate, so being discerning in evidence evaluation is essential to make sure that debaters read the best evidence available in their debates.

What follows are some general standards for what qualifies as good evidence, but it should not be taken as exhaustive, and there are times when even the most apparently obvious of these standards for good evidence could be counterproductive.

Correspondence

The primary role of evidence in debate is to provide external validation for the arguments that debaters make. This means that a good place for debaters to start evaluating the quality of a source is whether or not it actually supports the conclusion they are arguing for. This seems obvious but is a bit more complicated than it would initially seem. For example, often debaters find sources about the topic they will be arguing, but those sources do not share the conclusion that the debater is advocating. Can debaters use evidence from a source that supports their argument even if the author of the source doesn't share the debaters' conclusion?

The author observed a particularly stark example. A debater was arguing that left unaddressed social strife would tear the United States apart and a radical egalitarian shift in United States domestic policy was necessary. The source used to argue that social strife was tearing apart the United States was an extremely politically conservative academic that was explicitly opposed to the radical egalitarianism advocated by the debater. The author was left with a conundrum: was the debater's use of this evidence ethically sound? Certainly, the debater and their source agreed about the problem, but they dramatically disagreed about the solution.

A good rule of thumb in this sort of situation from the debater's perspective is to categorize evidence based on a correspondence principle. Meaning, how closely does the source adhere to the argument that the debater is making? A first-order correspondence refers to a source that shares the conclusion that the debater is advocating. The simplicity in defending this sort of evidence from criticism is obvious, and so it is generally considered to be of high value. A second-order correspondence would be a source that provides support for an argument but is not committed to supporting it. For example, a source might provide a statistic that supports the conclusion a debater is advocating, without taking a stance on the same conclusion. This sort of evidence is helpful but does require a bit more explanation to defend it as a helpful source because the correspondence is not so self-evident.

The third-order correspondence position is occupied by the hypothetical above. The source provides support for a claim the debater is advocating but reaches the opposite conclusion. For the debater avoiding this sort of situation is ideal. To the extent that a debater might choose to hazard the ethical dilemma, they must be prepared to explain to the judge why this source should be viewed as credible in its support of their argument. This is not impossible, the debater and their source do have an area of agreement, but it can be challenging, and if the difference is too extreme might create an additional problem.

Say the other team is aware of the disconnect between the debater and the source they are citing, they might respond in two ways. The first would be to argue that the source does not provide credible support for the argument, and so the judge should be skeptical of the claim advanced by the debater. The second would be to initiate an ethical challenge, alleging that a debater has deliberately used a source out of context with the intention to be deceptive. Essentially an allegation of a sort of plagiarism this argument is often treated in a similar manner. Different judges will handle such arguments differently, and some tournaments have explicit rules governing this process, but if such a claim is argued it can not only determine the outcome of the debate but damage the reputation of the offending debater.

When making determinations about the evidence they are defending debaters would be well advised to consider correspondence as a first criterion. More than a few students in college classrooms leave their papers for the last minute and work to pigeonhole the first sources tangentially relevant to their topic and manage to pass classes. Part of what makes debaters superior students is learning to research in an environment where competitors quickly pick up on such obvious errors. Taking the time to perform an honest assessment of source applicability is an essential part of the research process.

Expertise and Credentials

While debaters are ideally well-read and attentive to the world around them, they generally speaking are arguing about topics where they are not considered experts by a reasonable audience and so their claims lack credibility outside of the debaters own rhetorical gifts. So, to give their arguments a greater degree of credibility debaters rely on sources that are from qualified experts. For many judges, the relative expertise of the sources cited by debaters functions as a sort of tiebreaker in determining which side has won an argument, so the motivation to bring the most qualified sources to bear in an argument is very strong.

Expertise can come in many forms, and often what qualifies as expertise has more to do with the nature of the argument which is advanced. When the author is teaching public speaking classes he often has students deliver speeches about the importance of honey bees to maintaining agricultural production in the United States. These speeches almost universally begin with a quote from Albert Einstein which is almost assuredly not correctly attributed suggesting that without honey bees humans would go extinct.[9] The problem with attribution aside, despite Einstein's very publicly recognized genius as a physicist, his credentials as an entomologist (the title for someone who studies bees) are notably lacking. As might be imagined, the author is not especially impressed with such speeches.

In policy debate expertise tends to refer to one of two features that a source should have. The first is academic qualification (essentially advanced education that prepares the author of a source to perform research on the topic at hand) or experience addressing the issue at hand. The other is personal experience with the issue at hand. In the context of nuclear weapons policy, a nuclear scientist at a premier research institution might be a very good source if the question pertains to nuclear weapons technology, but a lack of experience working in or studying foreign policy means that on most of the issues around nuclear weapons policy, the scientist is not an expert. Balancing the need for academic qualification and experiential qualification is a common tension.

Some sources lack either experience or academic standing but nonetheless are used as sources in debates. A frequent example of this is journalistic writing. Journalists primary talent usually is in their ability to gather data and report a coherent story. As a result, interpreting their writing through the lens of expertise can be a bit misleading, in which case credentials might be a better way to think about expertise. For example, writing from a journalist in a major national publication is more likely to be considered well-credentialed than writing from say a student writing for their college newspaper. Although both writers are journalists, one of these publications lends a reputation to the author that increases the likelihood that their reporting would be trusted.

Of course, expertise can be overrated. Some sources are extremely well qualified, but turn out to be completely wrong in the long view of history. That said, absent hindsight and with a need to provide the best possible evidence, putting a degree of faith in the purported greater knowledge that an expert source has is reasonable. For debaters, finding the most well-qualified source is extremely valuable.

Objectivity

The question of objectivity in debate evidence is an extremely challenging one. The practice of debating, unlike the composition of essays or reports for most classroom purposes, requires advocacy because the role of evidence in a debate is to provide external validation for the position adopted by a debater. Sources which provide such validation often contain an explicit or implicit bias because the fact-finding process of the author of the source will naturally cause them to conclude that one side or the other is more accurate.. To the extent that an unbiased source exists, it likely is unbiased because it is trying to illustrate both sides of an issue without rendering a conclusion, not especially helpful if the evidence is supposed to provide support for a debater who is taking one side of an issue. Pursuing an idealized version of objectivity quickly becomes impractical.

When a debater is contemplating the objectivity of a source their goal should not be objectivity in the sense that the source doesn't have a bias. Rather, the source should be objective in that their information-gathering process is minimally encumbered by pursuit of the truth. For example, if a debater is arguing against a team that argues for a policy to limit climate change they might look for sources arguing that climate change is not a major problem. There are myriad sources that support that conclusion, but many of those sources are published and authored by think tanks which are supported by the fossil fuel industry. Because their funding comes from industries that would benefit financially from a lack of regulation to limit fossil fuel emissions which contribute to climate change, these think tanks are incentivized to minimize the problems posed by climate change.

The debater using evidence from a think tank that is funded by the fossil fuel industry is at a disadvantage, because while their opponent might not be able to articulate the specific inaccuracy in the evidence, the allegation of bias will cause the judge to distrust the think tank evidence. This does not on its own determine the outcome of the debate; there are generally more arguments involved, but by abandoning source objectivity, the debater who would use the evidence described above is behind not only in the comparison of evidence quality but also perceptually because it seems like their research practices are not representative of argument best practices.

This isn't to say such sources ought to be considered entirely off-limits. Biased evidence is often better than no evidence, and despite the apparent bias of the source, that doesn't make it inaccurate. Many debaters succeed in using evidence that has a strong bias by knowing how the source gathered its data and being able to articulate why that source's conclusion is sound. That said, objectivity is remarkably valuable.

Timeliness

Many policy debates are centered on very timely issues. For example, a debater might argue that a change in policy might impact an upcoming election that currently favors a desirable candidate. Because polling data, campaign strategy, and current events can change likely electoral outcomes overnight, winning this argument requires the debater to read the most timely evidence. Some debaters who rely on this strategy will even dedicate time in between debate rounds at tournaments to update their evidence and are well advised to do so because the time they spend updating this argument can often translate directly into winning debates.

All that glitters is not gold however. Often the sources that provide the most timely evidence are otherwise of low quality. For example, the most recent evidence that a candidate is winning might come from a poll that is released by that candidate's campaign to influence voters (called a push poll). This source would obviously have a strong bias and be less useful than older evidence. Often very timely sources are written by journalists who have little or no expertise and so they are not especially informative compared to more qualified sources. Finally, some issues change in small amounts day to day, but those small changes are not representative of a broader picture.

Consider a debater who needs to argue that the United States economy is doing poorly. They might find very recent sources that explain why a specific company declaring bankruptcy is a harbinger of a future decline in the United States economy. This might look like an appealing source, but if the majority of the news about the economy is positive leading up to the publication of that article, the conclusion it makes is unlikely to be representative. Older evidence that takes a broader view is likely to be more persuasive for many judges. So while timeliness matters, focusing only on timeliness can create problems in constructing a sound argument.

Cutting Cards

At this point a debater has developed a research agenda, put in their time gathering sources, evaluated it for quality, and is now ready for the last step of the research process colloquially known as card cutting. In this process what a debater will do is take the longer written sources that they have gathered and turn them into pieces of evidence stored in working files for each issue they have identified in their research agenda which can be turned into argument files which can be read in a debate. One of the persistent features of the most competitively successful debaters in the country is the ability to do this quickly, efficiently, and to retain the information in their evidence so that they can articulate it in a debate. For debaters looking for careers in research-intensive professions such as academia and legal practice, this is easily the most valuable skill provided in debate.

The card-cutting process for policy debate is defined by a balance of interests. One of those interests is in being able to use evidence in an academically rigorous manner, meaning that the sources that are used must be held to the same standards applied in a classroom. Another interest is argumentative, presenting the evidence in a way that lends credibility to the argument made by the debater. A third interest is accessibility, making the evidence a debater reads intelligible to their opponent and judge.

To begin card cutting a debater should develop a consistent template for presenting the evidence that is easy for the debater to read when delivering a speech, and easily shared with their opponents and the judge. A debater can use any approach for this they choose (there is no rule about what this should look like) but typically debaters use pre-existing templates. Typically these templates are essentially a series of macros that overlay a word processor, most commonly Microsoft Word.[10] What these templates do is enable more rapid processing of articles, websites, and scans of books into a format that is easy to read by debaters while delivering a speech and for the audience to follow along with while reading.

The first step is to read the source and identify a section that supports an argument that the debater believes it would be helpful to read from in the debate. These sections should always be kept in complete paragraphs, and often paragraphs below and after should be included. The reason for this is to ensure that there is no reason to doubt the context of the section which is being used in the debate. Otherwise, as a fellow debater or judge reads the evidence they may doubt that it is being authentically represented in the debate. Once a section has been identified it should be copied into the template that the debater has decided to use. Immediately upon copying the relevant section into the template, the debater should write a citation immediately above the text. That a citation should be created immediately upon copying a section of a source into a template cannot be stressed enough. Debaters have wasted countless hours copying sections of text into their template and then forgetting where those sections of text came from.

Citations for debate are a little bit different in format from most of the commonly used style guides (MLA, APA, Chicago) as a concession to the fact that debate speeches are delivered orally. As a result, the format will follow the model illustrated below:

Tannenwald 23

(Nina, Senior Lecturer in the Department of Political Science at Brown University; "It's Time for a US No-First-Use Nuclear Policy," in *The Sheathed Sword: From Nuclear Brink to No First Use*, Prakash Memnon & Aditya Ramanathan (eds.) 2023, Bloomsbury Publishing: New York, NY).[11]

In a debate, the speaker will read the top portion of the citation, which is the author's last name and year. In some cases, the qualifications might be read as well.[12] By setting the text at the top, the debater is helping make the citation easier for them to pick out, but by including other relevant citation information, the debater is making their source accessible to the audience. One addition to citations common to debate practice is the initials of the debater or coach who located the evidence. Although not always required, this is good practice so that if questions about the evidence arise, it is possible for the person who initially located it to be consulted.

After the debater has cited the evidence, they should perform a close reading of the text and underline all portions of the text relevant to the argument they are making. Doing this helps debaters quickly identify the relevant portions of the text more quickly and make necessary revisions. With this step completed, the initial processing of the source is completed, and the debater should extract more pieces of helpful text from the same source or move on to another.

After a debater has exhausted the sources that they have collected (or need a change from a repetitive task), the next step is to formulate their evidence into an argument. In the next chapter, there will be more discussion of what an argument entails, but in terms of completing the research task, it is simple enough to explain here. The debater will write above the citation a brief claim that they are advocating, which the evidence supports. This claim, referred to as a "tag," will likely be modified later, but now serves as a placeholder to help the debater know what argument the text supports. As a final step, the debater will identify the specific parts of the text (now known as a "card"), which they intend to read in a debate.

This last step, typically referred to as "highlighting" because debaters tend to use the highlighter function in their word processor emphasizes the contradictory needs for debaters to produce an argument efficiently while maintaining fidelity to the original piece of evidence. This can be a challenge because many authors will develop an argument over the course of several very long paragraphs and might write in especially challenging prose. The goal is to highlight it so that it can be read in a short period of time is difficult and there is a temptation to highlight single words out of whole paragraphs to produce an argument with any kind of efficiency. Standards for what sound practice looks like vary among debaters and coaches, with some teams developing a reputation for questionable highlighting of evidence that produces almost incoherent language when spoken.

A good rule of thumb is that when highlighting, a debater should always exclude language irrelevant to the claim they are making. Within the remaining text, a debater should always strive to speak a complete sentence, this does not mean the complete sentence is written (although it often does), for example, removing prepositions is not a problem because the meaning of the sentence is intact. In the sample card illustrated below, we can observe a simple example. Note how in this sample the debater is not reading each word in the selected text but is still delivering a speech that is intelligible and in keeping with the intent of the author.

INTERCONTINENTAL MISSILES ARE UNNECESSARY-SUBMARINES ARE PERFECTLY SECURE.

Snyder 18

(Ryan, Former Visiting Research Fellow at the Arms Control Association, "The Future of the ICBM Force: Should the Least Valuable Leg of the Triad Be Replaced?" Arms Control Association White Paper, March 2018, https://www.armscontrol.org/policy-white-papers/2018-03/future-icbm-force-should-least-valuable-leg-triad-replaced, ASH)

<u>A central</u>, if not the central, <u>**rationale for maintaining**</u> the <u>**ICBMs rests upon fears of vulnerability in the strategic nuclear submarine**</u> (SSBN) <u>**force**</u>.[8] If the SSBNs are unable to withstand threats to their survivability and deliver nuclear weapons to the homeland of an adversary, it is argued, then the ICBMs provide a backup to carry out that mission. **Absent any such threats, maintaining the ICBMs for the purpose of deterring nuclear attacks is** more **difficult to justify**. Concerns that technology may one day render SSBNs vulnerable have existed since nuclear weapons were first placed on submarines during the Cold War. And while U.S. SSBN vulnerability was last studied in the public domain several years ago, <u>**no prior scholarship has revealed any doubt about the survivability of the sea-based leg of the triad**</u>. Among these previous studies includes <u>**one**</u> 1983 <u>**paper**</u> by Richard Garwin that <u>**suggested the extraordinary demands of holding an SSBN in trail by passive acoustics**[9] **would not threaten the force, and**</u> in any case, that <u>**countermeasures would very likely deter the attempt**</u>.[10] Garwin further concluded that short-range sensors would be required by the "hundreds of thousands" to make the SSBN force vulnerable to attack.[11] A different study claimed that countermeasures are even easier to deploy against attempts to acquire an active acoustic trail and that such threats are easily neutralized.[12,13]

Beyond highlighting, there are other things that can be done to cue debaters on how to read evidence. Bolding text, boxing portions for emphasis, and shrinking the size of parts not being read are optional ways of adding emphasis that can help debaters read the evidence. What will matter most in the debate is that students are able to read an entire piece of evidence and that what they read will be accurately reflected when the evidence is shared with other teams.

After completing this process for the sources which have been gathered, the next step is to organize the evidence to have a complete working file so arguments can be constructed. At the top of the card in the illustration is a header that identifies the general topic of the evidence. The header corresponds to a tab on the navigation pane of the Word document (see the left-hand side of the illustration), allowing the debater to quickly identify pieces of evidence about the same topic and group them together. In the sample here, this is done by using a macro embedded within a template, but this same process can be done using the headings tool on most word processors.

A good step at this point is to use the navigation pane to identify places where the sources that have already been consulted might be a bit thin. Assuming the debater's file is a bit more filled out than the example here, they are ready to begin constructing an argument file. What is required for each argument is discussed at length in Chapter 3 for affirmative arguments and Chapter 4 for negative arguments. One helpful tip is to keep this working file separate from the arguments that will be produced from the evidence that has been gathered. Many pieces of evidence can help more than one side of the debate and can be used in several different arguments. Having a separate working file makes it easier to keep a more general version of the evidence handy for later tailoring to the argument needs of the debater.

Conclusion

By this point it has likely not escaped the readers' attention that this chapter on research is lengthy. One of the defining features of policy debate is that it emphasizes research and evidence-based argumentation. Although this can feel like a tedious process, it pays major dividends for debaters who are detail-oriented in performing their research. Some of these dividends take the form of competitive success, the debaters who have invested time to find the best available evidence to support their arguments win far more consistently. That said, it would be a mistake to think that competitive success is the only reason to invest substantial time in researching to prepare for policy debate.

Most topics that debaters research are outside the bounds of most collegiate classroom curricula, and as a result research is necessary not just to produce sound arguments, but to develop an understanding of the issues being debated. The research process provides debaters with an education that is more expansive than their peers in the classroom and includes the skills necessary to have a well-founded individual opinion, even on issues that seem unnecessarily pedantic. One of the author's former debaters has a particularly telling story.

As a debater they struggled with addressing a particularly obscure (to most people) French philosopher named Baudrillard. After graduation, they attended law school and found themselves working at a firm that argued before the Supreme Court. Much to this debater's chagrin, as a part of the briefs that this former debater helped prepare for the Supreme Court was an argument that drew on the same obscure French philosopher. There is of course an element of coincidence at play in this story, but it illustrates just how valuable the wide research net required for policy debating can be.

Notes

1 Alexander Hiland, *Presidential Power, Rhetoric, and the Terror Wars: The Sovereign Presidency* (Lexington Press: Lanham, MD, 2019).
2 Alexander Hiland, "Serving Our Students: Rethinking Novice Debate," *Argumentation and Advocacy 53*, no. 2 (2017): 120.
3 Some teams will begin research when the topic area is selected rather than waiting for a resolution. This approach can be effective in some cases, but the ability for the resolution to deviate from the focus in the topic paper can make this a risky strategy.
4 The student in question was not being facetious. They were completely earnest in their beliefs.
5 For legal reasons none of those will be discussed in this guide.
6 The Congressional Research Service is especially valuable for debaters because of its non-partisan public service role.
7 Easily accessed at scholar.google.com.
8 Shanara Reid-Brinkley, "Introduction: Celebrating the Legacy of the Louisville Project and Grappling with the Anti-Blackness Still Plaguing College Policy Debate," *Contemporary Argumentation and Debate* 38 (2023): 4–5.
9 Keith Delaplane, "On Einstein, Bees, and Survival of the Human Race," Beekeeping Resources, University of Georgia Bee Program, 2024. Accessed 4th March. https://bees.caes.uga.edu/beekeeping-resources/other-topics/on-einstein–bees–and-survival-of-the-human-race.html.
10 The most commonly used template is available at: https://paperlessdebate.com/verbatim/.
11 Nina Tannenwald, "It's Time for a US No-First-Use Nuclear Policy," in *The Sheathed Sword: From Nuclear Brink to No First Use*, eds. Prakash Menon and Aditya Ramanathan (Bloomsbury India: New York, 2023).
12 The most notable example of this is the American Debate Association National Tournament, which has a rule requiring qualifications to be read for all sources, although this rule is not necessarily the most rigorously enforced.
13 Ryan Snyder, "The Future of the ICBM Force: Should the Least Valuable Leg of the Triad Be Replaced?" Arms Control Association. March 2018. https://www.armscontrol.org/policy-white-papers/2018-03/future-icbm-force-should-least-valuable-leg-triad-replaced.

3
AFFIRMATIVE CASES

So with a sound understanding of the topic and the research process well underway, it is time to get started putting together the affirmative cases. The plural is used advisedly, as most students discover during their time in debate there is little in the way of absolute and incontrovertible truth. Moreover, the strategic value in tailoring arguments for diverse audiences suggests that rather than focusing on pursuing a single objectively true argument, most students eventually develop multiple different affirmative cases. That nuance aside, most debate teams begin by developing a single affirmative case, which can be expanded over the course of the season. The amount of time and effort required to put together an affirmative case, and the need for it to respond to the topic, rather than arguments made by other teams, typically means that writing an affirmative case takes much longer than putting together negative positions.

The affirmative case refers to the arguments that a debater is able to prepare for the affirmative side of the topic to be presented in the first affirmative constructive. Because, as will be discussed later, policy debating is focused on the desirability of the plan rather than the resolution, a case should represent a consistent set of arguments that do not contradict each other and will remain consistent over the course of the debate. For this reason, the best affirmative debaters have the ability to think not only about what the best first speech would be, but how that case can be improved over the course of a debate by responding to negative arguments.

This makes crafting a sound affirmative case uniquely challenging because it requires discerning and important choices to be made about a wide array of issues including how to rebut negative arguments while remaining consistent with the arguments presented in the first speech. Some other important considerations are the availability of good research, anticipated reactions from judges, educated guesses about the quality of negative arguments against a case, and in some important cases there are ethical components of the decision as well. Although as a rule this guide attempts to avoid taking a stance on those ethical decisions, many debaters will for good reason conclude that their cases should reflect their own reasoned beliefs. This is doubly true where the students wish to focus the debate on issues that are germane to the topic, if not necessarily the resolution (or for that matter issues that apparently have little to do with the topic).

In drafting this chapter, the author has deliberately attempted to provide a broad survey of how affirmative cases can and should be written. It does so because this chapter is intended to offer guidance not only in how to draft various different types of affirmative cases but also provide explanations of different types of affirmative cases for debaters to begin making sense of the cases other debaters have constructed. Despite the broad approach this chapter takes to case construction, debaters should view what is provided here as a starting point, rather than an all-inclusive summary. College debaters are remarkably clever and creative, and those who compete for long enough will surely devise or come across cases that are not covered here.

Understanding Arguments

The one rule that is true across all good affirmative cases is that they follow sound general principles of argument. For that reason, this chapter begins by offering a general guide to sound argumentation. It does so with a substantial caveat that it is an incomplete guide. Unbeknownst to many debaters, argument studies, rhetorical theory, performance studies, philosophy, informal logic, and countless other disciplines have valuable insights and theories about how arguments succeed or fail at persuading an audience. To put together a comprehensive guide to argumentation theory would require a herculean effort across multiple texts, rather than a single section in a guide that is geared towards practical preparation for policy debate.

The dominant model for argumentation used in debate is a simplified version of the Toulmin Model of Argumentation. Although it is exceedingly speculative to identify a single reason why this is the case, contrasting the Toulmin model with an alternative approach helps clarify why debaters find it useful. Suppose, for example, the goal was to ensure that an argument followed an idealized form, one strategy would be to present all arguments following the rules of formal logic.

In formal logic there are rules of inference that are required to be followed for an argument to be truthful, the two most common rules are described using the Latin titles "modus ponens" and "modus tollens." Both rules of inference rely on sequential reasoning, where one assumes that the statements of a premise are valid for the conclusion to be presumed. Below are two examples of arguments that follow such rules of inference.

Modus Ponens

Premise: If nuclear weapons are dangerous, we should disarm our arsenal.
Premise: Nuclear weapons are dangerous.
Conclusion: We should disarm our arsenal.

Modus Tollens

Premise: If nuclear weapons prevent war, then there will be no wars.
Premise: War continues to take place.
Conclusion: Nuclear weapons do not prevent war.

In both of the examples above, the formal rules of logic are followed. In the modus ponens example, while we can see that there are many reasons why disarming would be desirable if we grant the initial premise that the danger of nuclear weapons is sufficient to warrant disarmament, then those other reasons are inconsequential to the conclusion. In the modus tollens example, we see that the existence of war disproves the first premise that nuclear weapons prevent war. Arguments that other causes for war exist are immaterial to the conclusion that nuclear weapons prevent war. In both examples, what the reader quickly notices is that although this form of logic is present in many sound arguments, most people do not argue in such strict syllogisms. Instead, most arguments have more rich descriptive language and attempt to persuade through other means than appeals to formal accuracy of the syllogism. The reader will also note that determining the validity of these premises requires evidence, which formal logic does not account for. Instead, it assumes the accuracy of the premise to focus the analysis on whether the relationship between the premises of the argument and their conclusion.

This is not to say that formal logic is not helpful. Quality arguments are generally best served to follow the rules of formal logic to ensure that valid conclusions are reached. To illustrate this, consider how the errors possible in both rules of inference might produce a weak argument. For modus ponens, the error of inference is described as "affirming the consequent" meaning that the second premise affirms the second half of the first premise as illustrated below.

Affirming the Consequent

Premise: If nuclear weapons are dangerous, we should disarm our arsenal.
Premise: We should disarm our arsenal.
Conclusion: Nuclear weapons are dangerous.

The error illustrated above is illogical because while the conclusion may reflect reality, that reality does not follow the logic of the syllogism. Instead, the conclusion of the first premise is assumed even though the decision to disarm does not necessarily mean nuclear weapons themselves are dangerous. Indeed, there can be many reasons to disarm, of which the danger of nuclear weapons is only one. The inverse problem associated with modus tollens logic is described as "denying the antecedent" as illustrated below.

Denying the Antecedent

Premise: If nuclear weapons prevent war, then there will be no wars.
Premise: Nuclear weapons do not prevent war.
Conclusion: There will be war.

The error illustrated above is illogical because while nuclear weapons do not prevent war, it does not follow that war must necessarily ensue. In denying the antecedent, this argument would ignore the myriad possible causes of war that have nothing to do with nuclear weapons. In both of the examples of error illustrated above, the reader is tempted to accept the argument as accurately reflecting reality. Indeed, from a rhetorical perspective, they sound compelling even if their logic is unsound. Formal logic is helpful in that it can help an arguer think critically about whether the conclusion of their argument is derived from a true relationship between their stated premises. A useful activity for debaters as they compose cases is to sketch their argument as a syllogism like those presented above to test their validity.

The problem is that in practice most arguments do not follow a strict logical structure, or at the very least, trying to discern that structure can be challenging. Additionally, assuming the validity of the premises of the argument ignores the responsibility of the arguer to demonstrate that the premise is valid. To account for these problems while both enriching and simplifying the process of analyzing argument a field of inquiry known as informal logic has developed. The Toulmin model is a product of this field of inquiry that is intended to account for all of the common components of an argument.

In the Toulmin model, an argument consists of six essential components: A claim, ground, warrant, backing, qualifier, and rebuttal.[1] Astute readers will immediately notice that when they hear a person make an "argument," they almost never hear a speaker articulate all of these components. In part, that is because this model is designed to emphasize describing all the parts of an argument that can be made, and in part this is because there is a slippage between what we might colloquially call an "argument" and an "argument" in a more formal and scholarly sense.

In its most linear form, an argument following the Toulmin model begins with a claim, which is the truth proposition that the speaker believes to be true for the purposes of the argument. A claim on its own is not an argument, because it lacks reasoning to support it, and might best be understood as an opinion. To make this opinion into an argument, the speaker is obliged to provide what Toulmin describes as a "ground" meaning a basis for believing the claim. That a speaker is able to articulate a claim and a ground is not yet sufficient for an argument, as the relationship between the claim and ground must itself be rooted in some sort of reasoning. The explanation of the relationship between the claim and the ground is described as a "warrant."

Where these three parts are present, what otherwise might simply be described as an opinion is transformed into an argument. It should be noted, that present does not necessarily mean uttered. One of the often more confusing aspects of the Toulmin Model is that it was developed with a sensitivity to the possibility that audiences may be familiar with an idea before it is argued. So, an otherwise incompletely uttered argument might become complete through the audience filling in the blanks. This concept of an incomplete utterance, but complete argument is usually described as an enthymeme, an argument that does not need all of its logical premises stated because the topic is so well trod that the audience can induce the conclusion.[2]

That an argument has all of its necessary components does not mean that we have accounted for all that can be accomplished in an argument. For policy debate purposes, an especially important part of an argument is what Toulmin describes as "backing," which refers to evidence used to support either the ground or the warrant. In practical terms for debaters, backing is typically provided by the evidence used to support the argument. There are some potential other types of backing, for example, appeals to evidence such as historic examples, but to provide an added sense of credibility, most debaters would rather have a piece of evidence from another author explaining the historic example. Thus, for the most part, backing is used to refer to the external evidence provided to support an argument.

The last part of the model that is typically used in policy debate is the "qualifier," which is used to provide an assessment of an argument's likely certitude. Typically, a qualifier is expressed in the claim, where a debater will articulate the gravity of the argument. For example, the affirmative might make a claim that "strategic ambiguity is dangerous and increases the likelihood of conflict." In this example, the term "increases" is a modal qualifier that indicates that strategic ambiguity will make conflict more likely, but is not a guarantee. By extension, the affirmative is making a claim that the effort made to eliminate strategic ambiguity is going to probably decrease the likelihood of conflict. It is not a guarantee, but instead a probabilistic claim that is theoretically speaking more likely to be true.

It is worthwhile to ask the question, why use a qualifier of the goal of an argument is to present an absolute truth? The short answer is that rarely is an argument absolutely true, because the world is simply too complicated to hold to such absolute truths. As a result, there is a need to argue using probabilistic claims so that we are more likely to be correct. In our example, it would be easy for the other side to point to the fact that there have been very few wars between nuclear-armed powers, and so it is hard to say that strategic ambiguity makes conflict inevitable or unavoidable. The "increases the likelihood" qualifier has a better chance of accurately reflecting reality because even though that sort of conflict is infrequent, that does not preclude the possibility that strategic ambiguity increases the risk of conflict. Beyond the simple utility of making more accurate arguments, the qualifier really serves a protective function for the arguer's credibility. If the debater is perceived as arguing in an excessively polemic manner defending unrealistic claims, it undermines the perception that they are adopting a well-reasoned stance. The use of qualifiers addresses this problem by preserving the apparent thoughtfulness of the arguer.

Much to the frustration of more scholarly inclined debate coaches, policy debate has developed its own version of the Toulmin model. In this version, the ground and warrant are collapsed into the term "warrant." As a practical matter this condensation is not altogether unreasonable as in many arguments both inside and outside of debate the warrant is not explicitly stated. Moreover, to the extent that "warrant" is often used to connote having a reason, the condensation of terms is at least intuitive, if not especially dogmatic to the Toulmin model, which guides much of contemporary policy debate practices.

A further condensation common to policy debate is that the evidence read by debaters is responsible for providing not only the backing but also the warrant (in the sense of the term common to policy debate). This is especially true of the constructive speeches and first rebuttals, where debaters are trying to give evidentiary support for the positions they have taken. A dogmatic approach to argument theory might suggest that this means much of policy debating is an appeal to authority, and in a certain sense that is accurate but the negative connotation that might be attached to such appeals is misplaced. Policy debate as an activity requires debaters to argue about issues that they by definition have limited expertise about, so that they may become more expert. To rely on the insights of at least ostensibly more informed sources is a pragmatic solution to the lack of special qualification that most debaters have.

For this reason, most arguments made in the constructives in policy debate, and affirmative cases in particular, follow a consistent format. The cards that were produced during the research process described in the previous chapter are modified so that the "tag" is now rewritten as the claim for an argument, and then the evidence is read to provide a warrant. Each of these pairs of claims and cards constitutes an "argument" in the Toulmin sense, and when paired together are also an "argument" in the sense that they represent a series of claims that are intended to persuade the audience (in this case a judge) to reach a conclusion.

Stasis

In policy debating, there is one specific component to argument theory that is especially important. This concept, known as stasis, defines what claims an affirmative needs to make. The term stasis for argumentation theory diverges substantially from what is typically found in the dictionary. Originally derived from Aristotle's discussion of legal speech[3] where stasis refers to the nature of the argument contested, in policy debate, stasis is a term used to describe the specific claims that the affirmative must prove in order to win a debate (and subsequently what the negative must disprove). There is no universal agreement about what stasis entails for the affirmative (and for the negative). Instead, there is a collection of theories about what the affirmative must prove, which generally guide the construction of affirmative cases. Having a sense of what these theories look like can be helpful for making strategic decisions about how the affirmative case is constructed.

One approach that used to be supremely dominant argued that the affirmative had the burden to satisfy certain "stock issues" in order to win the debate. This approach has a dual heritage both in the debate tradition[4] and an academic tradition where it is used to analyze public address.[5] In traditional stock issues analysis, the affirmative was required to argue and prove favorably, five elements of their case. There has historically been some variation in what the title of these five elements are but today they are most commonly referred to as Inherency, Harms, Significance, Solvency, and Topicality.

Inherency arguments are claims that the status quo exists for a specific reason and that it cannot address the issues which will be raised by the affirmative case. These barriers are either a product of the law (termed structural inherency), persistent attitudes or beliefs (termed attitudinal inherency), or because of a lack of decisive action (termed existential inherency). Although at various times in debate history there have been arguments that the affirmative must convince the judge that the case satisfies all three inherency barriers, in modern practice it is generally assumed that succeeding at one inherency argument is sufficient to justify an affirmative ballot. An example within the topic that has been the focus of this text would be an argument that the current doctrine for nuclear posture in the United States is defined by strategic ambiguity, which makes a declaratory policy a dramatic redirection of beliefs about the role of nuclear weapons. In this example, there is no structural barrier at play, but the plan is nonetheless a radical departure, so an overemphasis on strict approaches to inherency is an impediment to reasonable debating.

Harms arguments articulate the problems that exist in the status quo or will exist without a change in policy. If the affirmative fails to identify a problem, then they have failed to demonstrate a reason why a change is desirable. When presented in a case, the harm arguments are usually presented alongside significance arguments. Significance arguments explain why the harm is substantial enough to make a change in policy desirable. This argument is included in the stock issues because otherwise the affirmative would not be required to illustrate a problem that is substantial and could win by defending a change in policy that is so minor that it is indistinguishable from the status quo. For example, the affirmative might argue that current United States nuclear policy relying on a nuclear triad is extremely expensive. That it is expensive is not necessarily a problem until the affirmative proves that this expense has created a substantial problem.

Solvency arguments are claims that the plan is sufficient to solve the problems articulated in the affirmative case. The term sufficient is used very intentionally because proving that a plan is necessary does not mean that the problem is resolved, and if the problem cannot be resolved, then the plan is not itself desirable. This is not to say that the direct action of the plan must always solve the problem. For example, the affirmative can argue that a change in United States nuclear posture will cause other countries to shift their own policies, which would solve for the harms presented in the case.

To this point, these four stock issues are typically presented in the affirmative case. The fifth stock issue, topicality, is typically not argued until the second affirmative constructive. As a stock issue, topicality is the expectation that the affirmative presents a case that affirms the topic. In a prior era, this would be accomplished by requiring the affirmative to read definitions and interpretations of the topic to demonstrate their case fit the topic. This practice has fallen by the wayside, as judges generally drifted toward an approach that required the negative to challenge the affirmative because the case was presumptively topical. Today, arguments that the affirmative plan affirms the topic are typically done less from a global perspective and more in refutation to specific arguments from the negative that the plan does not affirm the topic.

Topicality is a complicated issue for affirmatives because, as discussed in Chapter 1, policy debate resolutions are written very broadly to help sustain a year of competitive debating. For the affirmative to demonstrate all possible policies that can be imagined under the wording of the topic are desirable is unrealistic given how broad the topics are. As a result, the affirmative is allowed to interpret the resolution as a "parameter" or boundary for what the affirmative can advocate, a theory known as parametrics. When challenged by the negative, the affirmative is obligated to prove that their plan falls within the parameters of the resolution by either arguing that they meet the interpretation of the topic suggested by the negative or because their case meets a superior interpretation.

How affirmatives should construct their cases to satisfy these stock issues will be discussed in a later section. When considering a stock issues approach, debaters should be sensitive to the evolutionary arc that stock issues debating has undergone. In earlier eras, the debate focused almost exclusively on whether the affirmative had met their stock issues burdens, because if the stock issues were met by the affirmative, then the plan had been proven desirable. As a result, some negative teams eschewed even presenting reasons why the affirmative policy was undesirable focusing instead on arguing that the case had not satisfied the stock issues.

Over time, while the stock issues remained important, negative strategy diversified substantially. The reason for this is relatively straightforward, an excessive devotion to focusing on stock issues makes it very easy for the affirmative to win because they only have to prove their case, not address the problems that enacting it might create. So negative teams diversified their strategies to include arguing for disadvantages to the affirmative case, questioning philosophical assumptions of the affirmative case, and proposing alternative policies to the affirmative plan.

In response, alternative approaches to stasis developed to account for the fact that the completeness of the affirmative case was not the only matter to be debated. To account for this, other issues have come to be included in stasis, with the most common being loosely termed "desirability" meaning that the affirmative has the burden to prove that their policy is preferable to any alternative offered by the negative. This approach to stasis has had the obvious benefit of giving the negative more strategic options in the debate and also has pushed affirmative debaters to seek out the best policy to defend. This has created a general trend toward affirmative teams defending more expansive policies as a favored strategy because the affirmative can leverage more significant impacts in their arguments against policies advocated by the negative.

One of the artifacts in this shift has been an increased emphasis on debating whether the affirmative's policy suggestion should be adopted, rather than whether the suggestion could be adopted. The term used to describe this notion, "fiat," in practice refers to an agreement that the object is to debate whether the affirmative should be adopted, rather than its likelihood of being adopted. This is an important feature of policy debate given the various forms of gridlock and obstructionism that define politics in the United States. Using our current topic as an example, it is hard to conceive of the sort of political, popular, and military acquiescence necessary for the United States to disarm its nuclear arsenal ever coming about. Nonetheless, in order for a debate to take place, it is necessary to imagine that just such a thing could come to pass, and so policy debate accepts the notion that the affirmative team can "fiat" a policy into existence. The flip side of this argument is that the negative loses the ability to win the debate by arguing that the affirmative plan would never be enacted, but arguing that the policy is unworkable could still be used to call into question the ability of the affirmative to achieve solvency, as discussed above.

There are some debates where stasis changes significantly. Some affirmative teams will defend cases that either defend the general suggestion of the topic (but not the resolution), or argue about issues that are outside of the parameters of the topic (and by extension the resolution). Where this happens, the affirmative is tacitly arguing against a traditional approach to stock issues derived from the resolution and is suggesting a different approach to stasis. These cases will posit alternative criteria for determining when the affirmative has met its argumentative burden typically defined by satisfying a political, intellectual, or social condition that the affirmative team argues is of greater value. These cases are usually described as "critical affirmatives" and will be discussed at length in a later section.

A similar approach is found in affirmative cases, which tend to loosely go under the label of "performance" affirmatives. This title is a bit of a misnomer because all utterances are in a general sense a performance, but these cases differ in that they often will not use the explicit and didactic model of argumentation described above. Instead, debaters might use poetry, music, dance, or other modes of communication to attempt to persuade their judge. A common complaint about these approaches to argument is that there is no clear stasis for what the affirmative must prove to win the debate. This complaint is perhaps a bit hasty; in general, these debates tend to follow the same practices as those found in critical affirmative cases. Namely, after a challenge from the negative that the case does not affirm the topic, the affirmative team will identify a different stasis condition that they believe is of greater value, which is satisfied by their case.

Despite the importance of stasis and stock issues for understanding what the affirmative must argue, as a general rule, stasis and stock issues appear only infrequently as an explicit topic of discussion in debates. The primary reason for this relatively infrequent appearance is that as policy debating evolved there developed a tendency toward at least tacit consensus about how the debates ought to proceed. Rather than debating the sort of deep theory explicated in this section about what the affirmative must argue in a case, the trend has been toward debating the desirability of the plan presented in the case. There are exceptions, some of which will be spelled out in Chapter 4, but as a general rule understanding stasis and stock issues is most helpful in understanding how to compose an affirmative case.

Strategic Considerations

The composition of an affirmative case is a very time-intensive endeavor, and as a result, the decisions which are made in drafting the affirmative case are disproportionately weighty. In composing this guide, the decision to put research ahead of case composition was very intentional, because trying to write an affirmative case without knowing how it fits within the broader context of the topic can result in an immense amount of time spent pursuing arguments that are remarkably weak. For the same reason, before an overinvestment in a specific affirmative case is made there are some strategic considerations that need to be evaluated.

The first consideration is simple. Based on the research collected to this point, which affirmative case seems most likely to be true? This might seem exceedingly obvious, but in practice, this is both challenging to discern without recourse to prior value judgments on the part of the debater and less determinative than it might otherwise seem. Some of the most obviously desirable policies are difficult to explain in a timely manner, and so time limits for affirmative speakers make defending even the best policies a challenge. Some ideas are very good, but face so many different forms of criticism that defending them against all opposing arguments overextends a debater. Some policies are obviously desirable, but the research to support them is less well developed than the evidence to support them thanks to countermanding economic incentives. This is not to say truthfulness is not a valuable quality in an argument, but that from a strategic perspective, it is only one consideration.

The second consideration is the intellectual interests of the debater. Different cases raise different issues, and the personal interests of a debater are an important consideration as well because it is easier to invest time and energy learning about issues that a debater is interested in. For many debaters contemplating making arguments that fall into the category of "critical" or "performance" arguments which do not engage the topic from the policymaking perspective, this is a primary motivator and a perfectly sound one, but it may put the debater on the weaker side of some other considerations.

The third consideration is the scope of the affirmative case, meaning how many issues are organic to the case. For example, a case with a large scope may claim a more diverse array of advantages over the status quo, enabling the team to read many different versions of the same case to keep the negative team off balance. On the other hand, a case with such a large scope is generally apt to have a diverse array of disadvantages, which the affirmative must be ready to address. By contrast, an affirmative case with a narrow scope might only have a small number of advantages that it can claim, but the list of negative arguments is similarly small. This can help focus preparation on perfecting arguments, rather than preparing a large number of arguments. This is especially true for debaters who are interested in arguing for "critical" or "performance" style affirmatives because by eschewing the more predictable arguments focused on the topic, these affirmatives force the negative into debating the legitimacy of the affirmative as an argument, narrowing the scope of the debate substantially.

The fourth consideration is what the impacts of those issues are. For example, if an affirmative plan is only able to address issues with very long-term impacts, the case might not be successful at responding to negative cases which emphasize very short-term impacts. This is a common feature of cases that focus on the environmental impacts of a policy because although those issues are important, the adverse effects of poor environmental policy tend to be felt in the long term while the risks (usually described in economic terms) tend to be felt very quickly. Thinking about what impacts can be argued in a case is important to ensure that the case is competitive against likely negative arguments.

A fifth and final consideration is what judges pre-existing views of the case are likely to be. For example, if a debater chooses to argue a critical or performance style case, they may not be able to be persuasive to as many judges. A case that adopts an unpopular position on policy issues may face an uphill battle. None of these are reasons to reject a case out of hand, but they should be a part of the decision-making process. One example here is quite poignant. When the author was coaching on a topic that asked the affirmative to defend expanding energy production their team chose to defend expanding oil exploitation in the United States. This ran counter to the general preference held by many judges for expanding alternative energy, but the sheer volume of different issues and impacts that could be addressed by expanding oil production meant that even though it was a less popular policy among many judges, arguing that case was very easy and the team saw great success.

The Affirmative File

After a decision has been made about which case will be written, the next step is to pursue the research process necessary to complete the arguments. As discussed earlier in this chapter, the norm for most arguments is to have a piece of evidence that provides the warrant for each claim that will be made. If a debater is following along with this guide, they have already started this process and have compiled at least some evidence to begin constructing their case. From this point on, the research is more narrowly targeted to supporting the affirmative case that the debater has chosen to compose. This usually means alternating between finding evidence that the debater then turns into an argument, and the debater intuitively knowing what an argument should be, and finding the evidence to support it.

The aim at the end of this research process is to produce a file that has three parts that will constitute an affirmative file. The first is the affirmative case, which will be presented in the affirmative constructive. The second is additional advantages for the affirmative case, which can be read in the second affirmative constructive or be substituted into the first affirmative constructive. The third is the arguments which will be used to rebut the negative arguments which will be read in the second affirmative constructive, and if the affirmative team is well prepared, first affirmative rebuttal. The aim of an affirmative file is to create a "one stop shop" for all affirmative arguments which will be read in the debate.

In constructing the affirmative file, the most important task is to take the cards, or pieces of evidence, which have been collected and turn them into arguments. First, the cards from the working file are copied into a new document and re-organized by changing the headers to reflect the part of the affirmative file to which they correspond. Second, the tags that were created for the working file are rewritten as claims for the evidence so that when read sequentially, they constitute a complete portion of the affirmative case, an additional advantage, or response to a negative position. At this point, the affirmative file is completed.

To get to this point may seem like an arduous process for many debaters. In practice, it tends to go much more quickly than it seems, especially as debaters gain their own experience they will identify their own ways to streamline this process. The explanation provided here is intentionally step-by-step and broad to provide the best advice for new debaters without over-emphasizing differences in preparation for each of the case types. Nonetheless, the details of what an affirmative case looks like can vary substantially depending on the type of affirmative case that a debater chooses to advocate as well as rhetorical choices about how to present an argument.

Policy Cases and Files

Older debate textbooks geared toward policy debate emphasized fine distinctions between different ways that policies could be advocated, discussing topics like whether a case should be framed as a "meets needs" or "comparative advantage."[6] In contemporary debate, these distinctions have largely faded away, and now most policy debate cases are essentially similar in their organization. This is mostly a product of custom rather than a change in thinking on what constitutes a complete affirmative case.

The affirmative case is presented in the first affirmative constructive, and must at the same time be coherent as a speech while at least implicitly satisfying the stock issues described above. To do this, most debaters will use what public speaking teachers will describe as "signposts," meaning a title given to a part of the speech to help the audience. In the context of the sort of specialized audience common to intercollegiate policy debate, these signposts refer to the stock issues.

The first portion of the case is an inherency argument. Typically this is a very short part of the affirmative case because it is very rare that the negative will argue that the affirmative is not a change from the status quo. Usually, it consists of a single piece of evidence that articulates what the current policy under the auspices of the resolution is. For example, if the affirmative is advocating a policy of no-first-use for the United States nuclear forces, the affirmative might claim that the current United States policy is defined by strategic ambiguity[7] for the use of nuclear weapons and read a single piece of evidence to that effect.

The second portion of the affirmative case is usually signposted as an "Advantage" to signal to the judge that the debater is making a combination harm and significance argument. An advantage articulates a problem with the status quo, which the plan would purportedly solve. As a general rule, this requires a causal argument because what in public discourse might otherwise obviously seem to be a problem, debate sets a higher standard for articulating the specific consequences of that problem. For example, the affirmative might argue that a continued reliance on nuclear weapons to deter potential adversaries creates incentives for other countries to develop their own nuclear weapons. The idea of expanded nuclear arsenals worldwide seems intrinsically dangerous, but such an advantage doesn't have a clear consequence or significance. As a result, the affirmative case is obliged to articulate a specific consequence for the "horizontal proliferation"[8] of nuclear weapons.

So to extend our example, the argument might proceed with the following claims (and evidence providing a warrant for each). The United States current policy of strategic ambiguity for when it would use nuclear weapons serves to provide deterrence but incentivizes other countries to develop their own nuclear arsenals to defend themselves. The development of nuclear weapons is dangerous because the rapid development and deployment of nuclear weapons make it extremely challenging to put in place safeguards against the accidental use of nuclear weapons. The accidental use of a nuclear weapon will cause other countries with nuclear weapons to use their own arsenal because of a perceived need to defend their own populations. This would cause a large-scale nuclear war, which could threaten the future of humanity.

Critics of this line of argumentation might rightly point out that the consequence might be exaggerated, and it does sound like a slippery slope. The slippery slope charge is inaccurate, remember, in our hypothetical the affirmative has evidence for each claim. The exaggeration argument is perhaps more realistic, but let's say the negative succeeds in arguing that other countries would not respond to an accidental use of nuclear weapons by using their own arsenal. They are left arguing that a mass casualty event caused by the accidental use of nuclear weapons is of no consequence, a challenging proposition.

This illustrates the general tendency of advantage arguments, which is to rely on a causal chain and offer the affirmative the ability to defend the advantage even if they do not necessarily retain the ability to claim the most catastrophic consequences. It also illustrates a growing trend, where rather than having a separate part of the affirmative case which makes an inherency argument, the same claim that would otherwise be an inherency argument is articulated in the advantages. The reason for this is relatively simple that most affirmative advantages will be weighed against negative arguments that the plan has undesirable outcomes, described in the following chapter as a disadvantage. In the context of a disadvantage, the arguments about the current state of affairs are described as uniqueness, but serve a similar role to inherency arguments in that they describe issues as they are.

Here questions of argument strategy begin to enter into the picture. An affirmative which defends a single advantage carries a remarkable risk because if that one advantage is disproven, the negative would win the debate, as there is no reason why a change in policy is desirable. For this reason, most affirmatives claim more than one advantage and also strive to have each advantage claim more than one consequence so that even if the negative wins some arguments, the negative can still win the debate. While bound by time, the affirmative strategy is premised on articulating as many advantages as can be well defended in the nine minutes allotted to the first constructive while providing the third and fourth parts of the affirmative case.

The third component is the "plan." The plan is an articulation of what the specific affirmative policy will be. Historically, the affirmative was obligated to spell this plan out in great detail, including such issues as which specific agencies were responsible for enacting the new policy, what the specific mandates for the new policy would be, which agencies might enforce the policy, how it would be funded, and any additional provisions which might be required such as legislation that might have to be repealed.[9] In recent years, this sort of thorough plan explanation has declined substantially. There are at least two reasons for this. The first is that by taking a stand on any of those issues, the affirmative is granting the negative the ability to say that the plan is desirable except for those specific provisions. The second is that such specificity is rarely helpful in most debates because if the negative raises such questions in their constructive speeches, the affirmative can address them in a manner that is more strategic after the complete picture of the negative arguments is available.

The common practice today would have a plan read as follows: "Resolved: The United States Federal Government should adopt a no-first-use nuclear policy." The idea behind this simple sentence is to include the terminology of the resolution, to avoid claims by the negative that the affirmative is not relevant to the topic while retaining some flexibility to specify what the policy entails in later speeches. This approach is not without risk, the negative might argue that this plan is so vague as to be meaningless, which is unfair to expect the negative to dispute or would be impossible for the United States to enact as a policy. Such arguments are discussed more in the following chapter, but as a general rule tend to be less persuasive than might be imagined, and so most affirmatives err in the direction of vagueness.

The fourth part of the policy case is signposted as "solvency" and contains arguments about how the plan would solve the advantages. To continue our example, a claim in a solvency debate might be that "The United States adopting a no-first-use nuclear policy would reassure other countries that they are not immediately threatened, this would make developing a nuclear arsenal an unnecessary expense for other countries." These claims are warranted in accompanying evidence to complete the argument. In most affirmative cases the expectation is that at least one piece of solvency evidence would be read for each advantage. In many cases, it is strategic to make more than one solvency argument for each advantage so that if one of the arguments is disproven, another can be made.

Thus concludes the affirmative case, which would be read in the first constructive. An astute reader will note that this is a lot of argumentation to complete in 9 minutes. This is part of the reason for why many debaters develop a rapid delivery style, to allow them to make more arguments in the limited time available to them. A sample of this basic sort of affirmative case is available in Appendix A. In looking at this sample the reader will note that this abbreviated version has all the features of a traditional policy case but is not especially strategic in that it only has one advantage and has only a single impact and solvency card. A superior version would likely have a greater breadth and depth of arguments available.

The affirmative file is not yet complete; there are two steps remaining. The first of these is simple enough with the already extant information. Most affirmative cases are well advised to prepare additional advantages to be read in the second affirmative constructive. Such advantages serve two important strategic functions. The first is to provide additional reasons to vote affirmative should the negative effectively rebut those presented in the first affirmative constructive. This is a rare necessity but does happen from time to time. The second reason is more common, which is the negative proposes a distinct policy (discussed as a counterplan in the following chapter) that might address the same issues as those posed by the affirmative case. In this situation, the affirmative might choose to read a different advantage, which the negative's policy cannot address. The aim in constructing this additional advantage, or "add-on," is to provide a reason that is sufficiently different from those presented in the initial affirmative case that extant negative arguments will not address it, and so gain a comparative advantage.

The second more complicated task is called "blocking" and is addressed in Chapter 6. Essentially, this refers to the process of preparing the responses to the likely negative arguments against the affirmative case. It is important during this process to keep in mind that the goal of the affirmative is to in the last speech be able to persuade a judge that the plan has a comparative advantage. The best affirmative teams approach the negative arguments thinking about how the arguments embedded in the affirmative case can be leveraged against the best negative arguments. This means that in addition to preparing responses to negative arguments, good affirmative files will have evidence to provide additional warrants for their case, called "extensions."

At the end of this process, there is a file that contains the affirmative case, additional advantages, and responses to the negative arguments. This process is the same regardless of the line of argumentation that a debater decides to pursue on the affirmative. That said, other types of affirmatives require a different line of argumentation and by extension have to be organized and argued differently.

Critical Affirmatives

As discussed above, there are some affirmative cases that are not organized around or argued in the same manner outlined above. Going loosely under the category of "critical affirmatives," these arguments can be very similar to the type of affirmative above, or radically different. To the extent that they can be very similar they might defend a plan which affirms the topic, but the advantages are derived from a different intellectual milieu than most public policy literature. To the extent that they differ they may have little or nothing to do with the topic altogether. As a result, the term critical affirmative is decidedly loose, and a more precise categorization of these affirmatives and what they entail is necessary.

What unites critical affirmatives as a type of argument is that they draw on what is described as "critical theory." This is a loose term that at its most basic level is used to refer to theories that are critical of the current political, economic, cultural, social, etc. norms which define the world we live in. One way to think of it is in terms of academic disciplines. For every discipline, there are theories that constitute the generally received wisdom of that discipline, and then there are theories that are critical of that received wisdom. For example, there might be a theory of international relations, such as realism, which has a series of postulates about how countries will act. A critical theorist might argue that this theory is flawed because it overemphasizes the role countries play in international relations, and that this approach marginalizes ethnic groups who do not have exercise sovereignty in their own country. If there is a defining feature of these theories, it is that they are able to articulate the otherwise injustices of the world we live in and posit that continuing the norms of that world perpetuate injustice.

In the context of debate, critical affirmatives use the insights from such theories to warrant arguments that are most easily categorized by their approach to the topic. For a critical affirmative that seeks to affirm the topic through the traditional parametric approach, critical theory provides an evidentiary basis for the affirmative plan. This evidence stems from a literature base which is inflected by an ethically inflected approach to social issues that puts the negative

Affirmative Cases 51

in the uncomfortable position of defending an apparently unjust world. Because this affirmative otherwise holds with the norms for how affirmative cases are advocated, they are relatively easy to explain and avoid some of the complications posed by advocating other critical cases.

An example that one might see on the topic which has been discussed at length in this text would argue that the possession of nuclear weapons by the United States perpetuates a form of nuclear apartheid, allowing the United States to suppress the advancement of other nations through the impending threat of nuclear force. Such an affirmative might argue that unilateral disarmament of the United States nuclear arsenal would solve the problem. When the negative argues that this policy would collapse the deterrent capability of the United States, the affirmative can respond by saying that the arguments adopted by the negative are an example of the sort of nuclear apartheid that their case criticizes. By addressing the philosophical problem of nuclear weapons policy, the affirmative places the negative in the difficult argumentative position of defending the justness of the system, which the more policy-oriented arguments of the negative are ill-suited to do.

Another variety of critical affirmative will generally agree with the affirmative side of the topic but will eschew reading a specific plan of action. For example, one such affirmative might agree that the United States should disarm its nuclear forces because the nuclear weapons tests carried out by the United States to develop the nuclear arsenal destroyed indigenous lands. The affirmative proceeds to argue that a traditional approach defending a plan that prescribes United States Federal Government action would compel them to affirm the desirability of action by the government of the United States, which their very theory argues is unjust. When the negative argues that this case does not affirm the topic the affirmative can respond by saying that while they do not defend a plan their arguments align with the affirmative side of the topic, and so an affirmative ballot is justified.

A more radical departure from the topic might be a critical affirmative that holds that debating the topic is itself problematic. This affirmative might argue that the traditional nuclear policy discourses in the United States ignore the legacy of colonialism endemic to maintaining nuclear arsenals. It would be better for debate as an activity to focus less on the disposition of the United States nuclear forces, and instead, the focus should be on addressing colonialism. This affirmative might have what is called an advocacy statement, similar to a thesis that might be produced for an essay, which stands in for a plan, but generally would defend an intellectual stance toward colonialism rather than a specific change in policy. When the negative argues that the affirmative should engage the topic the affirmative argues that the value produced in their analysis of colonialism is greater than what would be produced by debating the topic, and so the affirmative side is preferable to the arguments made by the negative.

This effort to sketch critical affirmatives into categories is admittedly rough because part of the appeal of these affirmatives from a strategic perspective is that they allow the affirmative debater the opportunity to be more creative in their response to the topic. By definition, this means that affirmative cases are developed which slip between the cracks of this classification scheme. Nonetheless, these distinctions are helpful because they illustrate how critical affirmatives are typically constructed and how they differ from more policy-oriented affirmatives.

Critical affirmatives that defend a plan follow the same organization as a policy case, which has been addressed at length above. The two other types of critical affirmative discussed here, those that affirm a topic without a plan, and those that reject the premise that the topic should be affirmed, become more complicated. They are less bound to the organizational schema suggested by the stock issues approach found in policy cases. As a result, critical affirmatives are more diverse in their organizational structures.

To the extent that these diverse structures can be synthesized they tend to follow one of two organizational patterns common to what would be found in a public speaking course. The first is a "problem-cause-solution" approach which is generally speaking used for critical affirmatives that make the case that affirming the topic (without a specific plan) or adopting an ideological or intellectual perspective is capable of addressing a pressing issue (which may not be related to the topic). In this instance, the stasis question shifts away from stock issues in two important ways.

The first is in creating a separate test for what the affirmative must prove. Because the problems with the current system described in critical affirmatives tend to be extremely broad, affirmative advocacy is usually framed as a necessary response, but not a sufficient one in the same way that most policy cases are. This is usually justified on the basis that the demand for any single response to address broad problems is unrealistic and counterproductive to serious inquiry. Essentially, the affirmative becomes bound to prove that their affirmative is a proper response to a problem, rather than solving the problem.

The second stasis question becomes if the affirmative departure defending a plan that affirms the topic is permissible. In other words, the debate shifts away from the correctness of the arguments made in the affirmative to the legitimacy of the types of arguments made by the affirmative. These arguments are not always articulated in the first affirmative constructive, frequently they are articulated in the second affirmative constructive if the negative makes the claim that the affirmative should be forced to defend a specific plan that affirms the topic.

That the critical affirmative must demonstrate a smaller number of things to be true in order to affirm their case does not mean that these are easier cases to defend. They have some strategic advantages, but there are some weaknesses as well. The most obvious of these is that the affirmative must not only prove their case but prove that their case is a reason to vote affirmative. Consider that in a debate the affirmative only has thirty minutes of speech time, and the negative can eliminate nine of those minutes by arguing that no matter how accurate the claims of the first affirmative constructive are, they are irrelevant to the focus of the debate. This gives the negative a weighty strategic advantage that the affirmative must address.

To address this problem, developing the first affirmative constructive is generally built with an eye toward addressing this problem. When the negative challenges the appropriateness of an affirmative that diverges from defending a topical plan, it is called a "framework" argument. The first affirmative constructive is usually written with arguments and evidence that can be readily applied to these framework arguments. For example, a critical affirmative might argue that the public discourse on nuclear weapons is very technocratic, and even if the arguments are focused on reducing the role of nuclear weapons the language used privileges a central role for those weapons. This warrant can be used to claim that defending a plan that affirms the topic in the manner the negative is advocating forces the affirmative into the uncomfortable position of using arguments that are rhetorically opposed to the arguments that the affirmative is trying to make. A more in-depth discussion of these arguments is presented in Chapter 6.

There was a period when reading a critical affirmative was considered a risky choice because some judges' predisposition that they were not a sufficient basis to vote affirmative in a policy debate was so strong. In these judges' view, the role of the affirmative was to defend a plan, and the role of the negative was to negate it, and anything else was irrelevant. This description is still accurate for some judges, but there are many more today who have relaxed their expectations to give the affirmative leeway to argue as they see fit and put the onus on the negative to marshal a compelling response. The initial skepticism that debaters who were interested in critical arguments faced has been largely reduced.

There is one more note that should be attached to the discussion of critical affirmatives, which speaks to the politics of the argument. The diversity of critical affirmatives that debaters develop makes any effort to list them or categorize them by ideology a lengthy endeavor better suited to a book-length project. To the extent that there is a character that unifies these affirmatives, it is a skepticism of the current state of the politics of the United States. What these affirmatives offer is a space for debaters to explore and advocate from such skeptical perspectives. For many, this is valuable in a way that transcends strategic consideration and so this text does not preoccupy itself with the merits of such a choice. Nonetheless, to the extent that the time spent on debate is valuable, if a debater has a commitment to questioning their world it seems reasonable that advocating arguments that are equally skeptical is a reasonable choice.

Performance Affirmatives

The label "performance affirmative" is already a misnomer, because all affirmative cases are a performance. A policy case is a performance of argumentation in a style that mimics the sort of deliberative argument that might be found in speeches by politicians, lawyers, and public advocates. To the extent that a "performance affirmative" differs it is in the mode of communication used to express the argument, but not in the fact that an argument is being made. To illustrate what is meant by these alternative modes of communication a performance affirmative might entail a first affirmative constructive that does not read evidence or make the sort of explicit claim readily recognized by the Toulmin model. Instead, the first affirmative speaker may perform a piece of poetry, read a story, sing a song, rap, act out a scene, or any number of other performances to persuade a judge to agree with the affirmative team.[10]

A performance affirmative has much in common with the critical affirmative, in that it generally is skeptical of the current state of affairs in a more radical manner than most policy cases. Where the performance affirmative differs is that it has a broader view of an argument than what is generally adopted in critical affirmatives which generally differ in content from policy cases, but argue in a stylistically similar manner. Because performance affirmatives argue in a different manner from critical or policy cases, many debaters struggle with how to write such an affirmative. To make sense of this process it is easiest to begin with the ways in which performance affirmatives are similar to critical affirmatives. There are some which will use performance to provide reasoning to support a topical plan, some which will use performance to align their advocacy with the affirmative side of the topic, and others which will depart from the topic altogether. Depending on the answer to this question, what the affirmative is expected to prove will change as will how the speech is written.

Cases that conclude in the advocacy of a plan under the auspices of the topic typically will alternate between alternative modes of performance, such as reading poetry, with more explicit arguments following the Toulmin model. This type of affirmative will typically use the performative elements of their argument to provide a type of evidence that is particularly informative. For example, an affirmative advocating for disarmament might read a narrative from a person who was displaced from their home so that the United States could test nuclear weapons, arguing that the injustice this person experienced illustrates the fundamental wrong of the United States maintenance of the nuclear arsenal. In this case, the emotional appeal embedded in such evidence might be more compelling than the policy-oriented evidence that might otherwise be available for the argument. Nonetheless, by defending a plan such affirmatives typically are obliged to satisfy the stock issues associated with policy cases. As a result, the performance tends to be shorter and only occupies a part of the first affirmative constructive while the rest of the speech will seem much like what would be expected from the first affirmative constructive in a policy case.

Cases that align with the affirmative side of the topic but do not defend a plan would function in a similar way, with the caveat that without defending a plan such arguments tend not to address stock issues. Instead, they typically are pressed to demonstrate that their performance is a desirable way to respond to the topic. These affirmatives often will deliver their argument in their preferred mode for the entirety of the first affirmative constructive, and wait until cross-examination or the second affirmative constructive to clarify their specific position. For these affirmative cases there typically emerge two stasis components which are addressed in the second affirmative constructive. First, demonstrating that the mode of communication practiced in the first affirmative constructive is a sufficient basis to affirm the topic. Second, that the value in their departure from the norms of policy debate is substantial enough that negative arguments about the need for the affirmative to defend a specific policy are overwhelmed.

Where cases do not engage the topic, or have an unclear relationship to the topic, the performance typically serves the function of centering the focus of the debate on a separate issue that the affirmative argues is more valuable. Whatever the performance happens to be, the subsequent debate will focus on the merits of the performance, with the negative either arguing that it is undesirable because it doesn't engage the topic or has some undesirable feature. The first affirmative case will frequently not begin making arguments to defend the case until the second affirmative constructive, so composing the case is a relatively straightforward affair of developing a performance that fits within the nine-minute time limit.

Much like a critical affirmative the performance affirmative is typically composed with an eye towards the likely negative arguments that the affirmative should have to defend a plan of action that addresses the topic usually described as a "framework" argument. The affirmative rejoinder typically suggests an alternative framework that holds the debate should center on a different issue that is more important than the topic. This framework argument will be discussed more in Chapter 6, but for now, suffice to say that it is helpful for the first affirmative constructive to have some reasoning embedded in the performance which will advance the framework argument. A common theme for debaters who read performance cases is that although it is not always obvious during the speech they are providing warrants that will support more explicit claims later in the debate.

In the history of policy debating performance affirmatives are a relatively new phenomenon, only being a common practice for the last 20 years or so. As a result, they have less well-developed norms and expectations for how they should be argued. For debaters interested in treading less familiar ground they offer an intellectually engaging opportunity. Beyond self-edification, many of the changes that have occurred in debate to center marginalized voices have come from this stylistically creative approach. Because they depart from the strictures of more traditional policy-oriented argumentation, performance affirmatives create a space where perspectives and ideas that escape the focus of policy makers can be given voice.

Performance affirmatives are not for all debaters. For many judges, these arguments can be a tough sell, and in departing from more well-trod argument practices these affirmatives pose novel challenges which can make defending them confusing. These strategic weaknesses are a real concern for a lot of debaters, and so they tend to be less common. Nonetheless, some debaters win many debates reading them and some of the most impressive competitive accomplishments in recent tournament history have been by teams reading this style of case.

Conclusion

At the beginning of this chapter, it was suggested that most debaters preparing for a year of competition would be well advised to write more than one affirmative case. This seems like a tall order given how much work goes into preparing one. The reason for this is that as debaters develop their views and goals on debate limiting themselves to arguing a single case can be strategically disadvantageous and can constrain their academic goals in debate as well. Being able to tailor arguments to diverse judges, and to select an ideal strategy for the known tendencies for opposing teams, gives great value in flexibility.

Despite the value of such flexibility, writing the affirmative case is an extremely challenging task. Many debaters find themselves struggling with this process early in their career. Persistence and continued practice will make this process much easier and faster. Some debaters get so adept at the process that they might compose an entire affirmative file over the course of an evening of preparation, but for most debaters it is a slow process at least at the beginning. It is also an immensely rewarding process.

Most debaters end their formal education with the completion of their postsecondary degree. For many writing an affirmative case represents their most substantial scholarly project. When the author explains what an affirmative case entails he compares it to writing a master's thesis in terms of the amount of research, thought, and scrutiny that it will face. This is a bit unfair to writing an affirmative case, most graduate students only have to defend their thesis only once. Being able to select arguments that reflect their individual interests, become expert in those arguments, and have a platform to voice their view is a rare opportunity not just in the collegiate environment, but in the course of a human lifetime.

GLOSSARY

Enthymeme An enthymeme is an incomplete syllogism that relies on the audience to intuit sufficient reasoning to validate an argument.

Parametrics Parametrics is a theory of affirmation that holds that the resolution is a parameter for what the affirmative may defend rather than a statement that must be proven true in its totality.

Signpost A signpost is a public speaking device used to organize the arguments that are made for the audience. Usually, this is done by referring to what part of an earlier speech a debater is addressing their argument.

Stasis Stasis is the area of disagreement that must be resolved for one side or the other to win a debate.

Status Quo A shorthand term meaning "the way things are currently."

Stock Issues Stock issues are the necessary components of an affirmative case that must be proven in order to win the debate. These include Inherency, Harms, Significance, Solvency, Topicality, and Desirability.

Inherency Inherency is a barrier to a desirable change in a state of affairs which the affirmative will address. Inherency is one of the stock issues.

Harms Harms refers to the problems with the status quo which the affirmative will address.

Significance A claim that the harm is of substantial enough consequence that action is required.

Plan The plan is a statement of what the affirmative believes would be the ideal policy option.

Solvency Solvency is a term used to refer to the burden on the affirmative to demonstrate that the plan can sufficiently address the problems posed in the case.

Topicality The burden that the affirmative must defend a plan that falls within the parameters of the topic.

Toulmin Model The Toulmin model is the most commonly accepted description of an argument and its constituent elements. This model emphasizes how people argue in practice much more than the more strict models favored in formal logic.

Claim The first part of the Toulmin model, the claim is what the speaker believes to be true.

Ground In the second part of the Toulmin model, the ground is the basis for believing the claim to be true.

Warrant In the Toulmin model the warrant is reasoning that validates the connection between the claim and the ground that supports it. In policy

> debate, the term warrant is more expansive and stands simultaneously for what in the Toulmin model is both ground and warrant.
>
> **Backing** In the Toulmin model backing is external validation, usually in the form of evidence, which supports either the ground or the warrant in an argument.
>
> **Qualifier** In the Toulmin model a qualifier serves to modulate the initial strength of the claim.
>
> **Rebuttal** In the Toulmin model the rebuttal serves to address the inevitable response to a claim.

Notes

1 Stephen Toumin, *The Uses of Argument* (New York: Cambridge University Press, 1980), 97–102.
2 Aristotle, *On Rhetoric*, trans. George Kennedy (New York: Oxford University Press, 1991), 40–41.
3 Ibid., 104–5.
4 Policy debate students were engaging in argumentation focused on stock issues as early as the 1950s. An early treatment on the phenomena can be found in Ray Nadeal, "Hermogenes on 'Stock Issues' in Deliberative Speaking," *Speech Monographs 25*, no. 1 (1958).
5 See, for example, Kathryn M. Olson, "How Can We Address No Child Left Behind? The Importance of Inherency Analysis on Public Issues," in *Concerning Argument*, ed. Scott Jacobs (Washington, D.C.: National Communication Association, 2009), 580–89.
6 See, for example, Maridell Fryar, David Thomas, and Lynn Goodnight, *Basic Debate*. 3rd ed. (Chicago, IL: National Textbook Company, 1991), 119–34.
7 Meaning the United States is deliberately unclear about under what conditions it would use nuclear weapons.
8 This term is used to describe the spread of nuclear weapons to countries which previously did not have them.
9 See, for example, Austin Freeley and David Steinberg, *Argumentation and Debate*. 13th ed. (Boston, MA: Cengage, 2014), 238–43.
10 For a more contextualized discussion of performance debating, see Nicole Nave, "The Constant Pursuit of Inclusivity," in *Transcending the Game: Debate, Education, and Society*, ed. Shawn Briscoe (Carbondale: Southern Illinois University Press, 2024), 127–37.

4
NEGATIVE CASES

Most debaters fall into two categories: Builders and Breakers. Builders tend to believe that there is an ideal argument and focus on refining and improving that argument, a mentality well suited to defending the affirmative case. Breakers tend to have the opposite mentality, and when presented with an argument immediately look for inconsistencies, weaknesses, and poorly defended ideas that can be challenged. This sort of debater also frequently has something of a trickster mentality, looking for playful ways to intercede and challenge the arguments which the other side has made that are unanticipated. Breakers tend to be better suited to debating the negative side given their natural inclination to challenge arguments made by the other side.

This is of course a bit of an over-exaggeration; most debaters have elements of both personalities, and the task of an effective debater is to find ways to both build and break. Nonetheless, the best negative debaters do seem to take a special delight in coming up with a clever strategy to challenge what would otherwise seem to be a well-planned and thought-out affirmative case. This is especially true where the affirmative case defends something that seems to be universally desirable. That said, there are some structural forces baked into how debate is done that make the negative position very challenging even for the most skillful breakers.

Constructing a negative case is in many ways a more complicated proposition than the affirmative case because the negative position must rebut the affirmative, rather than the topic as a whole. As a result, a negative case is typically put together in a short period prior to the start of the debate, rather than prior to the start of the tournament. That is not to say that the negative side is not prepared prior to the tournament, but the focus is typically placed on preparing a broad set of negative arguments which then provide the negative side with a number of different arguments that can be combined and tailored in the preparation time before the debate to provide a complete case.

This chapter focuses on what arguments are available for the negative to make in rebutting the affirmative case. Taken as a collection and delivered in the first negative constructive, these arguments constitute a case. Unlike the affirmative, which may remain essentially the same from one debate to the next, the negative must change every time it encounters a distinct affirmative. As a result, the negative must prepare a great breadth of arguments and rely on discernment during the limited preparation time before a debate is announced to make the right choices bout which of the prepared arguments should be included in a case.

Negative Case Strategy

The way that policy debates are structured, where the affirmative gets to speak first and last and the negative has a large block of time in the middle, is nearly unique among debate formats because it is deliberately unbalanced to promote strategic decision-making on both sides. While the affirmative gains an immense advantage by defining the contours of the debate in the first speech and has the benefit of extended preparation, the negative has the ability to use the negative block to provide greater depth to their arguments. In putting together a strategy for a debate the goal of the negative is to take advantage of this imbalance so that even though the affirmative will get to speak last, the affirmative speaker will be fighting against a perception on the part of the judge that their arguments have already been largely refuted.

That sort of grand strategy is easy enough, the challenge is finding ways to accomplish this task for different cases in front of different judges. One helpful way to think about negative strategy would be to think of debate like a game of chess played simultaneously on three boards. A move made on one of the boards is going to move a different piece on each of the other boards, such that winning requires being away of the multiple impact of each of the moves. If we are to continue to follow this analogy, we might call those boards: judge predilections, argument quality, and policy implication. A decision by the negative to tailor their strategy to a judge's known preferences might mean that they adopt a weaker argument that has a less obviously desirable policy outcome than the affirmative case. Nonetheless, if the aim is winning the debate, pursuing a checkmate on the judge predilection board might be worth risking a weaker position on the other boards.

This extended analogy may not be helpful for debaters who don't play chess, but the implication is hopefully clear. Putting together a negative strategy requires carefully navigating multiple different considerations on the way to being able to give a judge the perception that the negative side has won the debate. Nonetheless, simply playing to a judge's preferences is not enough. As will be discussed in a later chapter, judges are not unintelligent and are looking to vote for the team that has defended the better arguments. This means that often times approaching a debate with an overly narrow focus on a judge's preferences is a recipe for disaster.

The first way the negative can win is by proving that the affirmative case is undesirable relative to the status quo or an alternative policy that is different from the affirmative case. This is the most common way that negative teams win, but it has distinctive challenges. The affirmative team, because they know their case more intimately and are used to defending it in approximately half of their debates, has a substantial advantage in knowledge and preparation. Nonetheless, the sheer diversity of arguments that can be marshaled to disprove the desirability of the affirmative plan allows the negative a degree of flexibility that can quickly turn the tables on the affirmative. It also carries the least risk of placing the negative in a challenging position relative to the presumptions of the judges in the debate.

The second way that the negative can win the debate is in many ways a corollary of the first, which is to critique the way the affirmative has engaged in the topic. One common example on foreign policy topics is to argue that the affirmative focus on maintaining the geopolitical position of the United States legitimates the aggressive use of military force, and while the plan may not explicitly state that the United States should go to war, such a decision is a logical extension of the claims made in the affirmative case. In this example, the strategy is not especially dissimilar from the first way the negative can win. Some critiques take a more controversial approach, which is to say that the arguments made by the affirmative, or their approach to the topic, or their relationship to their arguments, or some other aspect of their performance are sufficiently problematic that the affirmative should lose even if they successfully defend the arguments made in their case. In such instances, these arguments sound much like the third way that the negative can win.

The third way the negative can win is by proving that the affirmative case is not relevant to the topic. As will be discussed later, this is a more complicated endeavor than it may initially sound. This complication is made worse by a general tendency in recent years for judges to be more reticent to vote against affirmatives because they are not a part of the topic. Identifying a single cause for this trend is challenging, and perhaps impossible from an empirical point of view, but it is worth considering what this argument is asking a judge to do. Essentially, the negative is arguing that the weeks of preparation that the affirmative team has done is invalid, and essentially unworthy of debating, because a proper interpretation of the way the resolution is worded means the affirmative case is not a part of the topic. It is hard to ignore the sense that the negative is attempting to win on a technicality, and it is hard for many judges to reconcile themselves to voting on such a technicality. That isn't to say that it doesn't happen, or that judges won't do it, but there is a perceptual barrier that the negative must overcome.

The fourth and final way that the negative can win is to demonstrate that the affirmative case is incomplete in some important manner. This strategy derives from the stock issues tradition in policy debate discussed at length in the previous chapter and is generally based on proving that the affirmative has effectively failed to satisfy one of those stock issues. For example, as discussed in the last chapter, the affirmative must make an "inherency" argument. The negative can win by disproving this argument, or pointing out that the plan proposed by the affirmative is effectively the extant policy of the United States. The most common version of this strategy today relies on arguing that there is no advantage to voting for the affirmative, and if there is no advantage then there is presumptively no reason for change. Hence, the negative debaters are asking the judge to vote on "presumption." This strategy can be effective but is very challenging as most topics are written to allow the affirmative to address a pressing issue, making it easy to persuade a judge that it is better to try even a poorly defended change than to remain complacent with a problem.

Developing a negative strategy begins with an analysis of the affirmative case, and a subsequent judgment about which of the four ways for the negative to win is most realistic. From that judgment flows a decision-making process about which of the arguments available best allows the negative team to accomplish one of the strategies listed above. An apt analogy would be to solving a puzzle such as a Rubik's cube, where recognizing the different patterns suggests specific combinations of moves required to solve the puzzle. For example, recognizing that an affirmative is a central part of the topic and makes a complete case might foreclose the third and fourth strategic options, but makes the first and second much easier.

The decision about which arguments to include in the negative case for a debate reflects a balance between the optimal arguments to satisfy one of the ways the negative can win, a debater's relative knowledge and skill with advocating specific arguments, and judge preferences. This balancing of concerns means that hard and fast rules are elusive, but most debaters learn with practice and competition what works best for them. For this reason, the discussion of strategy in this text is limited to what is possible for the negative to accomplish. At the end of this chapter, some general suggestions are offered, but the preparation of the negative case has more to do with the individual debater and their skill than with any firm rule about the best way for the negative to argue.

Creating Negative Files

In policy debating there are a number of different ways to categorize arguments. Often this results in an immense amount of confusion for students who are at the introductory levels of debate. This chapter emphasizes categorizing these arguments based on what is most common in the parlance of contemporary debating, rather than what is most commonly seen in argument studies writ large. One productive approach to this chapter is to think of it as more of an extended glossary than a how to chapter like the chapter on affirmative cases.

The primary reason for this is that the process of researching and writing arguments for the negative is essentially the same as the affirmative. There is an initial analysis that is performed on the topic, which creates a sense of likely affirmative cases. From this list, decisions are made about which types of positions, described below are applicable to which cases. Most debate teams begin by developing the most generally useful positions, and then branching out into more narrowly tailored strategies to address affirmative cases that appear to be outliers.

In terms of organization the negative file only really differs from the affirmative file in that negative files generally have multiple different versions of the argument that can be selected for reading in the first negative constructive. For example, if the negative were to produce an argument that says restricting United States nuclear forces is dangerous because it decreases the deterrent capabilities of the United States, the file might contain different versions of the argument to be read against different types of restrictions that an affirmative would defend, rather than having a single more generic version of the argument. Beyond that difference, producing negative files is essentially the same. There should be additional evidence that can be read for each of the claims made in the first negative constructive, and prepared responses to the likely arguments the affirmative might make.

Because negative files tend to be less deep than affirmative files, the question is usually on preparing more different files. The open question is, what files should be prepared? The next section provides a summary of the arguments generally used by the negative in policy debate. From a preparation perspective, the goal should be to have a combination of these arguments below with each constituting its own file.

On Case Arguments

"On Case" arguments, or sometimes simply "Case" arguments is a blanket term for arguments that attempt to rebut a central claim in the affirmative case. Typically these are read toward the end of the first negative constructive to allow time for the negative to establish more complicated positions. One important strategic note for many debaters is that these case arguments are often treated like an afterthought because they tend to come toward the end of the first negative constructive, which is frequently a major error. Because they make it difficult for the affirmative to establish the factual basis for their case, these arguments are useful in amplifying the ability of other negative arguments to persuade a judge to reject the affirmative case.

These arguments can be further distinguished into two broad categories: defense and offense. Defensive case arguments attempt to prove that there is no advantage to voting for the affirmative case. That there is no advantage to voting for the affirmative case could itself be argued as a justification for the judge to vote for the negative. This is a relatively rare outcome. More commonly, these defensive arguments serve the strategic function of minimizing the apparent value of the affirmative case such that if the negative can establish that the affirmative policy carries a degree of risk then the judge would vote against the affirmative case.

For example, if the affirmative is arguing that the United States should adopt a "No First Use" (NFU) nuclear policy because it decreases the likelihood of an accidental use of nuclear weapons, the negative has a number of defensive arguments that it could attempt to prove. One example would be to argue that there is little risk of accidentally using nuclear weapons. After all, the only times nuclear weapons have been used it was extremely intentional. Another example would be to argue that adopting an NFU policy would not eliminate the risk of accidentally using nuclear weapons, because the cause of an accidental use of nuclear weapons is not our weapons posture, but rather our practices for handling nuclear weapons.

In both of these examples, it is important to note that the negative arguments do not eliminate the possibility that the affirmative argument is correct. Instead, what these arguments do is mitigate the affirmative claim that they are addressing a major and pressing problem. This is very common for defensive arguments and explains why winning a debate on the negative side using only defensive arguments is very difficult. Even if these arguments made by the negative are altogether conceded, if there is no additional problem posed by adopting an NFU, even a relatively minimal improvement in nuclear safety is better than leaving things as they are would be desirable, and the affirmative would win.

To address this shortcoming the negative is frequently best served by combining both offensive and defensive arguments. Offensive arguments claim that the opposite of a claim made in the affirmative case is true. This typically is done by arguing either that the causal logic in the affirmative case is backward, or that something the affirmative has normatively judged to be desirable is bad. In both cases, if the negative can prove their claim to be true, they have demonstrated that adopting the affirmative's policy suggestion makes things worse rather than better and the judge should vote for the negative side. These arguments are particularly important for negative teams because in many cases winning such an argument is sufficient to win the debate.

The simplest offensive arguments are that the affirmative has made an incorrect judgment about the desirability of an outcome of their plan. These arguments are typically referred to as "impact turns" because they argue that an impact the affirmative has deemed to be good is bad, or vice versa. Because most affirmative cases are typically designed around defending judgments that are apparently incontrovertible, many impact turns take polemical positions that can seem (or simply are) absurd. One example that has fallen out of favor in recent years is an argument drawing on the work of Malthusian economists that essentially argues that humans have overpopulated the planet and that an affirmative policy that saves human lives is undesirable because it will make overpopulation worse. This sort of position is no longer popular both because of its misanthropic character that is not appealing to many judges, and because its once ubiquitous nature has caused many affirmative teams to be especially well prepared to debate Malthusian theory.

More common in contemporary debates are impact turns focusing on unforeseen benefits that might accrue from an apparently counterintuitive position. For example, an affirmative team might argue that the United States should adopt an NFU policy because it will decrease the likelihood of other countries feeling pressured to develop their own nuclear arsenals to defend themselves (a process known as nuclear proliferation), which decreases the likelihood that an accidental or intentional use of nuclear weapons could take place. The negative might respond that if more countries had nuclear weapons it would actually create stronger disincentives for other countries to go to war for fear that the other side might escalate a conventional war into a nuclear conflict. Thus, nuclear proliferation is more beneficial because it would decrease the possibility of war taking place and save lives, meaning that the United States should not adopt an NFU.

To make this argument more effective, and offer the negative a fallback position it is often strategic to provide a defensive argument that supports the offensive claim. For example, the negative might argue that proliferation is inevitable given the geopolitical pressures facing smaller countries aligned against great powers. If it is the case that proliferation is inevitable, then regardless of its desirability the affirmative is unable to solve the problem.

This example might itself sound a bit far-fetched. That is not an uncommon feature of these arguments, but they serve an important pedagogical and strategic function. They force the affirmative to defend value judgments made in their case and provide an avenue for the negative to make general claims that are not reliant on knowing the exact causal logic of the affirmative case. This feature makes impact turns especially useful for teams that have more limited research capabilities or have little or no time to prepare responses to an affirmative case. Nonetheless, relying on impact turns is a bold strategy given the counter-intuitive nature of the argument and perhaps uniquely embodies the trickster ethos of many negative debaters.

The other offensive case argument asserts that the affirmative has a causal relationship reversed. Consider the previous example, but rather than arguing that proliferation is good, the negative argues that an NFU would make the United States appear to be weakening itself and create an opportunity for another country to proliferate without the fear of being on the receiving end of a nuclear strike before it has an arsenal to defend itself. Absent a reply from the affirmative, this bit of argumentative jiu-jitsu makes the affirmative plan appear to be undesirable because it has contributed to nuclear proliferation with the same risk of war presenting itself. To make this argument more effective, it is typically paired with an argument that the affirmative description of the status quo is inaccurate. For example, if the affirmative is arguing that their plan prevents proliferation of nuclear weapons, they likely have to argue that proliferation is already happening or will happen in a short period of time. If the negative can prove that there is no proliferation now, and the affirmative plan would make proliferation more likely, then the affirmative has created a new problem and carries a distinctive risk.

The notable characteristic of each of these arguments is that they strategically concede parts of the affirmative case, but argue that the opposite of other parts of the case are true. As a result, adopting the plan would be disadvantageous. There is an important cautionary note for negative teams in putting their answers to the affirmative case together. Let's say the negative is well prepared, and has both an impact-turn and link-turn prepared for an advantage and decide more arguments are better than fewer and read both. They have committed what is called a "double-turn" and essentially presented a new advantage for the affirmative case. To give an example, the affirmative case argues that nuclear weapons proliferation is happening right now, and creates a risk of nuclear war taking place, adopting an NFU would resolve this problem. The negative responds by saying, that there is no proliferation taking place, that adopting an NFU would cause proliferation, and that proliferation would eliminate the risk of war because of mutually assured destruction. Although all of the initial affirmative claims have been rebutted, the affirmative could concede that all of these negative arguments are true and that the plan would prevent war. A responsible decision-maker would vote for the affirmative team, because even though their arguments as initially presented were disproven, if the negative arguments are correct, then the affirmative proposal is a good idea albeit for the opposite reasons that had been presented.

This illustrates one of the greatest challenges in defending the negative side, which is keeping track of the arguments being made. This is doubly true in the context of the negative presenting its own arguments unrelated to the claims made in the affirmative case, which might have contradictions with the arguments the negative has made on the case. One of the most important parts of preparing negative arguments is making sure such contradictions are avoided, or at the very least do not prevent the negative from presenting a winning position. This becomes more apparent in the context of the off-case arguments that will be presented in the sections below.

Off-Case Argument: Disadvantage

Disadvantages are arguments that the affirmative results in an undesirable consequence that is not directly tied to a causal claim in the affirmative case. These are important arguments for the negative to have available because they allow the negative to shift the question of what is desirable away from the well-prepared arguments the affirmative has made about the reason why the plan is desirable to a more uncertain terrain of reasons why the plan is undesirable because of an effect not addressed directly in the affirmative plan. Despite this distinction, in its reliance on causal logic, the disadvantage is similar in its form to the affirmative advantage and negative attempts to turn an advantage. For this reason, at times the term disadvantage is colloquially used to refer to any negative argument that the plan is undesirable.

Disadvantages consist of at least three, but commonly four claims. The first of those claims is usually referred to as "uniqueness" and refers to a description of the status quo that is desirable (or at least more so than the outcome of what the affirmative is proposing. This argument is essential to provide context for the next claim, which is the "link" or change from the status quo that would result from the affirmative plan. The next claim is somewhat optional, because in some cases it is not necessary, but is generally common, which is an "internal link." The internal link is the next step in a causal chain, resulting in the final necessary claim, the "impact." The impact refers to the consequence of the disadvantage, which is argued to be worse than any problem purportedly solved by the plan.

One example of a disadvantage might present the following claims. Currently, the United States' strategically ambiguous stance on when it would use nuclear weapons reassures allies that it would use nuclear weapons to defend them from deterring aggressors (Uniqueness). The plan of declaring an NFU would clarify that only a nuclear attack would cause the United States to use nuclear weapons, which would cause allies to feel more susceptible to a threat (Link). Because of their perceived vulnerabilities, United States allies might decide they need to develop their own nuclear weapons (Internal Link). This proliferation, especially because it is done so quickly, is inherently dangerous and risks accidental or miscalculated use of nuclear weapons by allied countries (Impact). It should be noted, that simply asserting these claims does not make an argument. Instead, there must be evidence that provides reasoning to support these claims, but the structure of these claims represents a complete disadvantage.

Like an affirmative advantage, a disadvantage like the one presented above, is generally designed to use the shortest possible causal chain to defend the largest possible impact. The reasons for this, especially in the constructive, is twofold. First, because the negative must both respond to the affirmative and present the negative case, being succinct in constructing the argument is essential to using speech time effectively. Second, the negative strategy often relies on weighing the disadvantages against one or two advantages. A disadvantage with a smaller impact often struggles under these conditions because even if the affirmative does not have many substantive objections, they can prove that their case addresses a bigger problem. This is especially true if the affirmative can demonstrate in their case that the status quo is undesirable, a generally easy claim that is often assumed in the topic. While the example above might have some problems in demonstrating such a dramatic outcome, strategically it is helpful. For debaters looking to find other ways to address the strategic dilemma of the affirmative getting to point out the problems with the status quo that make the debate worthwhile, another argument is often a helpful tool to pair with a disadvantage.

Off-Case Argument: Counterplan

Perhaps the most complicated argument in a negative debaters arsenal is the Counterplan. A counterplan is an argument that an alternative course of action to the affirmative proposal can solve all, some, or none, of the problems raised by the affirmative while avoiding a disadvantage. The counterplan is arguably the most complicated argument made by the negative because the only real limit on the nature of the counterplans the negative can read is the imagination of the debater crafting the argument. For this reason, some judges have developed strong feelings that some counterplans are more or less fair for the negative to read. Fortunately, in terms of composition counterplans are relatively simple, so the elements of a counterplan will be discussed before turning to the more controversial aspects of this negative argument.

In the first negative constructive the counterplan consists of two essential elements. The first is a text, similar to what is presented in the affirmative case, outlining the specific actions that ought to be taken. The second is a solvency argument that articulates how those actions would address all, some, or none of the problems raised by the affirmative plan. As might be noticed, these arguments tend to be relatively short, which is part of their strategic utility. For example, if a counterplan can address all of the problems raised by an affirmative plan, it is a very short argument to present, which allows the negative team to focus much more time on explaining their disadvantage.

Brevity does not mean simplicity, however, and one important claim made in counterplans begins to illustrate this well. In presenting a counterplan the negative takes on two important burdens. The first is to prove that the counterplan is more beneficial than the plan. The second is to prove that it is "mutually exclusive" or "competitive" meaning that both policies cannot be adopted at the same time without consequence. Otherwise, if there is no reason to choose between either the counterplan, or the plan, the negative has not presented a reason to reject the counterplan, so presumptively the affirmative plan is still a good idea. In the affirmative, the argument that their plan and counterplan can be combined is referred to as a "permutation" a term roughly borrowed from mathematics to refer to a hypothetical way in which the plan and counterplan can be combined into a distinctive third iteration that can combine both elements.

Because of this burden, most of the debate that takes place around the counterplan is about the ability for two independent actions to take place simultaneously. There are a couple of ways for the negative to imagine this competition to take place. The first, and hardest to conceptualize, is what is called textual competition, meaning that the affirmative plan and the negative counterplan are not grammatically compatible. This usually is argued where the plan and counterplan differ primarily in the language used, rather than the substance of the action.

The second way that a counterplan can compete is through what is described as "functional competition." This mode of competition is premised on the idea that some actions, rather than grammar, are so opposed to each other as to be impracticable. For example, if the affirmative argues that the United States should adopt and declare a No First Use policy and the negative proposes that the United States should shift from a stance of strategic ambiguity toward an open declaration that it will use nuclear weapons first in defense of allied countries. This counterplan is the exact opposite of the affirmative plan, and so both cannot be plausibly done at the same time, and as a result, the counterplan competes.

The third, and increasingly most common means of competition is through "net benefits," meaning that while the plan and counterplan could be done at the same time, doing so would be undesirable, either because of a disadvantage to the plan that would result if doing both at the same time were attempted, or because there is a specific disadvantage to attempting both at the same time. This mode of competition is popular because it allows the negative to skirt discussions of process and definition in favor of relying on a more richly developed argument, the disadvantage, to assert that a combination is undesirable.

This illustrates the symbiotic relationship between the counterplan and other parts of the negative strategy. The pairing of a counterplan with a disadvantage and case arguments that are true of the plan but not the counterplan is a potent negative strategy because it stretches the affirmative very thin in terms of the number of arguments that must be addressed. Early on in the development of this argument many coaches and debaters argued that this strategy was so potent as to be unfair for the affirmative. While it is rare to find a judge who is unwilling to permit the negative to read a counterplan, the arguments that certain approaches to counterplans are unfair remains a potent one.

Consider the following, the negative reads two counterplans that are very different, and while the affirmative does answer one of them well, the other is answered poorly. The negative concedes the counterplan that is answered well is not desirable and advocates the other for the duration of the debate and asserts that the judge should not evaluate the counterplan which they have "dropped." If the judge follows the negative's reasoning, the affirmative has essentially wasted a large amount of speech time and might have a legitimate point that the debate is unfair.

This dilemma has led to a larger debate about counterplan "status" meaning what conditions under which the negative must defend the counterplan. In common practice, there are essentially three statuses that negative teams will adopt which influence how the argument is perceived by the judge which influence negative strategy. The most widely accepted status is an "unconditional" counterplan, meaning that the negative will continue to advocate the entirety of the counterplan no matter what arguments the affirmative has made over the course of the debate. For almost all judges this is perceived as a legitimate approach to counterplan strategy, as the negative does not have the ability to cease advocating the counterplan and maintains fairness in the debate. More controversial, and increasingly uncommon is a "dispositional" counterplan, meaning that unless the affirmative has read a disadvantage to the counterplan the negative is not obligated to defend it. This status is increasingly uncommon because for the negative it gives the affirmative too much control over the debate because by carefully selecting which arguments they make the affirmative is able to select the negative's arguments for them. Today, the most controversial counterplan status has become the most common, which is "conditional" meaning that the negative reserves the right to stop advocating the counterplan at any time, much like the example in the preceding paragraph.

For most negative debaters this controversy is not itself a problem. Most judges will vote for conditional counterplans, and their strategic value outweighs the risk that the affirmative team will convince the judge that the negative could be voted against on the basis of having read a counterplan conditionally. The calculus might start to change quickly for both judges and debaters where multiple counterplans are read, and especially where those counterplans make contradictory claims such that the affirmative would have to argue an issue both ways. For this reason, many debates at the high level focus on both teams arguing for what a fair debate might look like, and how the negative introduction of counterplan(s) has prevented this from happening. For debaters looking to avoid this problem, some of the other counterplan statuses look like more attractive strategic options.

Part of the reason for the controversial nature of the counterplan as an argument is their unpredictable nature, and how they can mitigate parts of the affirmative. For example, one counterplan which is commonly argued in contemporary debates is the "Plan Inclusive Counterplan" (PIC) meaning that the counterplan includes large portions of the affirmative plan, but differs in a specific or substantive way. For example, if the affirmative argues that the United States Federal Government should adopt a No First Use nuclear policy, the negative might respond by saying that the United States should adopt a No First Use policy excluding attacks from biological weapons, meaning that if the United States or an allied country was subject to a biological attack the United States would respond using nuclear weapons. The apparent benefit of this approach being that the counterplan would deter biological attacks while mitigating the risks associated with a more generally ambiguous nuclear weapons policy. For the affirmative, this counterplan is unfair because the negative is essentially able to defend that the thrust of the topic is desirable, and so most of the affirmative arguments against the negative side do not apply. For some judges, this is so compelling a problem that they might be susceptible to affirmative arguments that this counterplan is unfair, and would vote for the affirmative on the basis that the negative has essentially cheated.

Off-Case Argument: Kritik (Critique)

On a par for controversy with the counterplan is a third type of off-case argument known as a "Kritik" or "Critique."[1] The kritik is essentially an argument that the affirmative plan has an implicit or explicit premise that is so thoroughly flawed that the merits of the policy being advocated should either be disregarded or will be so thoroughly misguided in their enactment that a reasonable judge should reject the plan. In this way, the kritik positions itself as a prior consideration to contemplating the desirability of the plan.

From the standpoint of composition, a kritik consists of a mixture of components that are structurally an echo of the counterplan and the disadvantage. The first claim in a kritik is a "link" argument, which articulates a problematic premise embedded in the affirmative case (notably not necessarily the plan, as many kritiks are about an aspect of the performance of the affirmative case rather than the specific advocacy) which if taken as true produces a negative consequence. This negative consequence is the second claim, usually described as an "impact" which differs from impacts in many arguments because it is generally less specific. For example, a common impact is that the affirmative case represents an ideology that devalues human life in pursuit of an ideal, which makes violence in general rather than in a specific context, more permissible resulting in the loss of life. The third claim is termed an "alternative" which articulates what the judge should do rather than affirming the performance of the affirmative case, often simply suggesting that the affirmative should be rejected.

So a kritik might follow these lines. The affirmative team argues that the United States should adopt a No First Use nuclear weapons policy because it will reduce the incentives for other countries to develop their own nuclear weapons. The negative responds by arguing that the affirmative plan is premised on security centered a view of other countries as inherently threatening and not trustworthy in their own nuclear weapons development (Link). This view not only justifies the adoption of a No First Use policy but also the use of military force to prevent the development of nuclear weapons in a manner not dissimilar from the justifications offered for the use of force against Iraq making war more likely (Impact). The affirmative should be rejected for its reliance on security as a justification to begin a further interrogation of security discourse (Alternative).

In the example above what might be most frustrating is the Alternative, which does not necessarily post an opposed ideology, so much as using the act of rejecting the affirmative as a basis for an additional inquiry. From the affirmative perspective, this is remarkably frustrating. From the negative perspective, it is remarkably strategic in that the negative can win by saying the affirmative case is problematic, while not necessarily being burdened with providing an alternative. In fact, such a vague wording can be used to justify a controversial move in later speeches by the negative, to suggest that the plan could be adopted on a different basis which would address the problems raised by the affirmative while avoiding the problems raised by the perspective the negative is critiquing. This strategy is often described as a "Floating Plan Inclusive Kritik" because in some ways it is similar to the PIC described in the previous section, although the term floating is added because the negative is typically vague about whether they are actually advocating the plan without the problematic representation.

While the initial construction of the kritik is relatively simple, in the second negative constructive it can become immensely more complicated. One simple addition, for kritiks that are more pragmatically oriented, at times uniqueness arguments are made, with the claim generally focused on arguing that some aspect of the affirmative case assumes a condition of the world that is likely to change. The easiest example of this is for kritiks arguing that the current political economic system of the United States, essentially capitalist of one form or another, is not in the long view of history sustainable as a way to bolster the argument that some sort of a transition is necessary.

A more complicated addition is an argument that also attracts much of the controversy surrounding the kritik. Essentially it is the argument that claims made by the affirmative are demonstrative of an ideological bias which the judge should disregard. There are a number of different forms that this kind of argument can take, but their purpose is essentially the same, to make it so that the affirmative cannot leverage the benefits for their plan against the problem raised by the critique. This line of argument pierces the veil of one of the essential features of many affirmative cases discussed in the previous chapter under the term "fiat," that policy debate assumes that the affirmative is allowed to assume that their advocacy could be enacted for the purposes of debate. For some judges, this approach to the debate arbitrarily privileges the negative, and so they are skeptical of voting for kritiks.

Another complicated addition is the use of what are generally called "framework" arguments. Essentially, the negative argues that rather than voting for the best policy outcome, the judge should view their ballot as an opportunity to issue a referendum on an idea. This is justified either on a theoretical basis, meaning the apparent educational or competitive value of the idea suggested in the framework, or on the political or intellectual desirability of the idea suggested by the framework. The idea is essentially the same as the ideological bias argument described in the paragraph above, to argue that the judge ought not to evaluate the desirability of the affirmative policy, but instead to focus their decision-making on some other criteria that the negative is able to define.

In all of these additional arguments the negative strategy is intended to use the ideology embedded in the literature of their kritik as a way to avoid debating the affirmative case on their merits. For some judges, this is a sufficiently objectionable practice that they object to the kritik as a form of argument. There are others, although they are increasingly few in number, who object to the politics embedded in many critiques because they represent a substantial departure from the standard political coordinates of the United States political system. As will be discussed in Chapter 8, understanding which judges fall into this category is an important consideration for debaters who choose to read this argument. That said, the mere fact that a controversy exists should not be a reason to abandon the argument.

The argument that a source has a political bias is not itself representative of a kritik, and frankly is applicable to many sources read by both sides. Additionally, in its structure, a kritik is not altogether dissimilar from other arguments read in debate. The concern that many debaters express about reading kritiks is perhaps a bit overstated. The reality is that although the kritik might be best defined by having its arguments contextualized by particular ideologies, this true of all arguments, it is just that in cases where a kritik is not read the negative arguments concede the ideological assumptions of the affirmative case, and argue that their counterplan better satisfies that same ideology. For the negative, the kritik is a potent argument strategy because a team that has a well-developed version of the argument they can argue it in many different ways against many different affirmative cases. This strategic flexibility is very helpful for teams who might otherwise be overstretched to address the nuances of the many different affirmative cases that they may debate over the course of a debate tournament.

Off-Case Argument: Topicality

Consider the first debate tournament of the season. Unlike later tournaments, a debater has little idea what other teams might argue, and so you are not sure what your debates might look like. In this sort of circumstance, an argument about what the topic should be is essential. This argument is generally speaking referred to as "Topicality" and essentially is an argument that the plan advocated by the affirmative is not a part of the resolution. Unlike what is found in other debate formats, simply proving that the affirmative is not a part of the topic is not sufficient to win the debate, however intuitive that may seem. In policy debates the negative has the additional burden of proving that the affirmative not responding to the topic is sufficiently problematic that they ought to lose the debate.

This aspect of topicality is usually approached in one of three ways. The first is that the affirmative has failed to present a complete case, referencing the stock issues that the affirmative must prove in order to justify a judge voting for the affirmative case. At times, this is also done in reference to tournament rules, especially in the context of debates under the American Debate Association rules. The second is to argue that the negative is unfairly disadvantaged in the debate because it is difficult for the negative team to prepare for a case that is not a part of the resolution. Appealing to the value of competitive debate, the negative argues that the concern over fairness is more important than the value of considering the merits of the affirmative case. The third is to argue that by avoiding the topic the affirmative has limited the ability for an educational debate to take place because the other side is not adequately prepared.

This suite of arguments needed to persuade a judge to vote for topicality might come across as, to put it colloquially, a bit whiney. At times that description is accurate, but these arguments provide valuable training in many argument contexts. Consider, for example, an attorney arguing in defense of their client. Many of their arguments will have to revolve around the definitions of the language in the legal statutes in question, and arguing that their definition is superior to the opposing side. Indeed, many former debaters cite debating topicality as important training for professional careers, and not just in law. For example, in his capacity as an academic the author has spent many department meetings debating the proper interpretation of department policy, using a variation on the arguments outlined above.

A topicality argument generally consists of the following components. First, the negative articulates the proper interpretation of the topic, usually derived from definitions either from dictionaries or more contextual sources. Second, the negative articulates how the plan has violated this interpretation of the topic. Third and finally, the negative argues that the affirmative violation is either unfair or counterproductive for an educational debate. Unlike many of the other arguments, where the evidence provided to support every claim advanced, in topicality debates there are often only a very few pieces of evidence read to define the topic. This allows the negative to make an argument that the affirmative case should not be evaluated in a short period of time, hence, it's utility in circumstances where preparation is limited.

One of the important features of topicality causes it to be described as a procedural argument, meaning that it functions as a prior consideration to the affirmative case. If the case presented is not included within the topic, then the merits of the case are not relevant to the judges' decision. There are some similar arguments that can be made that follow a similar composition structure and role. For example, that the affirmative has written a plan that is not intelligible as a grammatically correct sentence, ergo it is undebatable or would not be enacted as a policy. Another common example is that some aspect of the plan, such as how it would be enacted, is vague and so cannot be debated. All procedural arguments share two strategically important features. First, that they are extremely brief, as the evidence used in any of these arguments is limited and might be only a sentence or two long. Second, that these arguments are able to win a debate even if the negative is inconclusive on all of the other relevant issues.

From a strategic perspective, brevity can have remarkable value. The ability to argue topicality quickly in the first negative constructive allows the negative to have a standalone argument that does not generally contradict or interfere with other arguments the negative might make throughout the debate. Many negative teams will take advantage of this by including topicality arguments that they have no intention of advocating at the end of the debate because it will take the affirmative more time to answer the argument than it takes the negative to make the argument, buying time for what the negative to elaborate on ostensibly more compelling arguments.

Procedural argument's ability to win the debate without disproving the merits of the affirmative case is a stunningly potent strategic tool. It means that the affirmative is no longer able to focus the debate on their strategically planned approach to the topic, and instead must debate the nature of the topic itself. It also means that, unlike other arguments, the affirmative proving that their affirmative is topical does not mean that they win the debate, merely that the affirmative does not lose prior to considering the benefits of the plan. The effect of these features is that many of the benefits that might otherwise accrue to the affirmative side can be mitigated by including topicality in the negative arguments.

Presenting a procedural argument is also helpful in that it can be used either to win a debate on the merits of the topicality argument or force a concession from the affirmative. Presume the affirmative presents a plan that has the

President of the United States declare a "No First Use" policy, but defends an advantage saying that the declaration would not be binding (essentially the President could lie) and so the plan might have both a benefit based on a perceived change in policy while not changing the policy in practice. The negative might argue that the plan is not topical because a restriction on nuclear weapons must be binding. This creates a "double-bind" where the affirmative must concede their plan is not topical and lose, or acknowledge that the declaratory policy would be binding and proceed without the advantage they claimed in their first constructive. Of course, the negative doesn't have to let the affirmative off the hook in this scenario, remember from the last chapter that plan texts are considered binding, and so the negative has the option not to grant the concession and continue working to persuade the judge that the plan as it was presented initially is not topical.

Despite this bundle of strategic advantages, many debaters in recent years have become more reticent about arguing topicality. There are likely a few reasons for this. It could be that this argument is less important with the increased potency of research tools discussed in Chapter 2. It could be that the features that make this argument a compelling strategic choice also make them challenging. Debating definitions can be challenging because they are often hard to warrant beyond the authority of the author, which in the case of reference materials like competing dictionaries might be hard to prove conclusively. That the arguments are often delivered without evidence makes can make it challenging to organize ideas and arguments so they can be presented in a clear manner for the judge.

Another possibility is that many judges are reticent to vote for it. Stacked on top of the challenges in the previous argument, topicality asks a judge to take a remarkably substantial step. Essentially, the negative is in the position of arguing that the judge should render a judgment that the affirmative case, painstakingly prepared over perhaps weeks or months, is not worthy of debate over what can feel like a mere semantic technicality. For a judge passing such a stern referendum can be a daunting task, especially if the arguments made in the affirmative case are compelling. Not all judges view topicality in this manner, but enough may openly or privately feel this way that investing in topicality in a serious way might cause a negative team to feel reticent about making the argument.

This should not be taken as a suggestion that topicality arguments are not strategically viable ways to win a debate, or that they should not be a part of the strategy. The best debaters have a degree of flexibility in how they approach the affirmative case. Topicality is often a helpful, and sometimes necessary, negative argument to test the affirmative case in a way that avoids the stronger arguments the affirmative can make. Instead, the aim is to illustrate that reliance on topicality as a sole strategy is not advisable in most cases.

Off-Case Argument: Framework

As discussed in Chapter 3, there are some affirmative cases that depart from the topic altogether. Under such circumstances, topicality may be an option, but if the affirmative case argues implicitly or explicitly that the topic should be completely disregarded, arguing that the affirmative does not meet a specific term in the topic does not help much. In such cases, the negative is often better suited to defend a vision of how the debate wholesale should take place. This argument is sometimes colloquially referred to as topicality, but is more aptly described as "framework."

A framework argument is structured in a similar manner to topicality in that it has an interpretation of the way the debate should proceed, articulates a way the affirmative has violated that interpretation, and reasons why the violation committed by the affirmative is sufficiently problematic that the affirmative should lose. That said, there are two differences that merit some special treatment. The first of these is how an interpretation is warranted. This often involves defining key terms in the topic, for example, "United States Federal Government" to articulate what the affirmative should be forced to defend. Although this part of a framework argument often reads like topicality, it serves a distinct function. Namely, to warrant a further argument about why it would be desirable for debate to be practiced a certain way.

In the example above the decision to define the term "United States Federal Government" would generally be made because the affirmative case which is being debated is antagonistic to defending action by the government. By defining the term, and arguing that the debate topic the affirmative to defend action by the Federal Government, the negative can make further arguments government-centered debates are good and desirable. Some of these reasons are similar to the appeals to fairness and education articulated in the previous section, but many of these are more philosophical in nature. For example, drawing on the pragmatist tradition in United States centric political theory, the negative might argue that government-focused debates better reflect the history of social progress in the United States. Thus, forcing the affirmative to defend government action produces debates that better align with many of the ideological commitments in the affirmative case.

From a strategic perspective the best case for this argument is that it is often necessary. Unless the negative team has a kritik which can be applied to the affirmative case in question, there are not many other argument options. Because most disadvantages are premised on the affirmative team defending government action, it is hard to generate a reason why the affirmative case is bad. Preparing case arguments can be difficult because if the affirmative is able to advocate abstract doctrine absent a question of implementation, there are so many positions for the affirmative to adopt that having compelling case arguments is a real challenge. Because the affirmative is not defending a plan, it is hard to argue a counterplan that is competitive. So, sometimes a procedural argument is necessary unless the negative team has more time to prepare arguments that are responsive.

There is a compelling case for framework beyond necessity, which is that it makes arguments which otherwise might not be especially relevant reasonably applicable to the affirmative case. Consider the previous example, where the negative is arguing that in order for the debate to proceed the affirmative must be bound to defending Federal Government action. Making an argument that debating government policy is good does of course disagree with the affirmative, but it is simple for the affirmative to point out that proving debating government policy is good is not a reason why debating other issues is not also valuable. Put differently, the negative's claims that debating government policy is good is not mutually exclusive with the value of debating the issues raised in the affirmative case. In arguing that the division of sides on the issues to be debated (often referred to as "ground") should be determined by the topic framework allows the negative to argue that the affirmative abdication of their designated role undermines the value derived from advocating policy change by the federal government.

The example of framework which has been explained in this section should not be assumed as the only way that it can be argued. For example, some teams argue for a more relaxed approach to framework which does not require the affirmative to defend government policy, but instead to align with the politics of a side of the topic. Others insist on the affirmative simply defend a concrete action rather than an abstract ideal without requiring a defense of the federal government. In these other approaches what the negative team is seeking to do is mitigate the extent to which the affirmative team can argue the ideas embedded in their case against the framework while retaining a sound justification for why the affirmative case is not a basis to vote for the affirmative.

There are some judges who are reticent to vote for framework. In many cases, this is the inverse of the problem that many judges have with voting for the kritik. Natural sympathies that judge may have with alternative approaches to debate than a focus on government policy, a reticence toward imposing a vision on how debate should proceed, and in some cases political sympathies coalesce to create a collection of judges for whom framework is an option. Earlier it was suggested that framework is in some cases an argument borne of necessity, this could be termed an exaggeration, because there are a host of kritik arguments that could readily be made responsive to most affirmative cases. Nonetheless, for negative teams framework can be a potent tool to address cases that avoid engaging with the topic.

Creating the Negative Case

The first negative constructive is much like the first affirmative constructive in that it is delivered from a script, and lays out the negative arguments that will take place over the course of the debate. This makes its delivery relatively straightforward, but also makes its preparation a challenging task to do well. The process is simple enough but requires some strategic thinking and decision-making which is notably difficult.

Deciding which combinations of the arguments outlined in the previous section is the most challenging part of constructing the negative case. Over time debaters develop their own approaches to this process, but one helpful approach is to create a decision tree that is premised on the types of affirmative cases that are likely to be read. The first step in this decision tree is determining whether this affirmative is responding to the topic or not. If the answer is no, the strategic options are generally limited, because if the affirmative does not defend a plan that affirms the topic the two options are to either critique some element of the affirmative case and argue that it should be rejected, or to simply argue that the affirmative should be rejected for failing to engage the topic.

As a result, the negative cases against affirmatives without a plan typically consist of first arguing either framework, a kritik, or both alongside case arguments. Unless the case arguments are quite robust and can prove the affirmative is thoroughly undesirable, the strategy is premised on giving the negative a strategic advantage by providing depth of argumentation on either the kritik or framework that the affirmative is unable to match. This is a challenging proposition because the narrow list of negative arguments means the affirmative is likely to be well prepared, but the negative has the advantage of a large block of speaking time in the middle of the debate to explain arguments in a depth that the affirmative is hard pressed to match.

If the affirmative defends a plan that affirms the topic there are more strategic options. The broadest possible strategy is called a "flex" strategy, where the negative will read at least one disadvantage, a counterplan, a kritik, and a topicality argument. The idea behind this strategy is that the negative will test the affirmative in many different ways, and will concede a number of arguments to focus on those which the affirmative struggles to answer. Assuming the negative arguments are relatively brief in their presentation of the first negative constructive, this can be fruitful in that the affirmative will struggle to adequately answer so many different arguments. However, it is hard to present so many different arguments without contradictions that the affirmative can exploit, and often the brevity of these arguments can make them unpersuasive.

Short of the "flex" strategy there tend to be two options. One of them is focused more on rebutting the desirability of the negative case. In this approach, the focus is on reading a combination of counterplans and disadvantages alongside case arguments to give the negative flexibility to either defend the affirmative as a worse policy than the status quo, or worse than a competitive policy option. The beauty in this strategy is that until the last negative speech, the negative can essentially defend two different positions, the status quo and the counterplan, and then focus on one of the options in their last speech. It allows for good depth on the negative, and if the case arguments include link turns or impact turns to the affirmative case can be especially effective. That said, these debates tend to be detail-oriented with competing claims, and being able to speak last can give the affirmative a great advantage in complicated debates.

The other common negative strategy is to use the kritik to serve the same purpose. Although it is often read with other off-case positions, topicality being the common example, the strategy is often constrained by the need to keep the negative arguments somewhat consistent. For example, a kritik of foreign policy decision-making would likely contradict a disadvantage which argues that the affirmative risks United States national security. The aim of this strategy is to avoid such contradictions and the more nuanced discussions of the merits of the affirmative policy to focus instead on arguing that the affirmative case has an unfounded assumption that should be rejected. This narrows the variety of negative arguments, but not the strategic goal. Case arguments, the alternative to the kritik, and framework arguments which preclude consideration of the affirmative casework to provide the same sort of flexibility available in the counterplan and disadvantage strategy.

There are numerous different combinations of arguments the negative can make and the list above is not intended to be exhaustive. These suggestions do reflect common approaches, that share a couple basic premises. First, the negative should present multiple different reasons to reject the affirmative in the first constructive to provide some flexibility because over the course of the debate, some arguments become more viable and others less. Second, the goal is to narrow the arguments over the course of the debate to better explain the most compelling arguments. Third, the aim is to focus argumentation around one of the ways the negative can win discussed in a previous section of this chapter.

In Appendix B a sample negative case is provided which would respond to the affirmative case offered in Appendix A. The reader will note that this negative case is written with the intention of providing a degree of flexibility for the negative team. Depending on the affirmative responses, the negative might choose to concede either the counterplan or the case arguments, while continuing to argue the disadvantage. The reader will also note that the negative case presented is abbreviated in the same manner as the affirmative case in Appendix A, and a more strategic case would likely present additional positions or arguments, especially on case.

After the decision is made about which arguments to make the process of constructing the negative case is easy. The debater simply opens the files with the prepared arguments and copies the relevant pieces of evidence and arguments into a separate document called a "speech document" which will serve as a script for the first negative constructive. Some additional small changes may be made, such as rewriting the claims for the arguments and rewriting the text of a counterplan or alternative to add clarity and specificity, but otherwise, the drafting of the negative case is simple.

Conclusion

This chapter has offered a broad survey of negative argument types which when presented in the first negative constructive represent a "case." The examples of the arguments presented here are generally representative, but they do not exhaust the diversity of ways these arguments can be constructed. Many debaters will notice over the course of their careers that there are arguments that blur the distinctions between kritiks and counterplans, disadvantages and case turns, framework, and topicality. Part of the value in debating is experimentation with argument form and style, and this chapter represents norms far more than rules for what form and style of argument are available to the negative.

Debating on the negative is a challenging endeavor because the affirmative is able to set the terms of the debate. It is also, after debaters develop some experience, incredibly fun. Studying an opponent's argument, coming up with a clever strategy, and persuading a judge that an apparently ideal policy or case is in fact a poor one is perhaps the most rewarding experience in policy debate. When a negative debater wins they know that despite all the ways the deck is stacked in favor of the affirmative, they were simply better in the debate and all of the preparation seems very much worth it.

GLOSSARY

Case Argument An argument from the negative which disproves a claim made in the affirmative case.

Link-turn An argument that the proposal of the opposing team would have the opposite of the intended outcome. For example, the affirmative might claim to solve the problem of nuclear weapons proliferation, and the negative could argue a link-turn that the affirmative policy would make it worse.

Impact-turn An argument that the opposing side is wrong in their conclusion about the consequence of an issue. For example, the affirmative might argue that nuclear weapons proliferation is bad, and the negative could argue an impact-turn that nuclear weapons proliferation is good.

Off-Case Argument A position argued by the negative which does not address an affirmative claim, but still refutes the negative case.

Disadvantage A position that argues that the affirmative case would result in an undesirable consequence.

Uniqueness A component of a disadvantage that argues that the current state of affairs is desirable.

Link A component of a disadvantage that argues the enactment of the affirmative plan would begin a causal chain.

Impact A component of a disadvantage that argues the end result of enacting the affirmative plan would have a negative consequence.

Counterplan An alternative policy to the affirmative plan that the negative argues would be more desirable.

Competition A term used to describe the test of whether adopting the plan and a counterplan or kritik alternative would be possible or desirable.

Textual Competition A test of competition that hinges on the question of whether the plan and counterplan or alternative could be combined in a grammatically sound manner.

Functional Competition A test of competition that hinges on the question of whether both the plan and counterplan or alternative could plausibly be enacted at the same time.

Net Benefits Competition A test of competition that hinges on the question of whether it would be desirable to adopt both the plan and the counterplan or alternative at the same time.

Permutation An affirmative argument that the plan and counterplan or alternative could be adopted simultaneously.

Kritik A position argued by the negative which holds that the affirmative case has a problematic assumption or belief embedded within it that should be rejected.

Alternative An alternative belief or perspective that the negative argues is preferable to the enactment of the affirmative plan.

Framework A negative position that argues that the affirmative has not engaged the resolution in an appropriate manner, and so should be rejected.

Note

1 By custom, debaters typically use the German spelling (kritik), a legacy of the early forms of this argument being developed largely from German philosophers. This guide will use the term kritik to delineate the specific type of argument from the term critique to avoid confusion about the multiple uses for the term critique.

5
CROSS-EXAMINATION

If there is a part of policy debate that reflects what most people imagine when they hear the term "debate" it is cross-examination. The term conjures equal parts the back and forth associated with presidential debates and the excitement of courtroom drama TV shows. In practice, cross-examination in policy debates looks nothing like political debates or TV shows, but there is something nonetheless dramatic about cross-examination.

The term cross-examination is derived from the courtroom practice of asking questions of a witness illicit answers from that would harm the case presented by the side that has called the witness. In policy debate terms, it serves effectively the same purpose. Following each constructive speech, the opposition is given the opportunity to ask the opposition questions. Although it differs from the more dramatic examples that a layperson might imagine, it is the only portion of the debate where both teams are actively communicating with the judge simultaneously. This unique feature makes it an immensely strategically important part of the debate.

Despite this importance, all too frequently debaters fail to take advantage of this important aspect of the debate. Part of this failure is a byproduct of not understanding what can and cannot be accomplished in a cross-examination period, but the greater part is that debaters rarely prepare themselves well for cross-examination. To properly prepare takes a large amount of time and energy, and many debaters focus instead on areas where the preparation is less time intensive with a perceived better payoff. Nonetheless, for debaters who take the time to practice and prepare for cross-examination they have a clear competitive advantage, and in close debates, they are far more likely to be successful.

DOI: 10.4324/9781003463078-5

The Essentials of Cross-Examination

The rules of cross-examination are closer to guidelines in practice. It's a bit unclear from a historical perspective why this is the case, but a reasonable starting place for the discussion might be the relatively late addition of cross-examination to collegiate policy debate formats.[1] Or it could be the experiments with using "flex-prep" where debaters are given blocks of time over the course of the debate to alternately prepare speeches or ask questions. Or it could be that at some indiscernible juncture debaters simply started to break the rules, and over time judges became more accommodating. Whatever the case, although there are rules the extent to which they are followed tends to vary.

Cross-examination takes place following all constructives. Cross-examination lasts for three minutes. During the cross-examination only the person who has just completed delivering the constructive should answer questions, and only the person who is not about to give the next speech from the other team should ask questions. This is the first place where the rules tend to get broken, as some debate teams use a more "tag team" approach, where the partner who is not designated by speaker order will "tag in" to ask a question or provide an answer. Although by a strict interpretation of the rules, this shouldn't happen, it is fairly common, and better thought of through the lens of how a judge will perceive the speakers.

For example, if the debater designated to answer questions is consistently deferring to their teammate, it would tend to give the perception that they are unprepared for the debate, and so would undermine their credibility as a speaker (and their team as a whole). For the same reason, if the debater designated to ask questions is persistently prompted or interrupted by their teammate it will tend to give the perception that their teammate doesn't trust them to ask the right questions. Although this sort of problem generally doesn't carry more weight with a judge than what can be conclusively demonstrated in speeches, where the important issues of the debate are not conclusively resolved these perceptual elements loom large in the mind of the judge.

So if only two debaters are supposed to be actively speaking during cross-examination, what are the other two debaters doing? Well, there are better and worse things that they can be doing. A very common usage that is quite bad might be described as "zoning out" where the nonparticipants watch the cross-examination to the exclusion of other tasks. Generally speaking, both debaters should be actively engaged in listening to the cross-examination period, taking notes, identifying issues being raised, and if necessary providing limited support for their partner. At the very least, appearing to be engaged gives judges the perception.

Beyond those tasks there is an additional responsibility that both debaters should be taking on. For the team asking questions, the person who is not supposed to participate should be using this time to prepare their next speech.

Essentially, as long as their partner is able to ask productive questions, their partner has free preparation time for up to 3 minutes. This is extremely valuable because it helps assure that their partner has adequate time to prepare the next rebuttal speech.

For the team answering questions there is a different task which must be accomplished. Namely, the debater who is not speaking should be copying their notes for their teammate. This topic is discussed in greater detail in Chapter 6, for now, consider the following. The person who just delivered the speech is unlikely to have a complete record of their speech. Without that record, they will struggle to put together their speeches later in the debate. So the job falls to the debater who is not speaking to transcribe their notes for their partner, a process called "backflowing." The question of how a flow works for the purpose of putting together speeches will be discussed in the rebuttals chapter, but for now, suffice to say that having a shared record of a debate as a team is essential to effective debating, and this requires the answering team to have the person not designated to speak working on this task.

All of which is a bit beside the point because the aim of cross-examination for both sides is to take advantage of this unique opportunity to try to gain a perceptual, strategic, or material advantage. While these side tasks are important, the focus in cross-examination for both teams has to be on making sure that the speakers are able to ask and answer questions effectively. Though there is a certain romanticism to the vision of a debater coming up with a clever question or quip off the top of their head, in practice effective cross-examination is far more likely to be the product of careful preparation than it is the product of pure inspiration.

There is one more very important general rule for cross-examination, the answers given are considered to be binding. Meaning, that if a statement is made in cross-examination that statement cannot be reversed or changed later in the debate. This rule is admittedly one which is somewhat malleable. Some judges are either inattentive or naturally more forgiving than others, and even the strictest might allow clarification later in the debate so long as the answer is consistent with what has already been stated. Nonetheless, what is stated in cross-examination can decide the entirety of the debate, which makes it an extremely valuable period of time that must be used efficiently.

Essential Cross-Examination Strategy

For both sides there are strategic priorities for asking cross-examination questions. They essentially boil down to three steps, with some variation in the particulars for each side. First, clarify important arguments. Second, attempt to gain a strategic concession, or at least force the opponent to defend an uncomfortable argument. Third, make weaknesses in the other sides argument clear for the judge.

For the team asking the questions this is easier to accomplish because they are able to direct the questions. That doesn't simplify the task of identifying the relevant strategic questions. A good place to start is doing an honest assessment of what parts of the opponent's speech were not understood. Was there a complicated wording to an argument? Was there some jargon that was unfamiliar and couldn't be parsed during the speech? Clarifying these potentially important issues should likely take place early in the cross-examination. That said, doing so quickly is important because other than understanding there is little gained by asking clarification questions and there are more valuable uses of this limited time.

Typically after the clarification questions the next essential step is to attempt to gain strategic concessions. Doing this successfully rarely looks like the dramatic conclusion to a courtroom TV show where the defendant is caught in a lie on the stand and admits they actually committed the crime. Instead, it usually amounts to a series of questions that sound only tangentially relevant which are revealed to be significant in the next speech. Consider a negative speaker asking the affirmative team questions about their case which argues that unless the United States were to disarm its nuclear arsenal eventually an accidental nuclear war would ensue. The negative speaker might ask if other countries have nuclear weapons, an apparently innocuous question to which the answer is obviously yes. The negative speaker might then ask if the safeguards for nuclear weapons in other countries are better than those used by the United States. The answer here is less clear, but if the affirmative agrees that safeguards are better in other countries the odds of accidental war look very low, the United States might have an accident, but there is no reason to believe other countries would follow our lead. If the affirmative disagrees, the negative can simply point out that the plan can't stop the risk of an accident on the part of other countries. In both cases, what the negative has done is use affirmative answers to innocuous questions to provide the reasoning for a negative argument. Because cross-examination is binding, the affirmative does not get to change their answer, at best the affirmative gets to disagree with the conclusion.

The third goal of cross-examination is to ask questions to give the judge an understanding of what the weaker parts of the affirmative argument will be. The aim of these questions is to use cross-examination time to illustrate the weakness in an argument so that in the subsequent speech it can be rebutted more easily. For example, say one debater realizes that a piece of evidence that has been read for an argument is out of date. They may ask how this older evidence is capable of accounting for a more recent turn of events. The affirmative answer is not especially important, the importance is in that the asking of the question shows the judge what the argument will be and so the argument can be made with less explanation later while remaining clear and effective.

Cross-examination is a valuable period of time for the debater answering questions as well as the debater asking them. That said, the goals are slightly different. When answering questions the most important task is to ensure that none of the responses result in a disastrous concession. Usually, where this happens, an apparently irrelevant question is asked, and the responding debater will give an extended response on the misguided premise that they are wasting the other sides time, only to realize that something they have said gives the other side an advantage.

One example that the author observed involved two teams debating energy production. One of the teams had suggested that developing small nuclear reactors would enable the use of desalination plants which could address water shortages in the Kashmir province which has a border between India and Pakistan. The other team asked a question about why there was a shortage of water in that region. As the affirmative expounded on the geographic and geopolitical reasons for this answer for approximately two minutes the other team patiently waited. At the end of cross-examination they asked how, with all of those problems, would a technology for removing salt from water address a problem hundreds of miles from the ocean? The affirmative's lengthy answer had essentially made it obvious that the plan they were proposing would be insufficient to solve their own advantage.

Beyond avoiding such a catastrophe, the team answering the questions has several other important tasks. The first of which is to clarify their position. As illustrated in the example above there is some risk in doing so, but every question is also an opportunity to provide the judge with a more direct and engaged explanation of the case which has just been presented. Unmoored from a script, the debater answering questions can read the judges' face and adapt or rephrase answers to improve clarity. This can be especially valuable where the arguments are particularly complicated or the delivery is less than clear.

Beyond clarification, in answering questions a debater is able to effectively pre-empt an argument. For example, a negative debater may be asked a question about how their counterplan would solve the affirmative plan. In response, the negative debater, knowing that in the first constructive their counterplan was not especially specific to the affirmative case, may begin to articulate a more specific argument. This strategy carries some risk in that it goes beyond what the negative has already defended, but it also strengthens the argument in the eyes of the judge by becoming more responsive to the arguments in question.

Although it is often underutilized by debaters, the opportunity to ask the opposing side questions is of remarkable value to a debater. Beyond the specific strategic goals, it is an opportunity to illustrate favorable contrasts with the opposing side. Asking the right questions to stress the other side, and demonstrating superior preparation is a way to project confidence that can influence how a judge interprets the subsequent argumentation. In a close debate, this can be enough to determine the outcome.

Good Questions

When cross-examining an opponent the aim is to accomplish as many of the strategic objectives described above as quickly as possible. This means asking questions that are generally speaking brief, and elicit brief answers. Otherwise, it is possible for the other debater to filibuster the cross-examination and use all of the allotted time to wax poetic about their arguments. For this reason, the best questions are asked intentionally and with a closed wording.

In an ideal world the cross-examiner would only ask yes or no questions. This way the opponent can only take up a very limited amount of time without giving the obvious appearance of filibustering. For example, say the negative is cross-examining the affirmative and is unclear about the significance claim in the advantage. Rather than asking "what is the significance of the advantage" which would allow the opponent the ability to explain the argument at length, a better approach might say "is it correct that the advantage is avoiding war" which would elicit a yes or no response. Thus, time is saved and more good questions can be asked.

The example above is a good question because the information is important for the cross-examiner to succeed in the debate. These clarifications, or in the case of the preferred wording, verification, questions are especially important for the affirmative side to ask. While either side can fall victim to confusion about an argument, there are more procedural questions that are unclear about the negative case. For example, the question of which arguments make the counterplan beneficial is often unclear, and so clarifying is especially important for the affirmative side.

The next important type of question is a probing question. A probing question is a question that seeks additional information. While the preference for a closed wording like the one above prevails, probing questions are often intended to elicit more information and so a yes/no formulation is not always readily available. One example of this approach is colloquially known as the "reverse pit of doom" where the cross-examiner asks their opponent a question that appears to be easy which can be used later. An affirmative debater may do this by asking a negative debater what the impact of their disadvantage is, knowing that in the next speech, their teammate will argue that the plan solves the disadvantage. As a result, the negative instinct to amplify the perceived importance of the disadvantage will ultimately work to the benefit of the affirmative. As the negative expounds on the disastrous concerns raised in their disadvantage, the affirmative gains a more significant advantage for their next speech.

The last type of question is an argumentative question. Argumentative questions test the respondent's ability to defend their argument. For example, perhaps a debater has argued that a change in policy will result in a nuclear war, a rather large claim. The cross-examiner might ask a question such as "if the risk of nuclear war is so high, why have nuclear weapons not been used for 80 years?" This sort of argumentative question does give the respondent the ability to give a longer response, but the time invested is worth it if the question cannot be answered well. Even if these questions are answered well they prime the judge for the argument that the negative is preparing to make.

Knowing the right types of questions to ask is a great start, but it is equally important to consider how to use those questions collectively. With experience, debaters tend to develop individual strategies for doing this, but one handy technique is to use what is called a cross-examination tree. In preparing for a debate, the cross-examiner will identify an issue with the opposing case that they believe would be valuable to challenge during cross-examination. The debater then formulates a yes or no question to test that issue. The debater will then plan separate follow-up questions based on both yes and no questions. This pattern will be repeated until the questions are at several degrees of remove from the issue. When the debate takes place, the order of questions is reversed so that regardless of the answers given by the respondent the cross-examiner can use a line of questioning to constrain the answers available to their opponent.

Another way to combine questions is to combine issues to produce a double-bind question. In a double-bind question, there are two possible answers, but both of the answers create a problem for the other side. A common place to find such opportunities is in a disadvantage. Say the negative reads a disadvantage that says currently the United States has robust deterrence against foreign adversaries, but the plan of reducing the role of nuclear forces would undermine such deterrence. A double-bind question would be "does the United States deterrence only rely on its nuclear forces?" This question forces the negative to either make the absurd argument that having one of the largest conventional militaries in the world is irrelevant or admit that there would be some degree of deterrence even if the plan were adopted.

Finding and deploying these sorts of questions is perhaps the most fun and exciting part of policy debating. From a strategic perspective, it is also incredibly valuable, by forcing the other side into defending uncomfortable positions the cross-examiner can force errors which can be exploited in later speeches. More importantly, a good cross-examiner will demonstrate the sort of aptitude and confidence that sets them apart from their opponent. In a close debate, such a narrow perceptual advantage can pay large dividends.

Good Answers

Cross-examination is as valuable for the responder as it is for the questioner. It is essentially an additional speech that can be used to both clarify existing arguments and demonstrate confidence and familiarity with arguments in a manner that is more interactive and engaging than is possible in many speeches. It is not without risk, obviously the aim for the questioner is to undermine the arguments made by the responder, but answering questions well and helpfully is no less valuable than well-planned and asked questions.

From a strategic perspective answering cross-examination questions serves three purposes. The first is to provide a robust defense against probing questions, providing answers to questions in a way that not only avoids the appearance of avoiding the issue at hand but also offers little in the way of advantage to the opposing side. The second is to clarify arguments for the benefit of the judge and the questioner. The third is to provide additional reasoning to support the arguments that have already been made.

In defending against probing questions there are essentially two tactics. First, rejecting the premise of the question. When the questioner pursues common yes or no questions answers that provide detail but do not fit into the yes or no schema both clarify the responder's argument while avoiding the intent of the questioner force a concession. The second tactic is to frame answers in reference to the preceding speech. So long as the answers to the questions asked do not take a stance beyond those articulated in the initial speech then there is little risk of inadvertently making a concession. At the very worst, a mistake that has already been entered into the record will be reiterated, and no special harm will be done.

Nonetheless, for less probing and more clarifying questions longer answers that provide more detail and explanation may inadvertently help the other team, but they also help the judge. It is worth remembering that the judge in a debate almost assuredly has spent less time thinking about the arguments in a debate than the debaters who prepared for it. As a result, the judge lacks a degree of context, and a rich answer can serve to fill in the gaps in the judges' understanding of the arguments. A good way to do this is to reference specific parts of the preceding speech as a part of the answer in order to help the judge connect the more deliberate and contextual delivery of the response to a question to the argument in the preceding speech which may be unclear.

The final tactic in answering questions is to provide additional reasoning for extant arguments. This does carry with it an element of risk, but the reward can be substantial. Additional reasoning does not, generally speaking, mean new evidence or even new arguments. Instead, the aim is to provide a greater depth of argumentation. A common way to do this is to provide an analogy or example that while avoiding the risks of producing an altogether new argument the affirmative is able to essentially provide an additional reason why the argument was valid. Say the affirmative has an advantage that is premised on the United States improving its relationship with a foreign country, in response to a question the affirmative might analogize it to an interpersonal relationship as a way to simplify the complex nature of foreign relations.

One tactic that is often tried but rarely a good idea is the filibuster. Essentially, the respondent provides an unnecessarily rambling and extended answer in order to waste the time of the questioner. Though this tactic is appealing in that it can limit the questioner from asking more questions it has a number of problems. The questioner can adeptly interrupt to ask their next question. The filibuster strategy is easy to spot for the judge who is apt to view it as, if effective, somewhat less than a charitable approach. Finally, in giving a needlessly extended answer the responder may inadvertently make a concession with dire consequences.

Answering questions is a challenging endeavor, but strategically valuable to the well prepared debater. Nuances of how to answer questions aside, a good rule of thumb is to have a reason for everything that is said in an answer, and only answer the question which is asked. Keep in mind, that this is an interactive speech, but the audience is the judge. Direct the answers to the judge, and answer questions in a manner that is persuasive to the judge, rather than the opponent.

Conclusion

Cross-examination is a remarkably important part of the debate, that is frequently overlooked by debaters. The focus on preparing speeches, evaluating arguments, and sorting through the strategic options available distracts many debaters from the one time during the debate when they are able to interact directly with their opponent. Setting aside the ability to clarify arguments and gain strategic concessions, there is an even greater loss in not diligently pursuing cross-examination.

From the perspective of the judge this period carries a great deal of value in illustrating which team has greater skill in argumentation. While most debates are not decided based on cross-examination, for many judges what happens during cross-examination colors which side is more right about the arguments in question. In close debates, this often means the judge must render a judgment about a contested claim where they lack compelling evidence that one side is more correct. In these situations, cross-examination, and especially the skill with which debaters handle it, provides a demonstration of competency that pushes the judge to favor one side over the other.

Note

1 Dating the exact origin of the beginning of cross examination in National Debate Tournament debating is difficult, but in the case of CEDA cross examination was a feature of the format at its founding in 1971.

6
ANSWERING CASES

Preparing the cases for the affirmative and negative can feel less like a debate than a competitive speechwriting project. In a certain sense, this is true, because the aim in both of those speeches is to present the most perfect form of the arguments for both sides possible. In a larger sense, the cases for both sides are merely claiming strategic positions in a game that is about to begin in earnest. In answering the cases, both sides attempt to advance their positions so that in the last speeches they are able to present a compelling summation of the issues for the judge.

Answering cases is the task of the second constructive speeches for the affirmative and negative and the first negative rebuttal speech. The inclusion of the first negative rebuttal might raise some eyebrows and deserve some discussion. Remember that the second negative constructive and first negative rebuttal are delivered subsequently, with only a cross-examination between them. As a result, the terminology used to describe this pair of speeches is the "negative block." Because both speeches respond to the first affirmative constructive, it is generally not helpful to ascribe to them different roles. Instead, they serve the same role but choose different arguments to address in their speech. Later in this chapter, the division of arguments between the negative will be addressed in greater depth; for now, suffice to say that the negative block and the second affirmative constructive serve a similar role in the debate.

That role is to selectively expand or contract arguments so that it will be easier to present the judge with a coherent justification to vote favorably at the end of the debate. What this looks like for both sides varies, but that variance has more to do with the speech structure than it has to do with the principles of sound argument. The choices that face both sides, which varied so much in the

DOI: 10.4324/9781003463078-6

construction of the affirmative and negative cases, become very similar when answering arguments, as the goals unite around mitigating the persuasiveness of the other side's argument while amplifying the persuasiveness of the debaters' own. Good arguments are good regardless of the side that makes them.

Flowing

One of the most essential steps to delivering any effective speech following the first affirmative constructive is an adequate set of notes which reflects the arguments made in the debate. Although any system of note taking could conceivably work, policy debaters generally favor a technique called "flowing." This system is distinctive in that it is not only a written record but a visual representation of the arguments that have been made so that their relationships are more readily identified. Essentially, a series of notes, known as a "flow" of a debate is a schematic, or map of the arguments which have been made. To produce this map, the longer form of the argument which is made is turned into a kind of short hand that the debater will recognize as standing in for the argument. The result is a sort of stenography that is intelligible to debaters, but somewhat enigmatic to most non-debaters, so much so that it featured in a 2009 episode of the popular TV program cold case. The reason for this specific note-taking system, which will hopefully become clear, is its usefulness in preparing speeches without a script, serving the same function as an outline would for a public speaker.

There are essentially two ways that flowing is done. The first approach is a traditional pen and paper approach. The other is done using a spreadsheet program, but essentially it recreates what historically was done on pen and paper. Both media can be made to work, but pen and paper have the advantage of allowing a greater degree of spatial organization, and so will be the primary focus of this guide. To adapt this guide to the spreadsheet method simply substitute the term tabs for pages and otherwise, the directions are effectively the same.

Every position for both sides in the debate is given its own sheet of paper. For the affirmative, this means inherency, each individual advantage, and solvency are kept on a separate sheet of paper. For the negative, this means every disadvantage, counterplan, kritik, and topicality is kept on a separate sheet of paper. Imagine, (or if preferred draw) a vertical lines so that there are columns that correspond to each speech that will be given in the debate, with the second negative constructive and first negative rebuttal sharing a column. In each of these columns, the arguments made in each speech will be recorded, with arguments that respond to each other placed adjacent to each other (some prefer to avoid this convention and draw arrows to connect arguments). This constructs the schematic representation of the arguments and allows the debater to see how the arguments from both sides do or do not respond to each other.

The notes that are taken consist of three parts. A brief indication of the claim, the name of the author, which is used to support the evidence, and the warrant provided for the claim. Because debate speeches are often delivered at something of a rapid pace, the emphasis is on doing this quickly and accurately without relying on the exact wording of the speaker. Every debater has their own very personal manner of doing this, and developing a system that works for an individual is more important than adherence to any specific rule, but there are some common strategies. Avoid any complete sentences, fragments are enough to convey the meaning of the argument. For that matter, complete words are unnecessary, abbreviating or eliminating vowels work equally well. Many debaters rely on symbols rather than whole words. Writing in smaller letters rather than larger letters can also save a surprising amount of time. All of this is a matter of personal preference, and over time debaters tend to develop their own particular style.

General Principles

In answering arguments, there are general principles that are fairly universal. The first, and in many cases most important of these is the "burden of rejoinder." Essentially, if an argument has been made, any disagreement must be expressed at the first opportunity; otherwise, it is treated as a conceded point. For example, if the second affirmative constructive does not address an argument made in the first negative constructive, that argument is treated as true for the purposes of the debate.

The merits of this principle are straightforward, it constrains judges from intervening against arguments that they dislike for their own idiosyncratic reasons and it prevents both sides from waiting until the last speeches to begin debates when their opponents have lost the ability to respond in a meaningful way. It also can be abused; some teams may focus their strategy on making a large number of bad or poorly evidenced arguments hoping their opponent will simply fail to respond or "drop" an argument. As a result, the debate can be of relatively low quality and rather than emphasizing competing arguments turn into a patchwork of unaddressed claims that look less like a debate and more like competing orations.

As a result, the burden of rejoinder is one of those principles that is important because it helps debate function, but like any rule in any sort of exercise can also undermine the purpose of the enterprise. When a debater is preparing to answer an argument their goal should be to first adhere to the principle, and challenge each argument that the other side has made which affects the arguments that their side must make in order to win the debate. Second, this burden would suggest that making more well-warranted arguments than the opposition is generally a strategic advantage. This is part of the reason why policy debate happens at such speed, to provide sound evidence for multiple arguments is challenging unless a debater speaks more rapidly than they might in everyday speech.

The speeches that are the focus of this chapter represent the turning point where the burden of rejoinder enters into the debate. The second affirmative constructive is the last speech where the affirmative side is empowered to enter new arguments in the debate, in the form of additional advantages to their case, or new responses to negative arguments. Subsequently, any arguments can only be made in response to new arguments the negative makes. For the negative, the question is a bit more fluid, but the general consensus is that new on or off case arguments are only permitted in response to new affirmative arguments. That said, the negative can generally expand existing arguments by presenting new components of existing arguments, for example, reading a new impact to a disadvantage.

An additional principle is stasis. Although this is typically discussed in terms of the affirmative case, it applies to the negative for the exact same reasons. In order to disprove the arguments which are made by the affirmative side of the debate, the negative must prove essential parts of their argument to be correct. This makes stasis a handy tool for both sides in that there are "checklists" of arguments that must be made for the affirmative to disprove the arguments made in a negative case and vice-versa. That is not to say that one side or the other must win all of the arguments made on their checklist, but rather that the checklist functions as a guide to which arguments are generally applicable.

What this approach helps avoid is committing a "red herring fallacy." Essentially, making an argument that is unrelated to the important issue in the debate. For example, if the affirmative is arguing for disarming the nuclear forces of the United States they may state that the arsenal has 5,044 nuclear warheads.[1] The negative might respond with a different number from a different source and say the size of the arsenal is 3,708 nuclear warheads.[2] There is of course a large difference between these numbers, and that difference might matter, but if the object of the debate is the desirability of reducing the size of the arsenal to 0 nuclear warheads the difference is irrelevant. What the checklist approach helps with is identifying what areas of disagreement are fruitful, and which are interesting, but do not in fact affect the argument at hand.

None of this speaks to what it means to actually answer an argument, which is a complicated and highly context-contingent issue. Perhaps the simplest approach is suggested by Perelman and Olbrechts-Tyteca's notion of "argument strength" which they loosely define around the adherence to the principles of the argument by the audience.[3] Taking their principle in hand, the goal is to impart to the audience a greater degree of adherence to a position than is found in the arguments offered by the opposition. This chapter is focused primarily on how this is done in the context of advancing entire positions rather than individual arguments, but delineating between the individual arguments and entire positions is not easily done, so delineating between different registers of argument is a productive starting place.

Answering Specific Claims

The first step in answering an argument is in recognizing the claims which the other side has advanced which seems weak and worthy of response. A relatively straightforward example might be that the evidence used to provide a warrant for a claim is from an obviously biased source. This weakness can be exploited to undermine the strength of the argument because of the source is biased then the argument itself may be rooted more in the personal interest of the source of the evidence than fidelity to reality. That does not mean that responding to that claim is always valuable. Remember that debaters have to deal with what quickly appears to be scant time, and so they may not respond to every claim in an argument. It may be the case that there are more important or pressing issues that must be addressed, and so this obvious weakness is ignored.

Assuming that responding to a claim is worthwhile, a debater will proceed systematically to undermine the relative quality of the argument. This systematic approach is important because debate is a verbal activity, and because the audience is listening and does not have the ability to re-listen the same way they might re-read, consistency in delivery is at a premium. So, the first step in challenging a claim is to use what is called a "signpost" to let the audience know which argument is being refuted. This is usually done by stating which position is being addressed and then stating which part of the position is the subject of the following argument. A signpost might read something like this: "On the proliferation disadvantage, the uniqueness argument." This signpost directs the judges' attention to the position which is being addressed, and subsequently which part of the position will be argued.

Subsequent to the signpost a counterclaim is made which articulates what is wrong with the signposted argument, and states the argument which will be advanced instead. From this point forward the Toulmin model of argumentation is essentially sustained with the caveat that depending on the nature of the counterclaim advanced there may or may not be a need for supporting evidence. A good rule of thumb is that if the counterclaim is about an error in the argument being questioned evidence is less important than it would be if the answer is trying to posit an opposing truth. For example, if the argument is that the other side has relied on a biased source, providing an alternative source may not be necessary if the aim is simply to weaken the argument. If the aim is to posit the opposite of the argument relying on a biased source, then supporting evidence for the counterclaim is more necessary.

In answering a specific claim the goal is generally speaking to weaken an argument by creating doubt. How much doubt is created depends on the nature of the claim and its role in a larger argument. In a debate that revolves around the definition of a term, topicality for example, the deterministic nature of the argument means that if the definition that the argument rests on is not applicable then there will be insurmountable doubt placed on that position. This works because arguments that hinge on definitions tend to be viewed through an "either/or" lens, more so than causal arguments which tend to be more probabilistic.

Answering Positions

In answering a position, the goal is to move beyond addressing specific claims to answering the argument as a whole. This means that rather than challenging a specific claim, the goal is to posit a separate set of claims which in the aggregate are stronger than what is offered by the other side. This is where the goals of the affirmative and negative diverge somewhat. The negative has already embarked on this task in the responses to components of the affirmative case presented in the first constructive, and so in the negative block, the goal is to provide greater depth to the answers to the affirmative case and address the affirmative responses to negative positions. For the affirmative the task is to provide new responses to the negative positions, usually relying on prepared responses. Hence, the emphasis is on the checklist later in the chapter.

For both sides, answering a position often means making a claim which does not counter a claim made by the other side, but nonetheless serves to weaken the position as a whole. As a result, the signpost must change. Usually, this is done by titling the argument. For example, if the affirmative is answering a counterplan, they might start by arguing that the plan and counterplan are not mutually exclusive, meaning both can be done at the same time and so the counterplan does not disprove the desirability of the plan. This argument is generally called a permutation, and so the signpost might say "First, permutation...." What this response does is help the audience by organizing the subsequent arguments by numbering, which will make it easier to direct the audience's attention to the appropriate argument later in the debate. Subsequently, the title for the argument lets the audience know what the following argument will be. Following our example, in the negative block, the signpost might be "Responding to the permutation" or "Responding to the first affirmative argument" both of which help the audience identify which argument the negative is responding to.

In answering a position, or expanding one, the goal is generally to present more reasoning than will be followed in the subsequent speeches. Because the later speeches are going to be shorter, the debating will tend to emphasize comparing the relative strengths of the arguments on a position collectively rather than addressing each claim individually. Having more distinct lines of reasoning or evidence for each argument is going to make it easier to make an argument appear to be stronger. It also helps if there are some parts of a position that do not favor your side to be able to acknowledge those weaknesses while arguing that other parts of the same position favor your side to create a comprehensive response.

This gets at the challenge of answering a position. A well-prepared team will always have more arguments prepared than they have time to make. This is in addition to identifying weak parts of a position that can be exploited as discussed in the previous section. The challenge is in both dedicating enough time to a position to provide robust argumentation that can be used for the duration of the debate, without dedicating so much time that other positions are unaddressed. Doing this well requires a good sense of timing, strategy, and thoughtfulness in approaching not only an individual position but also a case as a whole.

Answering Cases

Answering a case requires strategically assessing what the possible arguments in the last speech will be. Because over the course of the debate, many more arguments will be made than can possibly be answered, there is a need to think strategically about where speech time is spent. Recognizing when components of a case are more or less likely to feature in the last speech helps a debater spend time arguing important issues while spending less time on issues that are likely to be irrelevant.

For the affirmative this process is more pressing because the second affirmative constructive is a nine-minute speech that must stand up to fifteen minutes of negative scrutiny while addressing a nine-minute negative constructive. This time crunch places a premium on spending time efficiently and well. In putting together the answers to a negative case, the affirmative is best served by determining which arguments are most threatening and then making a decision about the order of issues to be addressed.

In general the second affirmative constructive will be ordered around the relative risks associated with the negative arguments. Because topicality is sufficient to win the debate on its own and if the negative wins a topicality argument the affirmative case is irrelevant, it usually is the first issue addressed. Because it is a challenging argument to win, it typically does not receive anywhere near the amount of time other arguments might because it is unlikely to be in the last negative speech unless the affirmative case is not a major part of the topic, which may reverse the general trend.

Subsequently, the affirmative should defend the case which was presented in the first affirmative constructive. How much time is dedicated to this can vary on a couple of important questions. First, how many arguments does the negative have against the case? Second, does the affirmative have offensive arguments such, as link or impact turns, against the case? Third, does the affirmative need to win every component of the case? The more yes answers exist to these questions the more time required. The aim of the affirmative should be to answer all negative arguments which prevent the affirmative from being able to claim an advantage at the end of the debate. This wording is deliberate, the affirmative does not have to win every claim made in the first constructive in order to win the debate. If the first affirmative constructive presented more than one advantage to their plan, conceding one of the advantages may save time if another advantage can be adequately defended. This approach, described as "kicking out" can save time, but generally is not an option if the advantage has been link or impact turned, because these offensive arguments prove the plan is worse than the status quo, and conceding them would prove the plan to be undesirable. If the negative arguments against the case are focused on the solvency of the plan, each of those arguments must be addressed because if the plan cannot solve the advantages then there is no benefit for the affirmative to claim at the end of the debate.

Experience is the best teacher, but a good rule of thumb is that the affirmative should work to limit their time spend on the affirmative case to less than what the negative has spent responding to the case in the first negative constructive. Ideally, this can be accomplished by applying evidence from the first speech to warrant reasons why the negative arguments are untrue rather than reading additional evidence. Where this isn't possible, the goal is to make the response to the negative arguments as brief as possible while still weakening it. In addition to addressing the negative arguments the affirmative must provide a brief statement, called an "extension" which summarizes the different components of their case, emphasizing the significance of the advantage that is claimed. This brief summary serves the function of clarifying for the audience what the affirmative is continuing to advocate from the first speech and also foreshadows how the affirmative case will compare to the negative arguments at the end of the debate.

Subsequently, the affirmative must determine how to spend time on the remaining negative arguments which can be complicated because while there are some rules, exceptions abound. In general, counterplans require relatively little time because they are defensive in that they prove the plan is unnecessary, not that it is bad. Disadvantages take more time because they prove the plan is bad and usually require reading evidence to disprove. Moreover, because a disadvantage is generally the benefit to a counterplan, answering a disadvantage effectively can make a counterplan irrelevant. Kritiks tend to take the longest because they require a similar set of arguments to a counterplan and disadvantage combined. Keeping these rules in mind, the affirmative must budget its time with an eye toward what the most likely negative arguments will be, either based on known proclivities of the negative team, or apparent effectiveness of the argument in disproving the affirmative position.

There is an important caveat to the suggestions made above for affirmative debaters defending a critical or performative case. Because these affirmatives are written to be prepared for framework and topicality arguments by the negative, typically the affirmative will defend their case first. The reasoning behind this is simple, by defending their case, the affirmative can apply the arguments presented in the first affirmative constructive to the topicality or framework arguments in a more efficient manner. Otherwise, for critical or performance affirmatives there is not much difference in addressing other negative arguments.

For the negative, answering a case is much simpler. The second negative constructive and first negative rebuttal has fifteen minutes of time allotted to address a nine-minute second affirmative constructive. While the rest of the structure of the debate favors the affirmative, this large block of time for the negative affords the ability to provide such a great breadth and depth of argumentation that the burden of rejoinder is changed from a principle of argument into such a potent weapon that the negative often has a distinct advantage. What this large block of time allows the negative to do is address all of the relevant affirmative arguments while adding new arguments that put more pressure on the affirmative.

To do this most effectively the negative will first divide responsibilities between the second negative constructive and the first negative rebuttal. This division of responsibility ensures that time is not wasted by having both speeches deal with the same arguments. There are many different ways this can be done, but a common approach would be to have the second negative constructive handle arguments that are defensive to the affirmative case, such as the one case arguments and counterplans, while the first negative rebuttal will handle offensive arguments such as disadvantages. Beyond the time advantage given in this division of labor, this approach also ensures that the most challenging arguments can be given to the first negative rebuttal which will have the benefit of not only the preparation time their teammate takes, but also their teammates' speech time and subsequent cross-examination time to prepare for the rebuttal.

Beyond dividing responsibilities, the negative will also make a similar calculation to the affirmative and might choose to concede certain positions to allocate more speech time to arguments which the negative believes will feature more prominently in the final speeches. This task is slightly more complicated because different types of positions require specific arguments in the position to be conceded for the position to cease to be relevant in the debate. Much like the affirmative advantage, if a disadvantage has been turned then the turn must be disproven before the argument is conceded otherwise the affirmative has gained an advantage. For counterplans and kritiks the initial question is about the status of the argument. As discussed in the previous chapter, if the argument is "conditional" then conceding it is generally not a problem so long as the negative is ready to defend conditionality as a desirable approach to negative advocacies. For the other statuses, the question essentially becomes whether the affirmative has made any arguments that the counterplan or kritik has a negative consequence. If the affirmative has made such an argument a dispositional counterplan must refute the argument before it is conceded. For unconditional counterplans or kritiks the answer is quite simple, no concession is permissible. If there is one argument that is most frequently conceded it is topicality, because even if the affirmative proves their plan is topical that is not sufficient to win the debate, and so unless the negative believes they will argue topicality in the last speech it is generally conceded in the block.

To concede an argument requires the negative to acknowledge an affirmative argument as true, which makes the position irrelevant. For example, if the affirmative argues that the disadvantage does not link to the affirmative case, the negative can concede that argument to make the disadvantage irrelevant. This should be done with some caution because most affirmatives answer a disadvantage with a combination of offensive and defensive arguments the negative must be sure that the defensive argument which is conceded would also disprove the offensive argument made by the affirmative. To extend our example, if the affirmative had argued that adopting the plan would solve the impact of the disadvantage the negative would need to disprove that argument in addition to conceding that there was no link. In the context of counterplans and kritiks the general approach would be to concede a permutation argument, that the counterplan or kritik and the affirmative plan could be adopted at the same time, so there is no need for the judge to evaluate the counterplan or kritik.

Subsequent to adopting time-saving measures to focus on the best negative arguments the rest of the debate becomes much more simple for the negative. The goal is to answer the affirmative arguments and provide additional reasoning for the negative positions. This is strategically important because it pressures the affirmative to respond to more arguments in the first affirmative rebuttal which is a mere six minutes long. For the affirmative, addressing a fifteen-minute block of negative speech time is an incredibly difficult challenge. Consider a disadvantage. If the negative not only answers the affirmative arguments but also offers several additional new reasons why the plan would link to the disadvantage, the affirmative may not have time to respond to them all. As a result, the negative will have to spend less time in their last speech establishing the truth of the disadvantage and can instead spend its time explaining why the disadvantage is more substantial than the purported benefit of the affirmative advantage.

There is no denying that the information in this section is intimidatingly complex. That is a reflection of the degree of nuance, sophistication, and strategy that goes into answering cases for both sides. Despite this complexity, after a little practice, it becomes intuitive and second nature. In the end, all of this maneuvering is in the service of giving debaters the ability to spend more time on what they perceive to be stronger positions and less time on positions that however valuable they were perceived to be at the beginning of the debate have been demonstrated to be less helpful.

The Disadvantage Checklist

For the affirmative side preparing to address negative cases usually begins with thinking through what the most substantial disadvantages to their case would be if it were adopted. On the topic which we have used as a model for this guide the most intuitive disadvantage would be that reducing the size or role of the United States nuclear forces would be undermining the goal of those forces, to deter potential adversaries. The affirmative could begin to address this disadvantage by designing their case around an advantage that argues, perhaps counter-intuitively, that reducing the reliance on nuclear weapons would boost deterrence, essentially presenting the argument against the most common disadvantage in the first speech.

That preliminary step aside, the affirmative is in essentially the same position that the negative would be in preparing responses to an affirmative advantage. A choice must be made between three strategies: defensive arguments, link turns, or impact turns. There are ways that these strategies can be combined, but thinking about them separately helps categorize the arguments that would be needed to satisfy the affirmative goal of proving that the advantages of the case they have presented outweigh the disadvantages to that case presented by the negative.

For defensive strategies the goal is to sufficiently weaken the disadvantage that the judge will either disregard it or conclude that it is of far lesser importance than the advantages in the affirmative case. Usually, this begins by arguing that the disadvantage is non-unique. If the negative is arguing that the plan would decrease the deterrence capability of the United States, the affirmative would respond by arguing either that United States deterrence is already at a low point, and so the plan would not be of unique consequence. A clever approach goes in the other direction, arguing that uniqueness overwhelms the link, meaning that United States deterrence capability is so robust that changing nuclear forces policy would be inconsequential. In both cases, the goal is to undermine the perception that the plan would have a meaningful impact.

Additionally, the affirmative would argue that the plan does not reduce deterrence. A version of this argument might be that a reduced reliance on nuclear forces would give the United States a more credible deterrent capability because it would be more willing to intervene early against potential adversaries. After all, the desire to use nuclear weapons is rarely there, but the United States has a more rich history of conventional military involvement and focusing our deterrence strategy around conventional forces might provide a more credible threat. This argument, combined with the non-unique claim above that the United States does not have effective deterrence now would be a link turn, effectively a new advantage for the affirmative. Because of the ability of this argument to be either offensive or defensive, it is a very popular approach with affirmative debaters because the rhetoric attached to the argument can change from one speech to the next to make it appear to be more offensive or defensive.

The affirmative might also argue that the disadvantage has no impact. A version of this might be that if the United States did not have deterrence capability it would be of little or no consequence. Afterall, if the United States could deter adversaries it is hard to explain why the United States uses its military so frequently, so it could be that deterrence is not very important. For a defensive strategy this approach would be fine, but if the aim was to argue for the link turn the argument that a decrease in deterrence is insignificant would also mean the affirmative's hard won advantage is lost. This problem means that if the affirmative is mixing defensive arguments with link turns, they will often concede the impact argued by the negative, in this case that deterrence is good.

An alternative approach would be to impact turn the disadvantage. In this instance that might mean arguing that deterrence is dangerous because if an adversary challenges the United States, it must use its military to prevent the perception of weakness. As a result, the United States is drawn into more conflicts than deterrence would likely prevent. This impact-turn approach can be effective, especially for more critical affirmatives because while these counterintuitive arguments may take longer to explain, you generally have fewer steps in a causal chain to demonstrate. The problem is that in conceding the thesis of the negative argument, the job of the negative debaters is reduced to defeating one affirmative argument, and with the negative block on their side, this can generally be accomplished relatively easily.

The biggest concern is to avoid mixing link turns and impact turns. As discussed in the last chapter, where this happens a double negative is performed. Consider if the affirmative had argued parts of all three strategies mentioned above. They would claim that deterrence is currently weak, but the plan makes it stronger, but deterrence is bad because pursing it creates more conflicts. That might not be the disadvantage the negative had intended to argue, but they can essentially concede it and only have to prove that their new disadvantage that the affirmative just argued on their behalf is of greater consequence than the affirmative case.

Answering disadvantages is the essential building block for answering all of the other negative arguments. While some negative positions have additional components that dictate different arguments are needed, if an affirmative debater can conceptualize their response to the negative position in terms of defense, link turns, and impact turns the other pieces fall into place relatively quickly. The goal for the affirmative against should be to produce arguments that are consistent with each other from one or a combination of these strategies to undermine the negative position at hand and leverage additional arguments to provide multiple reasons to reject the position.

The Counterplan Checklist

The counterplan checklist is a short one because counterplans themselves are generally a short argument. From the affirmative perspective, a counterplan is essentially a way to make it harder for the affirmative to argue that their plan is of greater consequence than the disadvantages posed by the negative. As such, when the position is presented in the negative constructive it is usually a one-sentence text that articulates what the counterplan would do, and a subsequent argument for how that would solve the case usually supported by evidence. An adjunct to this position is usually a disadvantage to the affirmative policy which provides a reason why the counterplan is net beneficial.

The first argument on the affirmative checklist is a permutation, or argument that the plan and counterplan are not mutually exclusive. If that is the case, then there is no reason to prefer the counterplan and a reasonable judge would vote for the affirmative. How a permutation is articulated varies a bit depending on the counterplan and how it relates to the affirmative case. Some counterplans embrace the entirety of the affirmative policy but suggest the policy should be enacted through a separate means than those suggested by the affirmative. These sort of counterplans are usually addressed with a permutation suggesting that both the plan and counterplan can be done at exactly the same time, a policy maker could "do both." This same permutation works where the plan and counterplan suggest entirely different policies that are not definitionally opposed to each other.

Assuming the affirmative is correct in identifying the counterplan and a "do both" permutation is argued the debate focuses around whether the benefit proposed by the negative is substantial enough to demonstrate the combination of policies is less desirable than adopting the counterplan on its own. The affirmative would then have two options (in addition to the arguments made against the adjunct disadvantage). One option would be to argue that the disadvantage would also apply equally to the counterplan, and so it is not preferable to the affirmative plan. Alternatively, the affirmative might argue that by doing both policies at the same time the disadvantage would be avoided. To give a common example, the negative might argue that adopting the affirmative policy through the Executive branch would cause political backlash, therefore the counterplan would be to have Congress enact the policy. The affirmative might respond that by arguing that having Congress enact a policy would also cause political backlash. The affirmative could argue at the same time that if both branches acted together it would signal unity which would limit any political backlash.

Some counterplans include all but a small part of the affirmative policy. These counterplans are generally themselves a more modest version of a topical policy, which is paired with a disadvantage arguing that the part of the affirmative plan that is not included in the counterplan is problematic. This counterplan is described as a "plan inclusive counterplan" because it includes at least a part of the affirmative policy. The affirmative might respond to such a counterplan with a "do the counterplan" permutation, and argue that the negative counterplan is sufficiently similar to the plan that it does not disprove the desirability of the plan. The negative responds that allowing the affirmative to cease defending part of their proposed policy (rather than an advantage to it) is bad practice because it allows the affirmative to arbitrarily change their plan to make negative arguments irrelevant. Subsequently the affirmative will argue that the plan and counterplan are not distinguishable, or that the benefit to the counterplan is so inconsequential as to make the counterplan and plan equally desirable.

There are other counterplans that are written to be resistant to permutations. If the affirmative argues for disarming the United States nuclear forces, the negative might propose a counterplan to expand the nuclear forces by developing new nuclear weapons. While the affirmative might try one of the permutations listed above, perhaps to waste the negative's time arguing an obviously not applicable permutation, there are more responsive arguments to make. For example, a permutation might suggest that an additional policy could be adopted that would address the reasons why the counterplan is superior, known as an intrinsic permutation. In response to the counterplan described above the affirmative might argue that as a part of the disarmament process the United States should develop other weapons technologies that would eliminate the need for an expanded nuclear force. The negative would point out that this is not a part of the affirmative plan as expressed in the first speech, and allowing such a permutation makes it hard for the negative to argue that the plan is in fact undesirable. A different approach altogether would have the affirmative cease to defend complete disarmament in favor of disarming a part of its arsenal. This is known as a severance permutation, and would likely prompt the negative to argue that allowing the affirmative plan to be changed mid-debate is unfair because the affirmative can simply avoid any disadvantage by ceasing to defend their proposal rather than address the negative argument.

As the examples above illustrate, often debates about the relationship between the plan and the counterplan feature arguments about whether a permutation is or is not a fair (or perhaps educationally worthwhile) argument for the affirmative to make. This is one of the features of a competitive enterprise without a rulebook, and the participants often litigate such questions among themselves. Essentially, there is a debate about debate, where the judge determines based on the arguments presented whether they should intervene to disregard the argument. These debates are notoriously unpredictable, but there are some areas of loose consensus about what permutations are and are not considered legitimate and merit consideration by the judge. The general consensus is that legitimate permutations include the entirety of the affirmative plan, and part or all of the negative counterplan. This means that, as a rule, the severance and intrinsic permutations described above are not considered legitimate. There are exceptions to every rule, and the negative generally has the burden to make the arguments for why this is the case. Nonetheless, relying on permutations that do not meet the rule described above is a perilous endeavor.

The second argument on the checklist is theory. Turning the tables on the negative arguments described above, the affirmative can and often should make theory arguments to the effect that the negative counterplan is unfair or not educationally worthwhile to debate. Consider a negative counterplan arguing that rather prior to adopting an affirmative policy of disarming the United States nuclear forces there should be a binding consultation between the United States and Japan. Such consultation is then argued to be desirable because as an ally that relies on the United States nuclear deterrence Japan would expect consultation and so passing a plan without a consultation would cause permanent harm to that relationship. The affirmative might argue that this counterplan is illegitimate because it would result in the wholesale adoption of the plan, and asking the affirmative to disprove the desirability of its own plan is hardly fair, and so the judge should reject the counterplan.

Although theory arguments often come across as a particularly whiney protest, they are an important tool for the affirmative. Remember from the last chapter that the only true limit on the policies the negative can propose is the imagination of the negative debater. For the affirmative to be expected to defend their policy against any conceivable counterplan is harsh, and so theory arguments provide a helpful check. Though there is little in the way of consensus about which counterplans are and are not legitimate in practice the arguments can be made quickly and so in responding to most counterplans it is an important option should the rest of the debate on the counterplan go poorly for the affirmative. The most common theory argument has to do with the counterplan status. As discussed in the previous chapter, counterplan status is a controversial topic among debaters, coaches, and judges, so when in doubt an affirmative debater is often well served to argue that the counterplan status should prompt the judge to disregard it or award the offending team a loss in the debate.

The third argument on the checklist is solvency, essentially that the counterplan does not solve the affirmative case. While the arguments listed above are important, the solvency question is typically the focus of most of the debate surrounding the counterplan. If the affirmative wins the counterplan does not solve the advantages of the affirmative case, then the affirmative will always be able to argue that the advantages of the plan outweigh the disadvantages. If the affirmative fails, then even a slight risk of a disadvantage would be sufficient to cause most judges to vote for the negative. Thus, even though it is the third item on the checklist, that has more to do with the fact that the other arguments listed above can be made very briefly, than priority. Putting the shorter arguments first affords the affirmative debate the ability to focus more time and arguments on this essential component of the negative argument. The ideal way to make a solvency argument is to use evidence from the first affirmative constructive to illustrate what the counterplan cannot accomplish that the affirmative plan does. Alternatively, new evidence might be read that the counterplan is unworkable. The easiest way to illustrate this is to consider domestic policy debate topics, where the negative often argues for state-led policy change as an alternative to the federal government taking action. There is a prodigious amount of scholarly evidence illustrating how ineffective states are at coordinating their actions in a manner that is comparable to what the federal government can do, and so the affirmative will argue that trying to adopt policies at the state level will be far less effective.

The fourth argument on the checklist is a disadvantage. Essentially, it is the same argument against the counterplan as what the negative would argue against the affirmative case. A simple version of this would be to argue that the disadvantage to the plan would apply equally to the negative counterplan. Alternatively, the affirmative could read a standalone disadvantage to the counterplan. This generally tends to happen less frequently because it tends to take a lot of time, and the advent of more lenient approaches to conditional counterplans has made it hard for the affirmative to gain an advantage by proving the counterplan is undesirable independent of the plans desirability.

The counterplan checklist is helpful because counterplans are unpredictable. There are so many different versions of the argument that trying to memorize the ideal response to all of them is impossible. What the checklist does is provide a template so that debater knows what the arguments should sound like, and what strategic purpose should be, so that when they encounter a new counterplan they generally know what they should be saying. It also helps because while any one of these arguments on the checklist could help the affirmative win the debate, having many different ones can help reverse the time advantage held by the negative side.

The Kritik Checklist

If counterplans are unpredictable by nature, it is hard to find words adequate to describe kritiks. Because their aim is to identify an often unconscious assumption in the affirmative case they raise issues that an affirmative debater might have a hard time foreseeing. When coaching novice debaters, the author often begins pep talks for debates where a kritik might be read by telling his debaters that it is like looking at an x-ray of your body. You know all of that stuff is in there, but until you can see below the surface you don't know what it looks like. In preparing to debate a kritik the best first step for new debaters is to be ready to hear uncomfortable and unfamiliar things said about a case, and then to trust their preparation to give them a start.

The checklist for a kritik is structurally similar to a marriage of the checklist for a disadvantage and counterplan. There are some distinctive features, but they tend to have more to do with accounting for subtle differences in argument content more so than a distinctive structural feature of the argument. Imagine an affirmative that argues for disarming the United States nuclear arsenal because continued reliance on nuclear deterrence is less effective than reliance on conventional weapons as a more credible deterrent. The negative might respond with a disadvantage that says a shift to conventional weapons would increase the likelihood of conflict because the nuclear taboo no longer prevents conflict. The negative might then propose a counterplan that advocates for a change in nuclear posture. An alternative strategy might be to kritik the affirmative's reliance on United States security interests as justification for disarmament, arguing that such justifications would also be used to justify preemptive war against other countries. Specifically, the affirmative's justifications are rooted in lowering the threshold for using military force, meaning that conventional conflict is more likely. A better approach would be to reject altogether the emphasis on security as a way to justify military policy decisions. In the hypothetical negative positions outline here the conclusions of the negatives argument are extremely similar, and structurally the arguments are the same. What differs most substantively is the way the debate is focused not on the desirability of the plan, but instead on the reasoning that is supposed to motivate the judge to favor the plan.

This is where the checklist starts, with an argument called framework. Essentially, framework is the title given to a collection of different arguments that essentially share the claim that the focus of the debate should be the desirability of the plan. It is intended to prevent arguments often made by the negative that the plan should not be evaluated. These arguments are discussed at length in the previous chapter, suffice to say for the affirmative all of these arguments are a problem because they make it so that the affirmative case is irrelevant to the judges' decision. So the argument must be made that the desirability of the plan should remain the focus of the debate otherwise the debate either becomes unfair or educational. An astute observer will note that this is a variety of the theory arguments described in the counterplan checklist. This is a correct observation, with the caveat that often framework arguments also include defenses of focusing policy discussions around probable outcomes.

Consider the following, the negative argues that the justifications for the plan demonstrate a bias that privileges the United States. The affirmative responds by saying regardless of that truth, the plan offers the best policy outcome. The obvious negative rejoinder is that such thinking promotes complicity with the effects of United States-centric worldviews such as (so the negative argues) islamophobia. For the affirmative to argue that their approach is superior because it makes debate more fair is not especially compelling in light of the very human appeal made by the negative. In response, the affirmative would be well advised to have prepared arguments that defend a pragmatic or utilitarian approach like theirs as an anecdote to the problems raised by the negative. So while framework entails a theory debate, it also can entail debates about the ideas embodied in argument practices.

The second argument on the checklist is a permutation. Again, similar to a counterplan, but slightly different because rather than combining two competing policies, now the argument is about the viability of combining two competing ideologies. There are two common permutations read against kritiks. The first is a simple "do both" permutation, arguing that the affirmative case is not exclusive with the ideas expressed in the kritik. Essentially, the argument tests just how true the negative's kritik is of the affirmative case. If the link to the kritik is relatively weak, vague, or unclear, the do both permutation can be effective in proving that the alternative idea expressed by the kritik is compatible with the policy proposed. To use the hypothetical case and kritik described in the top paragraph of this section the affirmative might argue that while the affirmative case entailed security justifications, the policy of disarmament would be the natural conclusion of eschewing national security as a justification for military policy. Given this natural agreement, the differences in justification are irrelevant.

An alternative permutation is to advocate for combining the affirmative case except for the specific parts which have been criticized. The idea here being less a test of the link to the kritik, and more a test of the alternative. The idea behind this permutation is to create what is called a double-bind, or argument that forces one of two conclusions. The premise of the double bind is that, because most kritiks are true of both the plan and existing United States policy, social structure, ideology, etc. the alternative must be sufficiently potent as an ideological shift to address all of those problems. Thus, the alternative can either overcome the problems raised by the affirmative case, or because it cannot solve those same problems it does not create enough change to warrant rejecting the affirmative case. This permutation is clever, but not insurmountable, because the inverse of the double-bind is also true. If the alternative can solve all of the problems illustrated in the kritik, including the affirmative policy or justifications can only create a risk that large systemic issues go unaddressed. Which side wins such a debate often comes down to how other issues in the debate play out.

The third argument on the checklist is a defense of the ideology in the affirmative which is being criticized. This is where most affirmative cases are at a disadvantage because they struggle in diagnosing what the kritik is actually about. The best place to start this process is in cross-examination by asking clarification questions about what the specific failings of the affirmative case are. Generally, these failings fall into one or more of three categories of humanistic inquiry: epistemology, ontology, and axiology. Epistemology is the study of knowledge, a kritik of this failing would argue that the affirmative is premised on inaccurate understandings of the world. Ontology is the study of being (especially of being a human), a kritik of this failing argues that the affirmative has misunderstood an essential feature of the human condition. Axiology is the study of ethics, and such a kritik argues that the affirmative has adopted an unethical position. Asking questions that clarify which of these three issues is the focus of the kritik is one way to know what sort of a defense is needed.

A kritik could of course include arguments in all three of these veins, but to illustrate what the affirmative response might look like consider an axiological kritik. The negative might argue that the affirmative privileging the United States security interests justifies the use of war to pursue United States interests, because war is fundamentally unethical the affirmative should be rejected. The affirmative might respond by arguing from a utilitarian perspective that while their affirmative may legitimate preemptive war, if it prevents larger conflicts then it would preserve more lives. To warrant the conclusion that their case is ethically sound, the affirmative would need a defense of this sort of utilitarian approach to morality. The problem with the approach outlined above is it remains general, and most kritiks are more narrow in their focus than this hypothetical. A better approach would require the affirmative to know more precisely the negative argument, and so have a more tailored defense of the ideology that lies behind the affirmative case.

Subsequently, the affirmative checklist more or less follows what would be found in debating a combination of a disadvantage and counterplan. Arguments such as the kritik not linking, not having a relevant impact, and not being able to solve the affirmative case or its own impacts constitute the relevant defensive impacts. On their own, these may not be enough to win a debate, and so typically some sort of offensive argument is needed.

One approach would be the link turn strategy. In this approach, the affirmative argues that their case would represent a substantial improvement in the issue raised in the kritik. In the context of the security-oriented kritik above, an affirmative might argue that a reduction in the United States reliance on nuclear forces is a practical approach that is more effective for addressing the problems raised by the kritik than the more abstract alternative proposed by the negative. This approach is essentially providing additional reasoning for a permutation because it demonstrates the compatibility of the affirmative with the kritik. This strategy of course relies on the affirmative already having a plausible alignment with the kritik, which is not always possible but can be effective under the right circumstances.

The other approach would be an impact turn strategy. Unlike most impact turns in other contexts which are counter-intuitive in the context of the kritik an impact turn is often framed as a more practical solution than the alternative. In the context of a security kritik the affirmative might respond by arguing that a commitment to security is desirable. Afterall, the affirmative might argue, the commitment to security had propelled the United States to position as a global power with a vast military and economy that has ensured a Pax Americana. Certainly, the benefits of this focus on security outweigh the risks of trying to revise the entirety of United States foreign policy. These arguments are similarly not intended to function on their own, they provide support for, as well as rely on, the framework debate to prove the focus should be on the desirability of policies rather than analysis of the case as an artifact of ideology.

Both approaches can be successful, the aim is to identify which approach can better take advantage of the arguments already made in the affirmative case. Some teams will even go so far as to prepare entirely different affirmatives to read when they know the team they are debating is likely to argue a kritik so that they can bring more responsive arguments to bear earlier in the debate. This is a sound strategy but does run the risk that a negative might not follow the script and read different arguments to take advantage of the change in affirmative strategy.

Many debaters find the kritik to be an intimidating argument. When the author became involved with collegiate debate over a decade ago, the kritik was not an uncommon argument but still something of a novelty, and many debaters of that era had almost an allergy to debating them. As they have become more common this sensibility has become less common. In the same way that the kritik offers the negative the opportunity to learn and debate a wider array of ideas, it offers the affirmative the same opportunity.

The Topicality Checklist

In addressing topicality arguments the aim for the affirmative is almost always to be as efficient as possible because winning that the affirmative is topical does not win the debate, it merely assures the debate is not lost. The exception to this rule is for critical or performance affirmatives, where this argument is a more substantive challenge to what the affirmative case purports to do. Nonetheless, for both types of affirmative case the checklist is essentially the same, with the primary difference being the amount of warrants offered for the same types of arguments.

The first argument in the checklist is a "we meet" argument. Essentially, the affirmative argues that it satisfies the interpretation of the topic or debate offered by the negative. Ideally, this can be done with evidence that contextualizes the plan as a part of the topic. If this argument is won, then the rest of the arguments are irrelevant, as the affirmative has demonstrated that it affirms the topic. Unfortunately, if a topicality argument is at all worth reading this argument is unlikely to be absolutely true. For example, an affirmative on the topic discussed in this guide might advocate adopting a no-first-use nuclear policy in response to biological weapons use. The negative might respond that this is not in fact a restriction because the United States would still retain a broad nuclear first use policy. This affirmative might plausibly argue that their plan is a restriction, albeit a narrow one, but it is not entirely clear that this is the case.

The second argument, termed a "counter-interpretation" is intended to solve this problem. The counter-interpretation essentially argues that the negative's topicality argument is premised on an undesirable interpretation of the topic. The emphasis on "undesirable" rather than, say, "inaccurate" is intentional, because often the affirmative is in the position of arguing that while multiple interpretations are grammatically correct, one interpretation is superior. To demonstrate why their interpretation is superior the affirmative will provide "reasons to prefer" their interpretation. The two most common of these go under the headings of fairness and education. A fairness argument essentially holds that the affirmative interpretation of the topic provides a more fair and equitable collection of arguments than the negative interpretation. An education argument generally claims that the negative interpretation narrows the topic so much that important issues are essentially off limits, and so important education on those issues is lost.

There is a third reason to prefer which tends to apply more for critical or performance affirmatives, that the interpretation proposed by the negative excludes arguments in a way which reflects a problematic social, political, and cultural norm. This argument differs in that incorporates the philosophical insights of the affirmative case into the discussion of how the debate should take place and what issues can be broached. For the negative, this line of argument is especially challenging because it is hard to find good evidence to support the conclusion that there is a substantial benefit to following the norms typically associated with policy debate relative at the cost of the political, social, and cultural analysis offered by the affirmative case.

The third argument on the checklist is that topicality should be evaluated on the basis of "reasonability" rather than "competing interpretations." The argument is essentially that if the affirmative is close to the topic, then they should not lose, the merits of debating the affirmative case outweighs the potential problems raised by including it. The negative rejoinder is that the judge should evaluate which interpretation of the topic or debate is best because the aim of topicality is to force the affirmative to defend a specific set of arguments which means a strict approach to best interpretation of the topic provides the greatest likelihood of this happening. This debate is rarely resolved in a determinate manner, but making the arguments well for both sides will tend to influence how the judge perceives the issues.

Resolving these three arguments consumes the overwhelming majority of the time spent arguing topicality. As a rule, if the affirmative wins any of the above arguments, they will not lose the debate on topicality. If the affirmative loses, or the debate is unclear, there are some additional arguments that may be helpful in tipping the scale, so the affirmative will often make them, but their utility should be appreciated as somewhat limited. To the extent that they play a role, it is often by giving the judge a perception that the affirmative departure from the topic is less important or worrisome than the negative would suggest.

For example, to mitigate the negative's protestations that the affirmative case was rendered too effective for a fair debate the affirmative will make a series of claims. "Cross-examination checks abuse" is a shorthand for the argument that the ability to ask questions would give the negative sufficient information to prepare more applicable arguments. "Disclosure checks abuse" is a similar short claim that in preparing for the debate the negative could have prepared arguments by asking what the affirmative would argue in the debate and thus the departure from the topic is no major concern. There are a number of other similar claims that could be made, but they essentially amount to the same conclusion. That the judge should disregard topicality as an issue because the negative could prepare arguments, so there is no problem in the affirmative not holding to the topic. Terming these utterances "claims" rather than "arguments" is intentional, because often they are simply stated without any further explanation or reasoning. The desire to limit the amount of time spent responding to topicality arguments is the primary motivation for this poor argument practice. That sensibility is not unreasonable, but most judges have a hard time taking such weak argumentation seriously.

Topicality is an argument that a lot of newer debaters struggle with. After spending so much time and effort to prepare their case, being told that the case is not worthy of being debated prompts a "how dare you" response that causes them to lose sight of the rest of the debate. It is helpful to keep in mind that topicality is merely an argument, and debating it is remarkably helpful. Many debaters who go on to pursue a legal career remember topicality debates as the best training they receive. Afterall, parsing the meaning of the text of the law differs from interpreting the resolution more because of the stakes involved than any difference in the task.

Composing and Delivering Answers

The aim of the checklist above is twofold. It of course provides the affirmative a list of the common arguments which can be made against the negative position, but it also directs the negative which arguments they need to be prepared to answer. In preparing for the debate tournament, the affirmative would add to their case files (or create separate files if they so wish) sections that pertain to each likely negative position and then use the checklist to prepare the arguments they intend to make against those positions. For the negative, each position should have its own file, but then have separate sections to respond to each of the arguments in the affirmative checklist.

The emphasis on the affirmative checklist in this chapter is also intended to help with speech organization. While the affirmative and negative can address each position or component of the affirmative case as they see fit, the order of the arguments on each of those positions is usually set by the second affirmative constructive. As discussed in the previous chapter, the style of note taking used in policy debates, the amount of information provided in a speech, and the need to recognize the connections between arguments means that the organization of a speech plays an outsized role in how debaters and judges understand what is happening in a debate.

The general rule is that the second affirmative constructive sets the order. This means that, in general, when the negative defends its position it does so by refuting the affirmative arguments in the order they were presented. There are times when a debater may decide to deviate from this course, for example, when the second affirmative constructive is especially disorganized as a speech, but they do so at the risk of losing the judge who will be attempting to align the negative and affirmative arguments. Following this rule also helps with composing the speech.

For the affirmative the task of composing a speech is as simple as copying the portions of the affirmative file that correspond to the negative positions into a separate speech document which constitutes their script. They may make changes to how arguments are worded to account for what was said in cross-examination or to include new ideas, but the blocks prepared prior to the debate form the backbone of the script. For the negative, the task is essentially the same with more files involved because each file corresponds to one position. In each file, there should be a section for each affirmative argument on the checklist, and the task is simply copying each section of the file that corresponds to the arguments the affirmative has made into a file.

Conclusion

Answering cases, positions, and arguments is the most technically complex, strategically sophisticated, and intellectually engaging component of the debate. This is not to say it is more important, most debates are neither won nor lost until the last speech in the debate. Nonetheless, a debater who has not invested in being adequately prepared to answer the first constructives may find themselves an exception to the rule.

Because of the difficulties associated with this part of the debate many newcomers feel like there are so many unwritten rules and nuance that they cannot hope to learn it all. Such newcomers should take heart, their peers are in the exact same place, and even the most experienced debaters will make mistakes. With time and experience these rules will become second nature and contribute to a rich intellectual engagement.

Notes

1 Hans Kristensen, Matt Korda, Eliana Johns, Mackenzie Knight, & Kate Kohn, "Status of World Nuclear Forces," Federation of American Scientists, March 29, 2024, https://fas.org/initiative/status-world-nuclear-forces/.
2 Hans Kristensen & Matt Korda, "Nuclear Notebook: United States nuclear weapons, 2023," Bulletin of the Atomic Scientists, January 16, 2023, https://thebulletin.org/premium/2023-01/nuclear-notebook-united-states-nuclear-weapons-2023/.
3 Chaim Perelman & Lucie Olbrechts-Tyteca, *The New Rhetoric* Trans. John Wilkinson & Purcell Weaver, (University of Notre Dame Press: South Bend, 2010): 460–461.

7
REBUTTAL SPEECHES

Despite the immense amount of time and energy invested in preparing them, the first two constructive speeches are generally the easiest to deliver effectively. They allow debaters to take best advantage of being able to think through issues before the debate, research, and dedicate time and attention to the rhetoric they use to persuade judges. An apt analogy would be to the opening moves in chess, which at the highest levels are essentially preplanned by both sides in an attempt to create a strategic advantage. Assuming nothing unforeseen happens, these are completed with a minimum of thought and effort in the debate. In this analogy, the second affirmative constructive and the negative block constitute a middle game, where both sides are making sacrifices and jockeying for argumentative position. The rebuttal speeches meaning, the first affirmative rebuttal and second negative and affirmative rebuttals represent an end game where each side attempts to prove that based on the foregoing arguments their side has effectively proven their case.

The analogy quickly reaches an important breaking point. Unlike in chess, there are no draws in debate, and the elegance of the execution of the moves serves as something of a tiebreaker if the arguments themselves do not resolve the debate. The best debaters are adept at delivering rebuttals that both satisfy the strategic demands of addressing the relevant arguments and using powerful and intentional rhetoric to amplify the apparent truth and significance of their argument relative to their peers. This requires preparation, but more importantly, creativeness in how they approach the arguments to be addressed.

One of the complicated and intellectually engaging features of policy debate is that each of the rebuttal speeches has important tasks to complete as a part of the effort to persuade the judge to favor their side. For debaters who are new to the activity, this sort of nuance is generally lost in the single-minded focus on responding to what the other side has said. More experienced debaters quickly realize that while responding to their opponents is important, of equal if not greater importance is framing the arguments that have been delivered by both sides. This chapter will provide a guide to what goals a debater should have for each speech, and how to tailor their arguments in order to be more effective.

The First Affirmative Rebuttal

For new debaters, especially those who are particularly attentive to the lessons of the previous chapter which emphasizes flowing and the importance of thoroughgoing and strategic responses to affirmative and negative cases, this is the hardest speech in debate. The author would hold that this interpretation is inaccurate, but this view is not altogether unreasonable. The challenge for the first affirmative rebuttal is that in the negative block, 15 minutes worth of argumentation took place, and must be addressed in a mere six minutes of speech time. This is a difficult task.

This task is made more difficult because the first affirmative rebuttal is handcuffed by a few important conventions that function as essentially unwritten rules. The first affirmative rebuttal is the first speech where adding new arguments is essentially impermissible. The reason for this convention is that if the first affirmative rebuttal were allowed to make entirely new arguments the negative would not have an adequate number of speeches to both address the argument and deliver a summation speech. The one caveat to this rule is if the negative makes new arguments in the block the affirmative is given the opportunity to respond using new arguments as it is their first opportunity to respond. Outside of this caveat, the affirmative is limited to arguing the claims already made in the second affirmative constructive.

An additional constraint is that the affirmative's short period of time for the speech makes it exceedingly hard to read evidence for the arguments that have been made. This means that if the negative has gained an advantage in the quantity and quality of the evidence read in the debate then the first affirmative rebuttal will need to surrender extremely valuable speech time to read new evidence or be very creative, neither of which is easy. Even where the evidence to make good arguments is present, the first affirmative rebuttal can only be used effectively if they have a well-organized flow that can tell them what was in that evidence, because it is simply too inefficient to locate a piece of evidence in the speech documents which have been exchanged.

Finally, the first affirmative rebuttal is a speech that has no script. Although most of the content of the preceding speeches is delivered using prepared materials, evidence that has been gathered, prepared arguments, by the first affirmative rebuttal the ability to use such preparation materials is effectively exhausted. As a result, the debaters delivering this speech typically need to have a certain comfort with improvisation, but bounded by the argumentation already presented in the speech.

In preparing the first affirmative rebuttal the speaker's first duty is to work with their teammate. Debates are not won in the first affirmative rebuttal, the negative will have its say and so the first affirmative rebuttal cannot have the last word, but the debate can be lost there. Where debates are lost in the first affirmative rebuttal the speaker has failed to defend a potentially winning combination of the arguments made by their partner. As a result, the speaker is best served to develop a relationship with their partner so that they are of the same mind about which arguments must be defended to win the debate. What those arguments are is explained in depth in the preceding chapters, and will be further addressed later in the second affirmative rebuttal section.

The aim for the first affirmative rebuttal is to give as efficient a speech as possible. This means first, avoiding the temptation to wax poetic about arguments, and to find word economical ways to make them. Where responding to a new argument made in the negative block the modified version of the Toulmin model discussed in previous chapters is required, but where the second affirmative speaker has already provided some reasoning a different technique is more efficient. This different technique could roughly be described as "meta-argument" or argument about the nature of the argument. In this technique, the debater relies on the attentiveness of the judge and their note taking to remind them of the existing argument and provide a reason why it is superior.

To do this, a debater first offers a signpost to direct the judge to the position, argument, and claim. A signpost might read for example, "On the disadvantage's uniqueness argument regarding deterrence" which would direct the judge's attention to the specific issue which the debater will argue. The next step is to clarify the difference in the claims by uttering something that may sound like, "they argue that deterrence is strong now because of the United States possession of nuclear weapons, the second affirmative constructive argued this is untrue because nuclear weapons are unlikely to be used which means nuclear weapons are an empty threat and not a credible deterrent" which clarifies for the judge what the competing arguments are. The debater then provides a reason why their argument is superior such as, "Our argument is superior because the leverage provided by nuclear weapons is irrelevant if a country lacks the will to use them, the nearly 80-year tradition of not using them has already degraded the perception of nuclear weapons as a credible deterrent." In this example, rather than disproving the initial negative claim directly, the debater has shifted the judges' attention to which side has more sound reasoning for their claim. This eliminates the need to address the specifics of the evidence read by both sides and reframes the debate around the perception of deterrence which would likely favor the affirmative side of the debate.

Another tactic is to take advantage of arguments not answered by the negative. To do this a debater uses the same sort of signposting technique described above and then points out the negative concession. The colloquial term used to describe a conceded argument is that it is "dropped," and the colloquialism used to describe an affirmative rearticulating this argument is "extension" derived from the physical act of drawing an arrow next to the dropped argument to illustrate that the debater is carrying it into the next speech. Such an utterance might sound as follows, "Extend the dropped affirmative uniqueness argument that deterrence is weakened by the reliance on nuclear weapons." What this utterance does is identify for the judge an argument which the affirmative has already won, which may still be contested by the negative, but only by nature of comparison to extant negative arguments. An astute reader might note that there is not much reasoning or explanation for this initial claim, which is a common feature. The debater is relying on the judge to have that reasoning at hand in their notes, and so are presenting an enthymeme.

In preparing the first affirmative rebuttal a debater begins by working systematically through each page of their flow and identifying which arguments need to be addressed, extended, and conceded so that over the course of 6 minutes no negative position which was defended in the block goes unaddressed, and at least one advantage is defended from the affirmative case. The reason for the "at least one" wording is that given the substantial time crunch, many debaters who have presented more than one advantage in the debate will choose to concede one of the advantages because the time required to defend it makes doing so less strategically sound. At the conclusion of this process, the debater has, spanning several pages of notes, an outline of their speech. All that is left is to deliver it.

The delivery of the first affirmative rebuttal, as the reader might have noticed in the examples of argumentation provided here, has little in common with the sort of grand oratorical style that one imagines when they hear the term debate. The reason for this is a sound one, what is being observed in the first affirmative rebuttal is the explication of informal logic in an oratorical form, rather than oration that has an informal logic. It is a speech in service to the later second affirmative rebuttal, far more so than a speech geared towards proving the oratorical brilliance of the debater, it demonstrates cleverness, efficiency, and decision-making skills.

The Final Rebuttals

The final rebuttals for both sides are tricky endeavors. They are in relatively equal proportion tests of decision-making, logical reasoning, oratorical brilliance, and rhetorical sophistication. For a debater who debates to learn these diverse skills, these are the speeches that test those skills the most. For a debater who craves competition, these are the most important speeches, because while almost any of the preceding speeches can lose a debate, only the last two speeches can win a debate.

What sets the last two speeches apart is that by this point the relative merits of each position are relatively clear, and while the arguments might not be altogether resolved they are at least explained in full. Neither side is enabled to make any argument that is entirely new, but both sides will need to make new arguments that give significance to the arguments that will be made. While both the second negative rebuttal and second affirmative rebuttal have distinctive features that will be addressed, both are essentially striving to accomplish the same task.

There are essentially three tasks that are required for both speeches. The first is clarifying the final position or advocacy for both sides in the debate. If the affirmative or negative wishes to concede a position so that they might either save time or eliminate an apparent contradiction, this is the speech where it must take place. The second is to provide the impact comparison for both sides on the issues that are most pressing in the debate. The third is to provide the judge with a cohesive reason to prefer their side in the debate.

To understand how these speeches are composed it is helpful to think about what has happened to the volume of arguments made over the course of the debate. Beginning with the first affirmative constructive through the negative block the debate expanded, and both sides were making more new arguments against the opposition in a manner that dramatically expanded the scope of the debate. Beginning with the first affirmative rebuttal the debate has narrowed to a relatively small number of positions for both sides in the debate. This trend will continue through the final rebuttals, and it is not infrequent that while the last speeches will include arguments on many positions which have been presented in the debate only one argument on one position will matter for how the debate is decided.

To make the decision about how to narrow the debate the single most important consideration is the impact, or consequence, of the arguments which have been made. At the end of the debate, the judge will determine who the winner is, and the single component that will most affect the outcome is the impacts that both sides can plausibly claim. From the debaters' perspective, this means conceiving of the debate in terms of what impacts they can convince the judge are real, and subsequently, will prove to be more consequential. In making this determination considering the nature of the impacts is a prominent feature.

Typically the impact of an argument is considered through three criteria. The first of these, and the most commonly emphasized, is magnitude. In its most crass form, magnitude refers to the number of lives saved or lost by a particular policy decision. This crass form has a certain appeal; obviously, mass death is a particularly deep and pressing concern that needs little additional explanation so it works well in the context of the debate. There are more sophisticated high-magnitude impacts, for example, if a team's argument has a climate change impact it is a very high impact argument because climate change would directly influence so many issues (as well as likely resulting in mass death). The problem is that high-magnitude impacts tend to fall shorter on the other criteria, and so an overreliance on such impacts can have some negative consequences.

The second criterion is probability, the likelihood that these impacts would come to pass. The probability of an impact is usually a balance between the events which are going to come to pass, and the likelihood that maintaining or changing policies would influence the outcome. For example, an argument that has poverty as an impact might seem highly probable because it is an ongoing problem that exists already, but might be proven unlikely because it is hard to imagine a single policy eradicating poverty. Other impacts may appear to be less likely but have their probability in debate inflated by the nature of being central to the policy discussions at hand. For example, the possibility of an accidental launch of a nuclear weapon resulting in a global nuclear conflagration that causes the extinction of humanity seems remote, until one is arguing about the relative security and utility of the United States nuclear forces.

The third criterion is the timeframe, how quickly and for how long the impact will take place. As a rule, it is better to argue that an impact will happen sooner rather than later on the premise that if an impact happens sooner it could influence subsequent events. A common example of this is that one team will defend an argument with an impact like economic decline which will happen quickly while their opponent will defend an argument with a slower impact like climate change. The team with the economic impact will say that there is more time to address the climate change problem, but the opportunity to avert economic decline is already at hand. Another common example is that a team will defend an argument that suggests they can prevent a specific regional war in the future, while another team will argue that they address ongoing structural violence caused by poverty, racism, etc. The teams will debate whether it is better to address an ongoing long-term impact or a future concern.

There are some other criteria that are at times discussed, one much less frequent but still valuable criterion is reversibility. For example, climate change may take a long time to make its worst effects felt, but those effects may be so irreversible that prevention is better than remediation. Sometimes moral side constraints are used as a way to focus less on the consequences of a policy and more on the morals surrounding it as a way to avoid the three primary criteria. In fact, the limit on the possible configurations of impacts is the creativity of the debater in articulating the significance of the impact. Nonetheless, the goal of a debater is to ensure that their argument is generally on the side of the impact with the greatest magnitude, which is the most likely, which happens the fastest.

The determination of which arguments will have the most important impact made, the next task is to establish what arguments must be defended to win that impact while mitigating the other side's ability to claim an impact. To do this requires referring to the concepts developed in the previous chapters. Has an argument become stronger or weaker over the course of the debate? Can a complete chain of causes be established for an argument? Does the conclusion of the argument satisfy the stock issues for the affirmative and/or the negative? In answering these questions, the debater will determine a set of priorities for which arguments matter more and less, and what must be proven in the debate.

The last universal feature of the last two rebuttals is how they would be best advised to approach their arguments. There is a frequent misperception of debate, which is that projecting confidence is superior to humility. This misperception is readily fostered by the debates between political candidates which frequently seem to be more about the appearance of faith to party positions, than reasoning to the ideal solution. Political candidates can be forgiven, the very format of their debates militate against the sort of nuanced discussion taking place in a policy debate, and their audience are audiences who have generally limited training in argumentation.

Policy debate generally features relatively expert judges, who by dint of their training are sensitive to the notion that typically both sides are able to make compelling arguments. As a result, projecting overt confidence is not always desirable. By the end of a policy debate, both sides are generally stronger on some arguments, conceded, or are at least perceptually weaker on others, and so they cannot simply defend their arguments as if they are won. Instead, these speeches are summations of the arguments, persuading the judge less on the content of the arguments, but more on the quality of the reasoning to support them. This means both professing the strength of an argument as well as acknowledging the apparent weaknesses of the arguments.

The Second Negative Rebuttal

In the opinion of the author, the second negative rebuttal is the most challenging speech in debate. The difficulty in this speech is that it must both present the judge with a reason to negate while anticipating the arguments which will inevitably be made by the affirmative. Not knowing what the affirmative will say places the negative at a distinct disadvantage because they often are in the position of giving not only a second negative rebuttal which explains why the negative has won the debate, but an implicit third negative rebuttal which disproves the most compelling affirmative rejoinder.

To do this the negative is best served to begin by identifying the best of the negative strategies available. The fourth chapter discussed at length what positions are available to the negative, what their strategic functions are, and what they must in proving to win the debate. In preparing for the second negative rebuttal the first decision is which positions are best suited to satisfy those functions. At the end of those debates, all of the principles discussed in that chapter remain true, but unlike the construction of the first negative constructive, which emphasized finding as many ways to challenge the affirmative as possible, in the last speech the negative has to select the best challenge.

This means first eliminating the positions that will no longer be the focus of the debate. In chapter five the process for this was already discussed, but the process for making this decision matters more in the last speech. With only six minutes left, the negative must aggressively pair down the number of positions it is defending. There are myriad ways that this could be done, but most debaters follow one of the suggested second negative rebuttal strategies below to present a coherent, consistent, and persuasive final speech against the affirmative. To parse how a debater might choose which positions to advocate in the last speech we will imagine a negative case has been constructed which included every type of negative position and all of them were present in the negative block. This hypothetical situation is rather uncommon but helps illustrate the decision-making process.

The first strategy for the second negative rebuttal is to reduce the debate to the desirability of the affirmative case. To do this, the second negative rebuttal would begin by conceding any topicality positions or kritiks. This means the negative will choose between a combination of case arguments, a counterplan, and a disadvantage. In most cases, this strategy is premised on winning a disadvantage, and then choosing between case arguments or a counterplan as a way to narrow the number of arguments that must be addressed. The simplest approach here is to begin with the counterplan and asking two questions. First, can it solve the affirmative case? Second, can the affirmative prove that the counterplan and plan be adopted simultaneously without consequence? If the answer to either question is yes, the counterplan is generally the weaker option, and so the negative would concede the counterplan (not withstanding questions of status or theory as discussed in the previous chapters) and use case arguments in combination with the disadvantage to prove that the plan has little benefit and a severe cost. All other variables being equal, this strategy works best when the negative has a more specific and compelling refutation of the affirmative case.

An adjunct to this first strategy would be to argue that the affirmative case has failed to satisfy a stock issues burden. Where this is done the arguments remain the same, but the difference is that more time is spent arguing that the affirmative has failed to demonstrate that the plan overcomes inherency, addresses a significant harm, or solves the harm that has been identified. The problem with this approach is that it is rare that an affirmative case is so thoroughly refuted that a judge can be convinced to vote for this argument. That said, if the strategy for the second negative rebuttal is to use case arguments and a disadvantage mentioning that the affirmative has failed to meet a stock issue burden adds minimal time because the arguments are essentially the same.

The second strategy is to advocate for a kritik of the affirmative case. This would require conceding disadvantages, counterplans, and topicality arguments so that the debate can focus on the relative merits of the kritik as opposed to the affirmative. This strategy works best where the affirmative has not produced a winning sequence of arguments against the kritik, and even if they have, the negative has the advantage of centering the debate around their arguments. Consider, if the negative can win that the alternative solves the case, or that the affirmative case should be excluded from consideration for reasons tied to a framework debate or is problematic in some other way, the negative may not address the claims of the case directly. This is a perceptual advantage and strategic one that should not be underestimated but does require thorough refutation of the affirmative arguments against the kritik.

The third strategy is to argue that the affirmative is not a legitimate part of the topic. Against critical or performance affirmatives this might be the only option in some cases, and so its relative utility is of small consequence. Against policy affirmatives, this option works best where it is at least apparently on the side of truth about the affirmative's relationship to the topic. Otherwise, absent an error in the affirmative it will be difficult to convince a judge that an apparently topical affirmative is not in fact a part of the topic. If the decision is made to argue for topicality there is little need to worry about the other positions, because if the affirmative is not topical then its desirability or problems with the negative arguments are irrelevant.

In the second negative rebuttal the first part of the speech is dedicated to conceding the arguments which will no longer factor in the debate. This should be done as quickly as possible, ideally within the first thirty seconds at most of the speech. The next part of the speech is generally dedicated to addressing the arguments needed to mitigate the ability of the affirmative to claim an impact. The reason for this order is that it allows the last part of the speech, dedicated to the reasons why the impacts claimed by the negative are more significant to provide a conclusion for the speech.

The composition of the second negative rebuttal follows the same approach as the first affirmative rebuttal where the flow is used as an outline, and the aim has shifted from refutation to argument comparison, emphasizing why the extant negative arguments are superior. What is added where a debater sees fit is an additional sentence or two explaining preempting the likely affirmative argument. Knowing what these arguments will be, and when preemption is needed is remarkably challenging, more a product of instinct honed through experience than through any systematic rule. Hence, the second negative rebuttal is the most challenging speech in debate.

The Second Affirmative Rebuttal

The second affirmative rebuttal is the last speech in the debate. It is the only speech that is not premised around logical calculation, predicting the evolution of arguments, or putting hours of preparation to use. This speech is instead about providing an effective summary of the arguments which have been made and finding the means to make that summary resolve in a vote for the affirmative side. Doing it well requires a degree of creativity, often humor, and more than a little charisma in addition to all of the argumentative skill required of the other speeches.

There are two registers of argumentation that must be present in the second affirmative rebuttal. The first is the individual argument register, which seeks to refute the affirmative arguments. The arguments in the second affirmative rebuttal mirror those of the negative in that some refutation must be done, but the refutation tends to be less about the arguments as they were initially presented and more about refuting the negative characterization of the debate. This means that much of the second affirmative rebuttal tends to track the arguments of the second negative rebuttal rather than the initial first affirmative constructive. Put more simply, the goal is not to restate the claims of the first affirmative constructive or the answers to the negative case, than it is to select the arguments necessary to win a debate.

The second register is the framing of the issues presented in the debate. What this looks like can differ across argument forms. For example, in a topicality debate the framing is generally geared towards making the negative interpretation of the topic appear to be unreasonable. A common approach to accomplishing this framing is to illustrate how arbitrary and capricious the negative interpretation is by listing the affirmatives that would be included or excluded to illustrate how narrow the scope of other debates would become. Another common approach is to illustrate just how essential the affirmative advantages are to learning about the topic. Both of these rely on arguments developed earlier in the debate, usually in this example the justifications for the counter interpretation, but offer a more substantive lens for the affirmative arguments and give a material character to the sense that the negative position is unreasonable.

In the context of the affirmative case against a combination of case arguments and disadvantages the common framing is that action is superior to inaction. The terminology often used where this is tied to extreme impacts such as human extinction is "try-or die" framing which emphasizes both the stakes at play and the apparent inadequacy of complacency. Alternatively, if the negative has opted for a counterplan and disadvantage strategy the common framing devices emphasize that the counterplan must not only be comparable to the plan but obviously superior, otherwise the negative has failed to satisfy its burden to disprove the affirmative. This approach is not altogether dissimilar to an" innocent until proven guilty" strategy reminiscent of legal argumentation, emphasizing that if the judge has reasonable doubt about the counterplan, then the affirmative deserves the benefit of the doubt.

In debates against kritik strategies the second affirmative will often emphasize the desirability of taking material action over abstract theorizing. Because the kritik is more of a philosophical objection, there is a (frequently false) assumption that the kritik is less concerned with taking concrete action. The affirmative frequently takes advantage of this assumption by asserting that the affirmative case represents a concrete response. The conceit in this framing is that there is not much that separates what the affirmative represents as a speech from what the negative represents, but to the extent that the affirmative case has a degree of specificity in its suggested course of action it appears to be a more substantive material response. This framing is productive because it takes advantage of the perceptual tendencies of the arguments, to prompt the judge to affirm a natural tendency toward action rather than inaction.

In composing the second affirmative rebuttal the most pressing challenge is to find embellishments, like those described above, which give the speech a distinctive character that can be used to persuade the judge. This requires a degree of creativity not found in most other speeches that give the second affirmative rebuttal its distinctive character. If the personality of the second negative speaker is the trickster, the personality of the second affirmative speaker is the artist. Diligent, and thorough in their craft, but possessing a vision which is the product of hard work but appears to the audience as more of a gift. If there is a speech that captures a romantic vision of debate which entails

Conclusion

The rebuttal speeches represent the culmination of hours of work. In the contemporary era competing in policy debate entails hours of preparation, intense thought, demanding performance, and cannot help but be exhausting. When a debater delivers their last rebuttal they offer the judge the product of an immense body of work distilled into a brief speech. These speeches test the skill of the debaters in a way that is not found in other parts of the debate. While the earlier speeches test preparation, and strategic thought, the rebuttals combine those skills with a test of creativity and oratorical talent.

With the conclusion of the second affirmative rebuttal the debate is ended. The hard work left at hand is to determine which team has won the debate. That the debate is over does not mean the debaters' work is over. Over the course of a debate, both sides discover strengths and weaknesses in their arguments, and the best debaters act quickly to put those lessons to use tweaking their prepared materials so that in subsequent debates they can improve their performance. In the pursuit of their competitive and educational goals, the best debaters are those who take advantage of every opportunity to get better.

8
JUDGING POLICY DEBATE

Making a decision in a policy debate is a complicated endeavor. In no small part this is because it requires a series of personal judgments about the nature of debate, and what, as an audience member, the judge considers to be important. At the same time, the judge is tasked with the challenge of rendering an impartial decision. This is no small task, as a judge approaches a decision with an individual set of personal beliefs shaped by their life experiences, cultural background, and knowledge base which means the total eradication of bias is impossible. Nonetheless, the role of a good judge is of incredible importance in maintaining a fair competitive experience for the students and educational opportunity for the students.

Consider a hypothetical from the author's experience. Debating by both sides has been remarkably even and comparable, and after half an hour of thinking through the debate, the judge is still unsure which side has proposed the best policy option. One of the teams hails from an august Ivy League university which has had a season-long record of competitive success. The other team hails from a small midwestern university with a direction in the title. If the debaters have not been able to resolve matters in a way that indicates a clear winner and loser, how can a judge divorce themselves from acknowledging which team has a better record of success and hails from an institution recognized for superior debating? Should a judge defer to the better team, or recognize the overachievement on the part of the underdog?

In our hypothetical the judge (who is not the author) has been faced with a complex task that has no clear answer. To help make sense of the situation in front of them the judge deferred to knowledge external of the debate to craft a narrative of what had taken place to give them a sense of what their decision meant. This is a tempting and all too human strategy for dealing with complicated issues, but not an ideal one for the debate. From the view of the debaters such an approach, even if it is extremely human, is flawed because it doesn't reflect the debating which has taken place which devalues the quality of thought and effort that they have expended in the debate. Even if the judges are seeking to avoid such an obvious bias, what standards or metrics can be used to guide their decision so that they can achieve objectivity?

Consider another hypothetical. One of the teams has obviously been better prepared and more practiced but has defended an argument that is explicitly racist. Their opponent, dumbfounded by the mendacity of their opponent, failed to respond in an effective manner. If the judge were to completely obviate moral judgment, they would vote for the team defending the racially biased argument. Should the judge make such a decision in the name of pure objectivity about which side has done the better debating? Should the judge impose their own views of morality to draw a line against voting for racist argumentation?

The thesis of this chapter is not that there is a magical theory or philosophy that allows the judge to navigate both hypotheticals equally well. What this chapter offers is a survey of different approaches to judging with the aim of balancing the tension between the demand for objectivity and acknowledging that judges are not robots, but human beings imbued with experience and knowledge that informs how they view debates. The aim of this chapter is to give debaters an insight into the intellectual positions that judges may occupy so that they can tailor their arguments to their audience. Equally, for debaters who find themselves in a position to judge debates, the aim of this chapter is to give guidance in evaluating debates. The aim of this guidance is not to impose a specific approach to judging on debaters who find themselves in the position of judging a debate, but to provide an a la carte menu that can be used to structure how a debater might go about evaluating which side has won a debate.

One of the interesting characteristics of policy debate is that judges are expected to produce a paradigm, or statement of their general preferences for arguments for debaters to consider as a part of their tournament and pre-debate preparation. This helps improve the performance of debaters by allowing them to tailor their arguments to the audience and, in turn, helps the judge to direct the debates they observe in a productive manner. Part of the aim of this chapter is to provide prospective judges with some guidance on how to judge debates so that as their views on debate develop they know how their views fit into existing policy debate norms.

Judge Philosophies

The topic of how to judge debates is much discussed among both judges and debaters. Indeed, many debaters will argue that the judge ought to use a specific philosophy to judge their arguments during the debate itself. An important part of pre-tournament and pre-round preparation for many debaters is reading the "paradigm" or philosophies of debate judges to see how their arguments can better take advantage of a judges' decision-making process. Although the effort put into drafting paradigms by judges is uneven, most judges do have something of a philosophy whether they know it or not. The philosophies described below are more strictly defined than what most judges follow in practice, with many borrowing elements from multiple philosophies to shape their approach to judging. Nonetheless, these categories are provided to give judges a starting point for thinking about how they will decide debates and to give debaters some insight into different approaches to debate judging to help inform their arguments.

Part of the exigency for describing the philosophies below is discussed at length in the next chapter. As a part of tournament procedure debaters are often able to exercise a degree of discretion about who might judge their debates through the use of preferences. To take advantage of this, debaters need to have a degree of knowledge and familiarity with the different judging philosophies.

Stock Issues

The stock issues paradigm has a resonance with how this guide articulates the approach to producing affirmative cases and to a lesser extent negative cases. Part of the reasoning for the approach taken in this guide is that a stock issues approach is helpful as a guide to composing affirmative cases because it articulates clear standards for what must be demonstrated by the affirmative as well as what the negative might consider challenging in order to win a debate. The philosophical stance taken by the stock issues paradigm in describing how debate ought to proceed has endured because it continues to be a productive approach to argumentation.

For a stock issues judge the fundamental question is whether or not the affirmative has met its burden to present a complete case justifying the adoption of the resolution as a truth claim. This paradigm places a premium on negative arguments that challenge directly the claims in the affirmative case but has difficulty accounting for negative arguments which do not refute the claims of the affirmative case. For example, a counterplan might test the necessity or desirability of the affirmative plan but does not disprove its ability to satisfy the other stock issues. As a result some more rigid stock issues judges might discount the counterplan as a reason to vote for the negative. Others might depart from a more rigid adherence to the paradigm and adopt aspects of the other paradigms to account for this weakness.

The dilemma presented above has caused most judges at the collegiate level to abandon the stock issues paradigm. Instead, they adhere to the principles insofar as the negative can attack those stock issues and win the debate, but are not expected to do so. For example, if the negative proved the affirmative case did not have a significant harm then the judge would vote for the negative. Where most judges depart is that they tend to be more open to negative arguments that do not speak directly to stock issues in rendering a decision.

Today at the collegiate level most judges do not adhere to this paradigm. To the extent that a debater would encounter a judge who adheres to this paradigm, they would be well served to make their arguments in terms of satisfying burdens more so than the desirability of the policy. This isn't to say that desirability is altogether irrelevant, but rather that demonstrating the case has (or in the case of the negative debater has not) satisfied its burden will feature more prominently. For debaters who are contemplating reading more critical or performative arguments on the affirmative or negative, this would be a remarkably difficult judge, because those arguments tend to operate outside of the stock issues paradigm, and so a debater may be well served to give them lower preference.

Tabula Rasa

Many debate judges of a bygone era described themselves as "tabula rasa" from the Latin term for "blank slate." A tabula rasa, or "tab," attempts to remove all pre-existing assumptions of what is true about debate, or the world which is being debated about, in order to render an objective decision based on the words uttered in a debate. Though many judges no longer identify with this philosophy, it still influences the way many judges think about the debates taking place in front of them.

Tabula rasa judges perceive their role as determining which side of the debate has done the better debating based on their ability to establish their arguments as true. The defining trait of a "tab" judge is that they determine the truth of an argument based only on the argumentation that has taken place in the debate. This means that assumptions about what is needed to present a complete affirmative case, how counter-advocacies should be evaluated, what the nature of the current policies are, and other assumptions are generally set aside. It also means that claims which are uncontested are treated as absolute truths for the purpose of the debate. Where competing claims exist, the number of warrants or the existence of warrants which have not been refuted tends to be preferred over more subjective criteria such as the rhetorical force of an argument. The easiest way to think about this approach is that it is a dogmatic attachment to the burden of rejoinder as a principle of argumentation. Arguments that are not addressed are true, and so contested arguments tend to be devalued because they are presumptively less true. As mentioned in Chapter 6, flowing is a term used to describe the system of notetaking common to policy debate. The noun form of the term "flow" refers to the collected notes which have recorded the debate. For a strict tabula rasa judge, this flow determines the outcome of the debate because the evaluation of argument quality is subsequent to the evaluation of what arguments have or have not been addressed.

Part of the reason why this philosophy has fallen from favor among many judges is that over time it became something of a caricature. Judges who rigidly adhered to this philosophy relied extensively on their flow of the debate to determine which side had won by adding up conceded arguments far more than evaluating argument quality. At times this required judges to decide debates on tedious questions of whether a single sentence that had been uttered was or was not a complete argument. It also meant that some relatively weak arguments by most other metrics won a large number of debates because a judge could not acknowledge that the argument had no correspondence to reality.

Nonetheless, elements of the tabula rasa paradigm have persisted. One of the features of this paradigm is that it has an extreme openness to argumentative styles by both sides. Most judges who vote frequently for critical or performance affirmatives that eschew the stock issues or emphasis on the resolution as the focus of the debate will tend to identify with the tabula rasa approach because they are more interested in evaluating the arguments as they are presented and rebutted than the fidelity that those arguments have to a theoretical standard. For other judges, the emphasis on a strict adherence to the flow, and which team makes more arguments, which arguments are dropped or advocated, what might be described as argument interaction, provides an avenue toward objectivity. A judge need worry about imparting their personal biases on a debate if their decision is based on the failure of a debater to utter a particular

The most redeeming feature of this philosophy is that it is remarkably open to alternative forms of argumentation. It minimizes the predispositions of the judges in terms of how the debate proceeds. As a result, debaters who are interested in alternative approaches to argumentation often favor judges with this approach. It is also popular with debaters who are adept at producing a large volume of argumentation and emphasize strategic approaches to produce mistakes by their opponents. There is a risk in this strategy which is not insubstantial. Namely, judges who adhere to this philosophy expect debaters to spell out their arguments with a degree of depth and precision which is challenging for many debaters. They are unable to rely on the judge to complete their ideas or arguments, and so the ability to use enthymematic arguments is lost.

Most judges who describe themselves in this manner today are more moderate than the dogmatic approach described in this section. In practice, it means that they try to avoid imposing their views on the debate and rely on the flow more than their peers in the decision-making process. As opposed to other judges, this is a difference of degree rather than kind but is worth noting in putting together strategies and arguments in the debate.

Hypothesis Testing

A hypothesis testing judge approaches the affirmative as a hypothetical example of the resolution if it were adopted as a policy. It represented an important evolution in the way debate judges and coaches thought about the topic, in that it lent credibility to the tendency for the affirmative to approach the resolution as a parameter for what the affirmative could defend rather than a statement that must be affirmed in total. It is also significant in that it expanded dramatically the scope of negative arguments that could respond to the affirmative case.

For a hypothesis testing judge the affirmative case is a hypothesis, much like what is found in the scientific method, and any test of the hypothesis is presumptively legitimate. This means that contradictions in negative positions, the use of multiple competitive advocacies, and critical and performative arguments are all equally legitimate. For the hypothesis testing judge the affirmative case has the benefit of selecting the terrain of the debate, but there are no rules on the negative argumentation. In practice, this gives the negative such wide leeway that most hypothesis-testing judges find themselves voting for the negative in a disproportionately large number of debates.

This tendency to vote for the negative has substantially reduced the frequency of judges who identify as hypothesis testers. Many more have adopted the notion that the negative has access to a wide array of arguments, but do not accept the notion that contradictory positions or all arguments are equally legitimate. Nonetheless, if a debater recognizes that a judge is permissible toward conditional counterplan or alternative status they have at least something of a residual sympathy toward hypothesis testing.

Debating in front of a judge who actively identifies as a hypothesis tester generally is not desirable for the affirmative, but very desirable for the negative. For the affirmative, it means that there is a general expectation that the case must defend a topical plan, and must defend against all possible permutations of negative arguments. For the negative, there is complete strategic flexibility, which makes this judge very desirable. As a rule, debaters need to worry less about adaptation for hypothesis testing judges and can focus instead on presenting the best possible arguments for their position.

Policy-making

The single most common approach to policy debating is embodied in the policy-making paradigm. In general, a policy-making judge envisions themselves as occupying a role where they have the ability to adopt or enact the policy proposed by the affirmative and view the negative role as disproving the desirability of that policy. This general predisposition is the most empirically common, but there is a fissure in the judges who identify as policy-makers that complicates that definition somewhat.

The fissure essentially centers around the perception of critical or performance argument strategies as a legitimate approach to affirmation or negation. One school of thought in this paradigm begins with the assumption that the focus of policy debate is matters of policy, and arguments that do not prove or disprove the desirability of that policy are not legitimate. For judges who ascribe to this view an affirmative may argue in whatever mode it prefers, so long as it results in an advocacy of a topical plan of action. This means that most critical or performance affirmatives will not be persuasive because they fail to satisfy the resolution burden of the affirmative. It also means that kritiks are unlikely to be a viable negative strategy for this sort of judge because they will tend to view them as irrelevant asides to the question of the desirability of the affirmative plan.

An alternative school is less dogmatic. Rather than demanding the affirmative defend a plan that affirms the topic, they view themselves as responsible for determining which advocacy is most beneficial. This means that the mandate of defending a plan that affirms the topic is gone, and the limitations on negative strategy are also gone. For both sides, this affords a maximum degree of flexibility, for better and worse. For the better, that flexibility ensures that any argument can be used to win a debate. For the worse, it means that debate preparation must be far more extensive and thorough because the debater must be prepared to address any argument at any time.

Where judges explicitly identify as policymakers they usually do to in order to signal that they fall into the first category. Where judges do not explicitly identify themselves with any particular paradigm they are almost assuredly in the second category. Beyond the important difference in which arguments are considered valid, they tend to approach debates in a very similar way. They begin by evaluating which impacts would plausibly result from voting for the affirmative or the negative. This means evaluating which side has won the individual positions in the debate. Subsequently, these judges determine which impacts are of greatest consequence using the same sort of impact comparison discussed in Chapter 7.

As a rule, these judges tend to be somewhat less flow reliant than a tabula rasa judge (in that they view arguments more holistically than relying on strict record keeping), more attentive to argument theory than a hypothesis tester (in that they are more skeptical of contradictory negative positions), and view stock issues (other than topicality) as secondary to determining what the ideal policy would be (but are extremely attentive to arguments about the harms, significance, and solvency issues in the affirmative). It would be reasonable to view policymaking as a synthesis of the other approaches, with the caveat that this approach to judging is less concerned with argumentation as such, and more about the policy issues discussed.

In preparing this guide, much of the advice was premised on the policymaking approach because it has become effectively dominant. In preparing for a tournament debaters will notice that most judges tend to fall into one or the other school of policymaking. In order to make their preparation effective a debater would be well suited to see how judges discuss how they approach specific arguments, but especially kritiks, to see which version of policymaking best describes their approach. Fortunately, other than selecting affirmative cases and negative positions there is little difference between these two paradigms. The major accommodation relative to the less prominent paradigms for this type of judge is the emphasis on impact comparison because a policymaking judge envisions themselves as responsible for the consequences of their decision.

The Critic of Argument

The last paradigm has relatively few adherents and arguably has the least clear defining features. The critic of the argument determines the winner of the debate based on which side has presented the best arguments. To the extent that this approach can be systematized, it is that the critic of argument seeks to award the side which has done the better debating. What this means is the product of what is argued by the debaters more so than an objective measure. For example, if the affirmative reads a plan which affirms the topic and the negative arguments are policy oriented, the judge will determine the winner based on which side has defended the best policy because the arguments by both sides explicitly or implicitly posit that this should be the focus of the debate. By contrast, if the affirmative reads a plan that affirms the topic and the negative reads a kritik, the critic of the argument would focus their decision more on which side better advocates their position than on the desirability of the plan. The difference here being that the judge would feel obliged to address the disagreement about what issues should be discussed in the debate in a way that a policymaking judge may not.

In general, the judges who identify as critics of argument tend to come from an academic background and view the lens through a more scholarly approach to argumentation. This means that principles of argumentation such as burden of rejoinder tend to play an outsized role in how they view the debate. For debaters who are more practically oriented in their argumentation, this tendency makes such judges somewhat unpredictable because they tend to be guided by rules that debaters are unfamiliar with. On the other hand, judges of this sort tend to be extremely flexible in their approach to what arguments debaters can make, because they are not beholden to a specific version of what the ideal debate ought to look like.

In preparing to debate in front of a judge who identifies as a critic of argument the first step is to be sensitive to what the stasis questions will be with the other team. Where both teams' arguments are focused on the desirability of the affirmative plan there generally is no need for adaptation. Where the negative is shifting stasis away from that question, debaters from both sides would be well advised to frame their arguments around how the argumentative burdens that come with both sides' arguments have or have not been met because the judge is evaluating arguments rather than policies.

General Principles in Judging Debate

In evaluating a debate the judge has countless variables which can factor into their decision. Quality of evidence, nonverbal communication, rhetorical sophistication, depth of refutation, concessions, and many more things can play a role for a judge. Judging a debate is also a largely personal endeavor, after all, to be a judge infers that a person exercises some judgment. Severing judgment from one's personal knowledge and expertise is challenging, perhaps impossible, and also not necessarily desirable. Complicating the issue for many judges is that they have relatively few opportunities to judge a debate, and so developing a sense of what they find persuasive from debaters can be hard due to a lack of experience. Becoming a good debate judge is a process, and what makes one judge appear to be good to one debater may make them appear horrendously bad to others. It would be arrogant to say that there is a single correct way to approach debate. That said, there are some common principles that can help a judge in making a decision.

In the previous section a number of paradigms were presented, each of which would provide some guides for which arguments will be interpreted as important and meaningful. Over time judges will determine which of the philosophical approaches suggested there in most applies to their particular convictions. For the sake of this procedural discussion, the principles which are discussed will be kept as general as possible. Over time and experience, judges will develop their own principles and beliefs, but some common principles work across all paradigms.

The first principle is non-intervention. This is an unattainable principle in many respects because a judge is always forced to render a degree of judgment that may not be entirely disentangled from their personal beliefs. Nonetheless, a good judge will seek to minimize the extent to which their decision in the debate is influenced by their own assumptions about arguments and focus to the greatest extent possible their decision on the arguments made by both sides in the debate. One strategy for minimizing the role of personal bias is for the judge to predetermine under what conditions they would vote against their predispositions. If those conditions are not within the taxonomy of reasonable arguments, then the judge is obliged to reconsider their predispositions.

The second principle is the law of non-contradiction. The principle of non-contradiction is that no one thing can both be and not be at the same time. For judging debate what this means is that the judge cannot believe both an argument and its opposite in the same debate. For example, if the affirmative argues that nuclear proliferation is dangerous in its case, and then argues that it is not dangerous in responding to the negative disadvantage, the judge must resolve the question in one way or another. Ideally, this contradiction would be acknowledged by the debaters, but in many cases it is not, requiring the judge to exercise judgment about which side of this contradiction is true. This principle is essential because otherwise the judge would find themselves in the position of rendering an unintelligible decision.

The third principle is the burden of presumption. Assuming all other things equal, and the debate is otherwise irresolvable, which side should win the debate? The conventional wisdom among such coaches would tend to conclude as follows. Presumption rests with the negative except where the negative has proposed an alternative advocacy. The reasoning for this is that to justify voting for the affirmative they must satisfy the demand to present a case that satisfies the stock issues of the debate, but in the instance where the negative argues a counterplan rather than defending the status quo the burden of the negative shifts toward proving the counterplan is competitive and of greater advantage. This principle is important because there are many debates that do not resolve themselves clearly, and so the judge must render a decision. Much the same way as the principle of innocent until proven guilty compels a prosecutor to prove their case, presumption burdens the affirmative (and perhaps subsequently the negative) to prove their case, and obviates the judge from rendering a decision that reflects their own beliefs. Instead, the debate is determined by the failings of one side or the other of the debate.

These general principles particular to the decision-making process are helpful guides, but there are some additional qualities that a judge should attempt to embody in deciding the winner of a debate. Beyond pursuing objectivity and avoiding intervention, a judge should work to be predictable in terms of their decision-making process. When a judge attends a tournament they are obliged to make a written statement of their decision-making process, called a paradigm, available to the debaters. In rendering their decision, a judge should make a good effort to adhere to this paradigm so that the decisions made by the debaters reflect to the greatest extent possible quality argumentation.

Making a Decision

The decision-making process begins during the debate, as the judge takes notes and begins interpreting and evaluating the arguments. During this time debaters are endeavoring to present the judge with the most compelling version of their argument, and the judge is obliged to be attentive to the choices in non-verbal communication, rhetoric, and argument framing. Following the debate the judge must be ready to request any evidence that they think they may need to consult as a part of their decision-making process. Increasingly, the custom is for debaters to provide a document with the evidence that has been read, but unless care is taken during the debate to be a dutiful audience the judge is unlikely to know which evidence is relevant to the debate.

In making their decision most judges follow a two-step process. The order of the steps tends to be a matter of personal preference more than any particular objective rule. One of the steps is determining which side has presented the better arguments on the relevant positions, the other is to determine which positions are of greater consequence in resolving the debate. For the sake of discussion, assume that a judge begins their process by determining which arguments are most important in determining the winner of the debate.

In determining which position has the greatest consequence for determining the winner the obvious first step is to exclude the positions not argued in the last speech. The next step is to evaluate arguments following a relatively fixed hierarchy. The first position to be considered is topicality because if that argument is won by the negative, the merits of the affirmative plan are irrelevant. Subsequently, any theoretical arguments that one side or the other has made the debate sufficiently unfair or educationally unproductive that the judge should assign a loss must be evaluated. Parallel to this evaluation would be any positions that the debaters have argued should be evaluated as a prior consideration to the consequences of the affirmative case. This usually happens in the context of the negative advocating a kritik that argues the affirmative is so problematic that the merits of the case should not be considered. Assuming that none of these issues has been featured in the last two speeches, the last consideration is the desirability of the affirmative case as argued in the second affirmative rebuttal against the position advocated by the negative in the second negative rebuttal.

In evaluating debates at this level the fundamental question is whether the plan is desirable or not. At this point, the judge will transition to the second step, of determining which side has won a position. Winning in this context does not necessarily mean that the argument is taken as an absolute truth for one side or the other; usually, it is more probabilistic. For example, the affirmative might have a well-warranted argument that a restriction on the nuclear forces of the United States would decrease the perceived need for other countries to develop their own nuclear arsenals, while the negative has a well-warranted argument that this same restriction would be viewed as an opportunity for other countries to develop their own nuclear arsenals. The judge might plausibly conclude that both claims can be true, albeit of different countries, so the affirmative would prove there is a likelihood that they solve their advantage, but that likelihood would not be a surety. The demand on the judge is to make a determination of which side's arguments on the respective positions are more compelling and to what extent they establish a probable truth.

The final consideration is the substantive consequence of those arguments. Assuming both sides have won that there is some likelihood that their arguments are true, the debate is usually decided based on the sort of impact comparison described in Chapter 7. Ideally, the debaters would perform the impact comparison for the judge, but where this has not occurred often the judge must perform this comparison on their own to ascertain which side has won the debate.

Subsequent to the judge making a decision about which side has won the debate they will need to submit a ballot. On that ballot, they will need to identify a winner, assign speaker points for each speaker, and rank the speakers. The norms for speaker points change relatively quickly, but the most common scale is a 30-point scale. The norms for what speaker points are appropriate fluctuate quickly, but as of the time of this writing, it seems that most judges rarely assign a score lower than 27.5 points for any debater. Traditionally ballots were filled out on paper. Today this is typically done using a web-based platform. The most ubiquitous of these platforms today is Tabroom, which provides additional space for the judge to provide feedback to the debaters and to explain the basis for the judge's decision.

Subsequent to completing the ballot the norm at most tournaments is for the judge to discuss the debate with the competitors. The custom is to begin with explaining which team has won the debate and why followed by feedback for the debaters. It is common, but by no means a guarantee, that debaters will ask the judge questions. This is often the most challenging part of the judging process because debaters' emotions might reasonably run high following a debate, and so the judge is obliged to both manage the feelings of the debaters and provide them with the feedback they need in order to improve. There are no hard and fast rules for how this is to be done, but it is incumbent on the judge to handle this task with a degree of seriousness and maturity. The aim of debate is to provide an educational experience, and in rendering a decision and explaining it the first obligation of the judge is to the debaters.

Conclusion

This chapter is intended to be as helpful to debaters as it is to judges. Understanding how judges are apt to perceive their arguments, the paradigms, and principles that guide their decision-making is invaluable. One of the most beneficial features of the debate community is that it is small enough that a debater might have the same judge numerous times over the course of their career, and so develop familiarity with how a judge thinks and decides who has won a debate.

This is important because while there are some aspects of judging that are relatively universal, it is also a remarkably personal endeavor. As judges accumulate experience they develop and refine their thinking about what good debating looks like, and how debates are won or lost. As judges develop these sensibilities they should be attentive to how they describe their predispositions about arguments to debaters, and update their paradigms accordingly.

9
PRACTICE AND TOURNAMENT PREPARATION

Over the course of a debate season, the most actively competitive and successful debaters would be hard pressed to find themselves in more than 60 debates. Most debaters find themselves competing in far fewer debates, generally around 40 over the course of an academic year. In the course of those debates, it is rare that two debates are in fact the same, even if they are at times similar, and learning from experience in debates can be frustrating because the test comes before the lesson. This makes practicing and tournament preparation an essential part of learning how to be an effective debater.

Why Practice

Despite the importance of practice, many debaters eschew giving this necessary part of tournament preparation its due. Some prefer to spend their preparation time researching, or refining their arguments. Others find themselves more excited by the prospect of scouting their opponents and identifying new strategies for dealing with the arguments they are likely to hear. Some adopt the perspective of now-retired NBA All-Star Allen Iverson who, after a conference finals loss, responded to a question about his preparation for the game with exasperation saying, "Practice. We're talking about practice?" Although he was a hall of fame caliber player, Iverson eventually retired without an NBA championship.

One way to understand the importance of practice is to think of the mind as a computer. During a debate, competitors only have so much hard drive space available to process data. If a debater has to spend a large amount of their hard drive space on relatively routine tasks, it is easy for them to overload their mind and crash. Or failing a crash, miss the big picture of the debate because they have to focus on trying to manage the relatively simple tasks that practice would turn into essentially mental muscle memory. This is true even for experienced debaters because while the aim of practice is always to make many of the routine elements of debate simple and easy to manage, it also affords the space for perfecting arguments in a way that is challenging during competition.

There is an additional reason to practice, which is especially true for new debaters. After the initial research for the affirmative and negative positions has been completed, the relative value of research begins to plateau because the time it takes to produce new arguments is very large, and the number of debates where a different argument could change the outcome tends to be relatively small. What will change the outcome of more debates is effective debating, which is only possible by engaging in the extensive practice.

Practicing Individual Skills

At the beginning of their careers, one of the most obvious stumbling blocks for debaters is that they have not developed basic skills. The result is that while debating, they are too focused on the tasks needed to perform to focus on the nature of the arguments being made. The best way to get around this problem is to dedicate time to turning unfamiliar tasks into second nature. The most simple tasks to develop are reading skills, flowing skills, and word economy skills.

One of the features of policy debate is that a combination of time limits and emphasis on providing quality evidence for the positions that a debater is advocating produces a trend toward rapid delivery. While this is not appealing to all debaters, and is not required to be successful, the drills used to develop rapid delivery have uses beyond policy debating. For debaters looking to improve their public speaking skills, these same drills also improve pronunciation and eye contact. When the author teaches public speaking students, he uses these same drills, because the trick to developing rapid delivery is being able to read text more quickly than it is spoken. For public speakers, this allows the use of a script with longer periods of time looking away from the script to make eye contact and engage with the audience. So, while the rapid delivery of policy debate may not be appealing to the debater, the drills used to develop it are still useful for general public speaking skills.

When performing these speaking drills, the point of emphasis is to have a sequence rather than simply doing one particular drill continuously. The reason for this is that each drill develops a different aspect of speech delivery and mixing different drills allows the debater to be more efficient with their practice time. When the author is coaching he errs on the side of performing each of the following drills for about one minute in the sequence.

The basic drill is to read a text forwards as quickly as possible, to mimic the delivery most common to policy debate. To develop the ability to read more quickly, the next drill is to read backwards while speaking as quickly as possible, which will help the debater develop the ability to read ahead of the words they are speaking. A similar strategy which also pushes debaters to move their mouths more quickly and emphasize pronunciation is to select a vowel or word that will be used in between each word in the text. This forces the debaters' mouth to move more slowly relative to their eyes and will train them to read ahead of where they are speaking.

To improve pronunciation, a debater will use what is called "the pen drill." A version of this iconic drill was featured in the 2007 film *The Great Debaters,* which chronicled the 1935 Wiley College debate team. In this drill, a debate places a pen (or something similar) crosswise in their mouth in a manner like a dog with a bone. They then read a text as fast as possible while attempting to have their lips touch around the pen. Over time this drill develops the muscles in the lips such that pronunciation becomes more crisp and can help debaters overcome background noise. This is not the most photogenic drill, it tends to produce a fair amount of drooling and incomprehensible sounds, especially for new debaters, but it is very effective. For debaters who prefer not to have anything in their mouth, an alternative is to overexaggerate the movement of the lips while reading a text.

Many debaters find themselves running out of breath or having trouble projecting their voice. In general, this is because debaters are not effectively breathing or speaking from their diaphragm. One drill that helps this problem is for debaters to lay on their back while reading a text, which isolates the diaphragm and requires the debater to breathe deeply in order to speak at volume. Another drill is to speak while holding an object such as a chair at chest height to develop upper body strength. An additional drill to address this problem is an endurance drill, which is simply reading for a longer period of time than would be used in a debate, say 10 minutes at once.

One final drill that helps with dexterity and pronunciation is to perform tongue twisters. Most tongue twisters are designed to trip a speaker up around certain common sounds in the English language. As a debater discovers a weakness in pronouncing certain sounds, they simply find a tongue twister that stresses that sound and practice it until it is no longer a problem.

While these drills are valuable individual activities, they are far more fun when they are done in a group. There is no way to do these drills and not have them feel humorous, and humor should be shared. That said, these drills are some of the best ways for a debater to improve on their own time, and a good rule of thumb is to spend a little bit of time every day doing it, especially for new debaters who need to improve their delivery skills.

The other remarkably valuable skill to develop individually is flowing. When the author was a student, a common suggestion was to practice flowing rap music from the fastest rappers of the era, Twista, Busta Rhymes, and Tech N9ne were common suggestions. This is still sound advice because the aim is to develop rapid notetaking ability which the rapid delivery of many rappers certainly offers good material to practice with. A slower, but more relevant to current events approach is to practice flowing news stories, or for that matter, lectures in class.

All of this is aside from the optimal option, which is to practice flowing debates. One of the most helpful changes in recent years has been the accessibility of recordings of debates, frequently posted on platforms such as YouTube, which are readily accessible. A simple search using obvious terms such as "college policy debate" will return many viable options. Alternatively, when attending a tournament watching debates by peers during elimination rounds offers a valuable opportunity. To get the most out of these opportunities, debaters should go a step further and render a decision on who won the debate and compare their decision to the judges.

A final skill that can be developed individually is word economy. There are two ways to make more arguments in debate: one is to speak faster, and the other is to speak more efficiently. Of those two options, efficiency is always the best option because the debater doesn't need to worry about a physical limitation on their ability to convey more ideas.

There are two drills that are helpful for improving word economy. The first is to write out word for word an ideal rebuttal speech. Then the debater will attempt to cut out a certain number of words from that speech (say, 30 words) and repeat the process until the speech cannot be further shortened. What this drill will do is reveal the tendencies that a debater has to use repetitive or unnecessarily wordy phrases to make their arguments. The second is to use the same procedure with speech time. In this approach, the debater will use a flow, rather than a script, with the aim being to learn how to use their flow more effectively while also developing a more efficient use of language. The place where this is most apparent is in the practice of signposting, which typically takes debaters far more time than necessary.

Similar to speaking drills, word economy drills work best when they are consistently practiced. Building good speech habits is the product of repetition and attention, and consistent practice makes dramatic improvements. A good practice for debaters to make improvements from one tournament to the next is to perform these word economy drills using speeches from debates at recent tournaments. Not only does this practice develop skills but also provide the opportunity to reflect on the arguments which were made, and how they might be improved for future debates.

Practicing Team Skills

Policy debate is a team activity, and to be effective debaters have to practice with their partners. Not only does this develop the individual skills of the debaters, but they also develop a degree of understanding and trust, which allows them to support each other during the rigors of competition. The skill and interpersonal components of this sort of practice aside, practicing with a teammate develops clarity about the arguments that both debaters will be making over the course of the debate, which is invaluable for competitive success. The two best skills to develop with a teammate are cross-examination skills and refutation skills.

Cross-examination drills are simple affairs. One debater shares a position with another debater and then is cross-examined on that position for three minutes. This replicates the experience of cross-examination, but in delivering the answers in front of their teammate, they are able to receive feedback on the quality of their answers. Together, the team will develop a "party line" about how to address the various lines of questioning.

A variation on this approach that pushes the questioner as much as the respondent is to limit the questioner to three questions to either receive a concession or illustrate an argument. Because the questioner is generally speaking interrogating an opponent's position rather than their own developing the ability to use questions to test an argument is uniquely challenging. What this drill does is push debaters to think through their questions not individually, but instead in a sequence that forces their opponent into a concession. This is one of those skills that can only be developed with practice, and so this drill is remarkably valuable.

Refutation skills are a cornerstone of effective debating but are hard to develop on one's own. The most straightforward drill for developing these skills is to have one debater present an argument (not a whole position) and have the other debater present three responses to which the first debater must respond. The aim of this drill is to develop the ability to respond to specific claims with more than one response so that in competition, when a debater identifies a specific important argument, they are able to provide more in-depth responses.

To give debaters an experience that better mimics the broader context of a debate, a popular drill is the "mini debate." In a mini-debate, one debater presents a position, for example, an affirmative advantage, and the other debater rebuts that position. In this drill, the debaters have time limits which mimic what might be expected in a debate. To continue with our example, the first speaker may have three minutes to present the advantage, and the second speaker may have two minutes, with gradually declining time limits succeeding through what would be the second affirmative rebuttal. One genre of argument that is particularly valuable to practice in this manner is theory arguments. Because many of them, especially debates about counterplan status, tend to be the same from one debate to the next. Practicing these debates in this way allows both debaters to handle these issues far more efficiently in competitive debates. What this drill offers is the ability for both debaters to test specific positions without the inefficiencies that come from practicing a full-length debate. What otherwise might be a two-hour investment can be reduced to a half hour.

Another drill, which can be practiced with a teammate or coach, is the rebuttal redo. This works well in the context of teams because for the first affirmative and first negative rebuttal the speaker is setting up their partners' final speech. This allows the last speaker to let their partner know which arguments they think are essential for their final speech. With a coach, the emphasis may be less on which arguments should be made or not made, and more on technique and time allocation. This is especially helpful for practicing the last two rebuttals to get feedback on the framing of the arguments in the final speeches.

Practicing Debate

Practicing a debate is an extremely important but also time-intensive endeavor. It is hard to get four debaters and a coach in the same place, at the same time, for the large block of time required for a policy debate. When it can be accomplished, it is important to maximize the value for these practices. Although the temptation is to make debates as close to competitive debates as possible, there are two different approaches that make better use of this extremely valuable time.

One approach is to have the coach give guidance during the preparation period for each speech, as well as feedback after each speech. What this does is make sure that the speech that is about to be given does not have a flaw that causes one team or the other to get too far ahead of their opponent. It also means that rather than waiting until the end, a debater gets immediate feedback so that they do not lose their state of mind about their arguments during the intervening half hour or more between a speech and the end of the debate. This is an especially helpful strategy for newer debaters to learn how debate rounds work.

An alternative approach, which takes a great deal of time, is a "stop and go" debate. In this approach, the coach will interrupt the debate as they see fit to explain what mistakes are being made, and then have the debater redo that component of the speech. This means that a regular debate which might take 90 minutes or so uninterrupted might instead take several hours. That said, for debaters who are past the stage of finding out the very basics of debate, it is an excellent opportunity to teach more advanced skills, especially for the later rebuttals in the debate where students cannot rely on prepared materials and need to think for themselves.

What to Prepare for Tournaments

After hours of research, writing, and practicing, a debater finds themselves ready for competition. In preparing for a tournament there are a few steps that a team must undertake to provide themselves with the best opportunity to reach their competitive goals. Without giving the impression that debate is necessarily unpleasant, one trend that the author has noticed as a coach is that many debaters are frustrated with their tournament experiences. If there is a consistent explanation why it is because the debaters have not mentally prepared themselves for what a tournament entails.

A debate tournament entails essentially nonstop debating for two days, and if a debater is successful three or four depending on the size of the tournament. This is strenuous mentally and physically, and debaters who are not taking care of themselves often suffer during the tournament. Getting ready for the rigors of a debate tournament is not overly complicated, paying attention to diet, getting sufficient sleep, staying hydrated, etc. are all fairly obvious. The problem seems to be that debaters underestimate the extent to which they must be intentional in taking care of themselves.

The mental component is equally important. The most important consideration is setting goals that are appropriate for the debater, the debate team, and the debate tournament. The aim in setting goals is for them to be at the same time attainable, and challenging. If a goal is unattainable debaters as individuals and as teams quickly become discouraged because they sense that they are failing expectations. If a goal is too easy a team will not invest in their preparation and will underperform their expectations. These goals should not only be competitive, debate is an educational activity and having goals for what debaters should learn over the course of a tournament is healthy and also in many ways much more attainable. A debater does not always control the outcome of a debate, but they do have control over what they learn from it.

To set reasonable goals and guide their preparation, debaters should perform a basic analysis of the tournament. This means scouting to identify trends and tendencies in arguments favored by teams attending the tournament, as well as judge proclivities, and nuances of tournament rules. Debaters are helped in this effort by the shift toward online platforms which provide teams with easier access to more data that can help them understand how best to prepare. Currently, the dominant platform is called tabroom, and offers information that in a previous generation was only available after a team arrived at a tournament. Data such as team records, judge voting records, and tournament rules, all being stored in one place offer modern debaters far more information than was available even a decade ago.

Tournament Scouting

The single most intimidating tournament is the first tournament of the year because no debate team knows what the other debate teams are going to argue. After the first two rounds of the tournament, there is an expectation that teams will begin disclosing information about what arguments have been made in past debates to help each other prepare. This happens before each debate, but similar information is generally expected to be placed online in what is called a "caselist." In a prior era, the caselist was a booklet that a tournament would furbish to attendees to let them know basic information about what teams were arguing.

Today, policy debate teams publish this information online. In preparing for a tournament, a team will look at the entries on the tournament registration page (generally hosted on tabroom) and cross-reference it with the caselist, which is now hosted on a web platform. Based on the cross-reference between the registration page and the caselist, a team knows at least in general what cases they are likely going to debate. There are layers of preparation that can be done with this information.

The first layer of preparation is determining what the optimal strategies would be for the cases which the teams in attendance have read in previous debates. A secondary layer would be to interrogate the quality of those arguments. With the shift toward online platforms, there has also been a shift toward "open-sourcing" evidence, meaning that teams will post the entirety of their cases including evidence. This allows the debaters to produce more precise and exacting strategies, and interrogate the quality of evidence for their opponents' arguments. Of course, there is limited time to prepare for each tournament, and so preparing for every team equally is not necessarily a reliable strategy. Part of the aim of tournament scouting is also to help make decisions about which teams merit more attention in preparing arguments. The general goal for a team would be to identify and prepare to debate against teams with comparable records, as they are the most likely opponents over the course of a debate.

Managing Preferences

One of the important features of policy debate is that debaters have a degree of control over which judges they debate in front of. The reason debaters are given a degree of control over judging is twofold. First, it helps to address the problem of potential judge bias by allowing debaters to exclude the judges who are ideologically predisposed against their preferred positions and arguments. Second, it allows debaters to maximize the odds that the judge in their debate will be relatively unbiased by the preference for the other team. There is no perfect system for judge selection, and even the most sophisticated tools do not guarantee a team will receive their favorite judge. Nonetheless, debaters who are attentive to this process can gain an important strategic advantage.

The first step in this process is to review the paradigms, usually available on tabroom, of the judges who will be at the tournament. Based on this review, debaters should identify which judges they believe to be most desirable given the positions and argument styles the team prefers. A good way to approach this task is to begin by categorizing judges into categories that describe judges who are extremely undesirable, permissible, and favorites. The reason for this categorization is because most of the ways tournaments select judges for debates track a similar categorization scheme.

The next step is to understand the tournament procedure for judge placement. There are essentially three systems in place, with some nuance and variation within the three models. The simplest system is a "strike" system. In a strike system, the tournament is allowing debaters to designate a certain percentage of the judges available as unacceptable. The debaters then identify which judges they do not wish to be judged by, and any judges not named could potentially judge a team. This system is simple but does mean that often debaters are placed in the tricky position of debating in front of a judge which may not be a good fit for their arguments. It almost always seems that when tournaments use this model, the debate teams never have quite enough strikes to get to the judges they want.

The more common system is what is called "mutually preferred judging" (MPJ). In this system, each team ranks all of the available judges. Then judges are selected based on the similarity in the rankings of the two teams that are debating. It is rarely the case that two teams would turn in the exact same preference sheet, and the need to pair multiple debates means that usually, judge selection is more of a matter of determining who fits best, not who fits perfect. There are two different ways a tournament might approach determining which judge fits best. One approach favors mutuality, meaning that the judge who is selected must be ranked in an extremely similar place for both teams. The alternative favors preference, meaning that a greater tolerance for differences in ranking is allowed so that both teams can benefit from having a judge who is more highly ranked.

There is a vibrant debate about which of these approaches is superior, and which procedure is used differs from one tournament to the next. Knowing which approach the tournament uses can dramatically improve the odds of receiving favorable judging, but there are some general rules that help guide the process. The first rule is that regardless of the difference between mutuality and preference, judges who are ranked higher will tend to judge more debates. Both systems are designed to give debaters better judging and rely on the premise that debaters will rank judges based on their desirability. The second rule is that the first is wrong. If a debater wants a specific judge they should consider where the other teams would rank that same judge, and make their rankings similar so that their odds of receiving that judge are improved. The third rule is that judges who are listed as being available for more debates will judge more, and so if a particular judge is very good, but only available for one debate, ranking them at the top trades off with a higher ranking for other desirable judges who are present for more debates.

For debaters who are unfamiliar with judges and so are unsure about their ranking, the best place to look is their paradigm and voting record. Things to consider, is the judge being placed in a large number of debates? Do those debates include competitively successful teams? Do they judge elimination rounds? Does the way the judge decides the debate play to the team's advantage? Do they have any predisposition toward an argument that would be advantageous? The more yes answers that are present, the more likely it is that the judge is highly ranked by other teams and should by extension be ranked highly on the team's preference sheet.

A final note on managing preferences. It is important for teams to take notes on the decisions judges render, not just so the team can improve the quality of its arguments, but also to enable the team to evaluate if the ranking that had been assigned to the judge was appropriate. Often in explaining their decision, a judge will disclose a predisposition that is not mentioned in their paradigm which might make them a better or worse judge than the other available data would suggest. Teams that keep track of their debates and what is learned about judges and opponents are building a body of knowledge that can be exploited in later debates and improve the quality of their tournament preparation.

Conclusion

That skill development and tournament preparation translate into competitive success is obvious. What often goes unnoticed is all of the additional benefits that are derived from the pursuit of competitive success. Debaters who are diligent in their practice and preparation will improve their speaking skills, refutation ability, and decision-making skills. All of this is valuable and good on its own.

What makes debate a pleasant activity is that the labor of preparation is shared. There are few academic endeavors that are essentially team events. The close bonds that develop over five-hour practice debates, contentious cross-examination practice, and the collaborative parsing of judge philosophies tend to last long after a debater's career is over. Much of this guide is focused on individual preparation for debate because much of the preparation is done individually, but if there is a lesson from this chapter it should be that learning how to work collaboratively with a peer is one of the most important and rewarding aspects of competing in policy debate.

CONCLUSION

Policy debating in the United States has changed substantially in the last several years. Like all intercollegiate activities changes in funding structures of the University, the lingering effects of the COVID pandemic, and changes in the collegiate environment have posed some pressing questions. For debaters, these issues have manifested themselves in ways that are often obscure to coaches. In committing to debate, a student impacts their ability to maintain a social life, adds an additional burden to academic work, and can impact the ability of a student to work while attending school. These issues have been at the forefront of a number of discussions among collegiate debaters and coaches, and while those concerns are pressing, recent efforts to address them offer a telling example of what is most impressive about the collegiate debate community.

With the beginning of the COVID pandemic in 2020, the debate community swiftly responded by taking steps to protect students, including suspending the National Debate Tournament for that year. Subsequently, the coaches and debaters rapidly adapted to the new situation by finding ways to make online debate a viable alternative for the following year. In the 2020–2021 debate season, a full slate of tournaments existed, and debaters were able to compete in national tournaments, unlike many of their peers in athletics and other intercollegiate activities. COVID also spurred the 4th National Debate Development Conference, which produced a number of reforms intended to address not only issues associated with COVID but also issues which had long festered such as the topic selection process, gathering data about debating, and addressing resource disparities between Universities.[1]

This period illustrates the best in the collegiate debate community. The inability to travel and compete in person during lockdown posed an existential threat to policy debate, indeed, some other formats and their supporting organizations have not recovered. While many of the reforms discussed at the National Debate Development Conference have not come to pass, others have, and many more have benefitted from the publication of the proceedings, including the author who is currently using it to advocate for the creation of a new policy debate program. While there remain pressing issues for the future of policy debate, the response to the COVID pandemic demonstrated a level of commitment on the part of the policy debate community that should instill some confidence in the sustainable future of policy debating.

Policy Debate Issues Facing Debaters

Policy debate continues to face a number of criticisms. As the reader of this text might have noticed, policy debate as an activity very much emphasizes technical competency, which some have argued trades off with a more public orientation for debate.[2] Aspects of debate, such as the notion that debaters should switch sides, have been criticized for undermining debate as a performance of conviction.[3] Others have pointed out that there has also been a declining emphasis on debate reflecting the aims of the communication studies discipline in particular and academics more generally.[4] The competitive nature of debate has been criticized for creating a narrower view of good argumentation, which does not reflect argument practices outside of debate.[5] There have been numerous such arguments made over the years that call into question the continued desirability of debate. Amusingly, it turns out that for policy debate, the call is largely coming from inside the house. Almost all of the research that is critical of policy debating is written by current or former debaters and coaches. For debaters, this brief mention of some of the criticisms of policy debate should not be interpreted as an attempt to warn them off. The aim is to give debaters the sense that policy debate is an example of a community that is more willing and capable of self-critique than most.

A second aim is to be realistic. In the introduction, policy debate as it is practiced today was described as the product of an evolutionary process within a community of human practitioners. Any activity with such a history is going to have its problems, and it is also going to have the opportunity for repair. For a student considering debating, it is important to both avoid the experience of jarring disillusionment that comes with realizing that the empirically present practice of policy debating does not live up to the romantic vision the student has in their head. Policy debate is a helpful and productive activity, but it is a human activity and like all such things, has aspects that are in need of repair.

For today's college student policy debate can be a costly endeavor. Traveling to compete in weekend tournaments means that social time on campus is lost. Time spent practicing trades off with time working a job, studying for class, or recuperating from the stress attached to college life. Too often debate coaches are insensitive to these expenses because for the coach it wasn't a concern. Equally, too often debaters find themselves unaware of those costs and look back on their college experience frustrated that they were not able to strike a more reasonable balance. There are also many debaters who do not discover the activity until their last year in college and regret that they did not have the time for the debate career they wanted.

That policy debate has its critics from an academic perspective is probably not a major concern for students considering engaging in policy debate. That debate is a human activity and flawed in much the same way is also probably not an earth-shattering revelation, nor for that matter is the point that college life is stressful and challenging. So why the enumeration of these issues? Simply put, it lays out the concerns which must be navigated in pursuing a policy debate career. They are not insignificant, but they also are not so dire that they should avert a debater considering a career.

Navigating Debate

Years ago the author was coaching a debater who came into college debate with a stunning record of success at the high school level, and that this debater could win a national championship seemed not just plausible but likely. After joining the team, this student immediately showed signs of alternate boredom and frustration that prompted a conversation between debater and coach. The debater felt they had little left to learn, and that competition for competition's sake was simply not satisfying. While the author disagreed with the little left to learn sentiment, clearly the debater would not enjoy debate if the model was purely competitive. The debater and coach agreed that they would only compete at tournaments with low stakes, and the debater would become a de facto coach for new students rather than pursuing competitive excellence.

Arrangements like the one above illustrate a feature of policy debate that too many critics overlook. Policy debate can serve many purposes. While this guide is designed to help students along the path of competitive success, its role is to facilitate and make accessible the more obscure features of debate so that the panoply of other opportunities becomes more readily available. Some use policy debate to explore issues that can hardly be discussed in any other forum. Others use it as a way to build a social network among their competitors. Many debaters use policy debate as a competitive outlet.

Without adopting an excessively soapbox-sounding position, the author would offer a suggestion. In embarking on a debate career, a collegiate student should consider what it is they want from debate. For example, if they want to experiment with ideas and arguments that don't generally find a home in the classroom, then debate can satisfy that desire. It may not be the winningest strategy, but if that is not the debaters' interest, then losing is not a problem. If a debater is motivated by competition, then policy debating certainly can provide that, but the debater shouldn't at the same time expect that they will have a large number of public-facing debates. A student may find that what they want is not available to them in policy debate, and that is ok as well. No activity is for everyone, all the time. That said, there is usually more flexibility in how to approach debate than most debaters realize.

After developing a sense of what a student wants out of debate, they should begin making choices that align their career with those desires. This means determining how many weekends should be given to tournaments, how much time is scheduled for practice and research, what goals for competitions should be, and what adjacent activities to tournament competition should be included in the debate experience. A good coach will offer advice and suggestions to guide the debater in determining how to align all of these interests and goals, but even without such a coach if a debater is intentional about what they want out of debate the odds of success are substantially improved because what counts as success is aligned with the desires of the debater.

When the author was a senior they qualified for the National Debate Tournament. This was uncommon at the author's alma mater at the time and a particularly supportive professor said, "you can skip class for the next month or so until after the NDT." While those six hours a week would certainly have helped with preparation, the author went to every class. Many debaters would make a different decision in that situation, and if that is what their goals for debate happen to be, then that is a fine choice. What is most important is that the debater is able to make that choice for themselves.

Navigating the Debate Tournament

While this guide has emphasized understanding the rules and norms of debate and debate tournaments, a brief note on how to handle tournaments themselves is merited. Specifically, it is merited because a debate tournament usually runs Friday through Monday and those days start at 8:00 A.M. and might run until 10:00 P.M. (or later). Over the course of those days, there is almost continuous activity debating or preparing to debate. This sounds intimidating, but if debaters take care of themselves is incredibly fun.

Debate is a physical activity as well as a mental one. This means that debaters should take care of their bodies as well as their minds. Sleep is essential, and while it is tempting to stay up late preparing for a debate, being properly rested can be equally valuable. Eating right is equally essential. This can be challenging when traveling because the temptations of indulgent fast food are particularly potent, but a large burger with fries and a milkshake from the fast food place we all know about is hardly the sort of nourishment required for debating. Being physically fit, however, a debater decides to define that goal for themselves, is equally important.

There are not many sports that require constant activity for an entire day, and a debater who is in their proper form is far more likely to have the sort of endurance required to be mentally sharp for the entire day of competition.

Parental scolding aside, there are some other features of the debate tournament that merit some explanation. One feature is the distinctive lack of a dress code for policy debate. While some debaters will dress somewhat more professionally, most choose to wear the same clothes that they would wear to class. For debaters used to the strict dress codes associated with high-school competition, this is a refreshing change. While this may strike some as exceedingly informal, it is worth bearing in mind that if dress mattered, it would put the judge in the awkward position of evaluating students based on appearance, which hardly seems reflective of an activity that is supposed to emphasize sound argumentation.

There is a social component to debate as well. Because debaters see each other many times over the course of a year of competition, it is natural that they would develop relationships with their peers and judges. This is part of the fun in debate, developing relationships with peers across the country. Debate offers a social network that if maintained can follow a debater for the rest of their life. Of course, there is a flip side as well, where gossiping or bad-mouthing peers or judges is a temptation, especially in the frustration that follows a lost debate. So debaters should take care to comport themselves in a manner that reflects the virtue they would like others to perceive in them. What this means of course differs from one person to another, but in general, debaters should avoid the temptation to think of debate as an altogether separate world where the way people treat each other doesn't matter because they don't see each other every day.

A place where this dynamic is often at play is after the debate when the judge is delivering their decision. The custom is to allow debaters to ask the judge questions about their decision, and that these questions are at times pointed is a perfectly reasonable expectation. What debaters (and especially judges) must avoid is losing their composure and sustaining their empathy for the person they are addressing. One never knows all that is happening with the other outside of the debate, but none of it can be helped by responding to a dissatisfying decision or a sharp question with aggression. By contrast, handling those same situations with patience and grace makes future encounters less anxious and might even ease the situation.

One final note on the tournament is not so much about conduct as about appreciating what the tournament offers. Debaters are given the opportunity to see more of the country more regularly than almost any of their fellow college students and to engage in a self-edifying activity that offers little return for their school. Supporting a debate program is remarkably resource-intensive for any school, and debaters should take seriously the investment that is being made on their behalf, and represent their school in the best possible way while ensuring that they make the most out of the school's investment in them.

Conclusion

Relative to most guides, this one might appear to have been rather fast and loose with its superlatives in describing its subject. If that is the case, then it is only because debate has the possibility to do so much for its participants. There are other debate formats, forms of intellectual exercise, and competition that are of immense value, but the combination of education, content focus, competitiveness, and fun found in policy debate is incontrovertibly unique. So, a few superlatives are at least warranted.

Notes

1 Kelly Young, "Introduction," in *Reimagining the Future of Intercollegiate Debate: Pedagogy, Practice, and Sustainability,* eds. Kelly Young and David Cram Helwich (Chestnut Hill, MA: American Forensic Association, 2023), 1–3.
2 Michael Bartanen and Robert Littlefield, "Competitive Speech and Debate How Play Influenced American Educational Practice," *American Journal of Play* 7, no. 2 (2015): 159–60.
3 Ronald Walter Greene and Darrin Hicks, "Lost Convictions: Debating Both Sides and the Ethical Self-Fashioning of Liberal Citizens," *Cultural Studies 19,* no. 1 (2005): 100–26.
4 Matthew Brigham, "'The Need for Research,' Revisited," Contemporary Argumentation and Debate (2017): 98–106.
5 Stephen Llano, "The Counterfeit Presentment: An Early 20th Century Model of Intercollegiate Debate As Civic Education," *Argumentation and Advocacy* 53, no. 2 (2017): 91–93.

BIBLIOGRAPHY

"2023–2024 Resolution," Cross Examination Debate Association, Accessed March 1, 2024, https://cedadebate.org/2023-2024-resolution/.
"About the Center for Arms Control and Non-Proliferation," Accessed March 1, 2024, https://armscontrolcenter.org/about/.
Aristotle, *On Rhetoric*, Trans. George Kennedy. Oxford University Press: New York, 1991.
Bartanen, Michael, and Robert Littlefield. "Competitive Speech and Debate How Play Influenced American Educational Practice." *American Journal of Play* 7, no. 2 (2015): 155–73.
Bartanen, Michael, and Robert Littlefield. *Forensics in America*. Lanham, MD: Rowman & Littlefield, 2014.
Brigham, Matthew, "'The Need for Research,' Revisited," *Contemporary Argumentation and Debate* (2017): 91–128.
Delaplane, Keith, "On Einstein, Bees, and Survival of the Human Race," *Beekeeping Resources*, University of Georgia Bee Program, Athens, GA. Accessed March 4, 2024, https://bees.caes.uga.edu/beekeeping-resources/other-topics/on-einstein–bees–and-survival-of-the-human-race.html.
"Fact Sheet: The Nuclear Triad," Center For Arms Control and Non-Proliferation, Accessed January 21, 2021, https://armscontrolcenter.org/factsheet-the-nuclear-triad/.
Freeley, Austin, and David Steinberg. *Argumentation and Debate*. 13th ed. Boston, MA: Cengage, 2014.
Fryar, Maridell, David Thomas, and Lynn Goodnight. *Basic Debate*. 3rd ed. Chicago, IL: National Textbook Company, 1991.
Gidley, Ned, Jacob Justice, Allison Harper, Mikaela Masin, and Tripp Rebrovick, "Topic Selection Process Reform." In *Reimagining the Future of Intercollegiate Debate: Pedagogy, Practice, and Sustainability*, edited by Kelly Young and David Cram Helwich. Chestnut Hill, MA: American Forensic Association, 2023.
Greene, Ronald Walter, and Darrin Hicks. "Lost Convictions: Debating Both Sides and the Ethical Self-Fashioning of Liberal Citizens." *Cultural Studies 19*, no. 1 (2005): 100–26.

Hiland, Alexander. *Presidential Power, Rhetoric, and the Terror Wars: The Sovereign Presidency.* Lanham, MD: Lexington Press, 2019.

Hiland, Alexander. "Serving Our Students: Rethinking Novice Debate." *Argumentation and Advocacy 53*, no. 2 (2017): 118–26.

Kristensen, Hans, and Matt Korda, "Nuclear Notebook: United States Nuclear Weapons, 2023," *Bulletin of the Atomic Scientists*, Accessed January 16, 2023, https://thebulletin.org/premium/2023-01/nuclear-notebook-united-states-nuclear-weapons-2023/.

Kristensen, Hans, Matt Korda, Eliana Johns, Mackenzie Knight, and Kate Kohn, "Status Of World Nuclear Forces," *Federation of American Scientists*, Accessed March 29, 2024, https://fas.org/initiative/status-world-nuclear-forces/

Llano, Stephen. "The Counterfeit Presentment: An Early 20th Century Model of Intercollegiate Debate as Civic Education." *Argumentation and Advocacy* 53, no. 2 (2017): 90–102.

Merriam-Webster.com Dictionary, s.v. "nuclear," Accessed March 1, 2024, https://www.merriam-webster.com/dictionary/nuclear.

Merriam-Webster.com Dictionary, s.v. "triad," Accessed March 1, 2024, https://www.merriam-webster.com/dictionary/triad.

Nadeal, Ray. "Hermogenes on 'Stock Issues' in Deliberative Speaking." *Speech Monographs, 25*, 1, 1958.

Nave, Nicole "The Constant Pursuit of Inclusivity." In *Transcending the Game: Debate, Education, and Society*, edited by Shawn Briscoe. Carbondale: Southern Illinois University Press, 2024.

Olson, Kathryn M. "How Can We Address No Child Left Behind? The Importance of Inherency Analysis on Public Issues." In *Concerning Argument*, edited by Scott Jacobs, 580–589. Washington, D.C.: National Communication Association, 2009.

Perelman, Chaim, and Lucie Olbrechts-Tyteca. *The New Rhetoric Trans.* South Bend: John Wilkinson & Purcell Weaver, University of Notre Dame Press, 2010.

Plato, *Meno*, Trans. Benjamin Jowett, Champaign, IL: Project Gutenberg, 1999.

Reid-Brinkley, Shanara "Introduction: Celebrating the Legacy of the Louisville Project and Grappling With the Anti-Blackness Still Plaguing College Policy Debate," *Contemporary Argumentation and Debate* 38, (2023): 3–10.

Snyder, Ryan, "The Future of the ICBM Force: Should the Least Valuable Leg of the Triad Be Replaced?" *Arms Control Association*, Accessed March 2018, https://www.armscontrol.org/policy-white-papers/2018-03/future-icbm-force-should-least-valuable-leg-triad-replaced.

Tannenwald, Nina. "It's Time for a US No-First-Use Nuclear Policy." In *The Sheathed Sword: From Nuclear Brink to No First Use*, edited by Prakash Menon and Aditya Ramanathan. Bloomsbury India, 2023.

Toulmin, Stephen. *The Uses of Argument.* New York: Cambridge University Press, 1980.

Vergun, David, "U.S. Nuclear Umbrella Extends to Allies, Partners, Defense Official Says," U.S. Department of Defense, Accessed April 24, 2019, https://www.defense.gov/News/News-Stories/Article/Article/1822953/us-nuclear-umbrella-extends-to-allies-partners-defense-official-says/.

Young, Kelly, "Introduction." In *Reimagining the Future of Intercollegiate Debate: Pedagogy, Practice, and Sustainability*, edited by Kelly Young and David Cram Helwich. Chestnut Hill, MA: American Forensic Association, 2023.

APPENDIX A
Sample Affirmative Case

Below is a sample affirmative case. It is intentionally kept short for demonstration purposes, but it has all of the essential parts of a case that would be read in the first affirmative constructive. The aim of composing this speech is to balance making a coherent speech while maintaining a high degree of fidelity to the research that is being used. For this reason, the bolded text refers to the debater's original contribution, while bolded and underlined is used to designate the parts of the piece of evidence that will be read. The portions of the evidence that will not be read are neither bolded nor underlined but are available so that the other team and judge can assess the quality of the evidence that is being presented. In this sample, as in most debate cases, great care is taken to both maintain the original context of the text that is being used in the evidence. For example, numbers placed in the paragraph correspond to the footnote numbers located in the original article. The reader will note that this is not the most rhetorically oriented speech; the emphasis is placed on presenting the evidence to support arguments, with the aim being to provide a more thorough explanation of the ideas over the course of the debate.

An additional note here is that the different sections of the affirmative case have headings attached to them. The purpose of these headings in the document is to help the reader organize the speech and know when they are transitioning to a new section. In compiling the affirmative file, similar headings are used for the arguments and evidence, which will be read in the later constructive speeches. To compose those speeches, a debater will simply copy the relevant headings into a separate document, which will be used to deliver a speech.

Inherency

The first affirmative contention is inherency. The 2022 Nuclear Posture Review walked back President Biden's promises to clarify and curtail the role of the United States Nuclear Arsenal. There is a pervasive attitude that the United States cannot risk a shift away from an ambiguous nuclear declaratory policy that prevents the adoption of a No First Use nuclear policy.

Kimball 22

(Daryl G., Executive Director of the Arms Control Association, "Biden's Disappointing Nuclear Posture Review," Arms Control Association, December 2022, https://www.armscontrol.org/act/2022-12/focus/bidens-disappointing-nuclear-posture-review, ASH)

<u>Since the end of the Cold War, every U.S. president has conducted an</u> in-depth <u>review of the nation's nuclear strategy. Each study, including President</u> Joe <u>Biden's 2022 Nuclear Posture Review</u> (NPR)<u>, has produced disappointing results.</u> That is <u>because they all maintain a dangerous reliance on the threat to use nuclear weapons to deter and, if necessary, respond to hostile attacks, including non-nuclear attacks,</u> "that have a strategic effect against the United States or its allies and partners." <u>The broad, ambiguous nuclear declaratory policy in the 2022 NPR walks back Biden's pledge to narrow the role of U.S. nuclear weapons. In 2020 he wrote "that the sole purpose of the U.S. nuclear arsenal should be deterring and, if necessary, retaliating against a nuclear attack.</u> As president, I will work to put that belief into practice, in consultation with the U.S. military and U.S. allies." <u>As far back as</u> 1990, Biden, then a U.S. senator, argued that the "military rationale for 'first use' has disappeared." <u>But the Pentagon-led 2022 NPR claims that the administration conducted a "thorough review of options for nuclear declaratory policy, including both no-first-use and sole purpose policies, and concluded those approaches would result in an unacceptable level of risk."</u> In reality, policies that threaten the first use of nuclear weapons carry unacceptable risks. Russian President Vladimir Putin's nuclear threats in the war against Ukraine and a Russian policy that reserves the option to use nuclear weapons first in a conflict with NATO underscore the dangers. As Biden himself declared on Oct. 6, "I don't think there's any such thing as an ability to easily use a tactical nuclear weapon and not end up with Armageddon." Nevertheless, his NPR, released two weeks after his "Armageddon" remark, leaves open exactly that possibility.

Harm and Significance

The second affirmative contention is crisis management.

The first subpoint is harms. The current norms against nuclear weapons use are weakening amid national rivalries, increased regional tensions, and arms races while nuclear weapons are being relegitimized.

Tannenwald 18

(Nina, Senior Lecturer of Political Science at Brown University, "The Great Unraveling: The Future of the Nuclear Normative Order," In "Meeting the Challenges of the New Nuclear Age: Emerging Risks and Declining Norms in the Age of Technological Innovation and Changing Nuclear Doctrines" By Nina Tannenwald and James Acton, Academy of Arts and Sciences: Cambridge, MA., 2018. P. 6, This text is available at: https://www.amacad.org/nuclearage, ASH)

With the end of the Cold War, nuclear weapons appeared to recede as a central feature of security relations among the nuclear powers. Responsible political leaders widely accepted that these were weapons of last resort. Concern shifted to nonproliferation and terrorist acquisition of nuclear weapons. The Nuclear Nonproliferation Treaty (NPT) was given a permanent extension in 1995, while the United States and Russia embarked on dramatic reductions in their nuclear arsenals. **Today,** however, **a new nuclear era is emerging, one of multiple nuclear powers, intersecting rivalries, increased regional tensions in Europe and Asia, and new technological arms races in both nuclear and nonnuclear weapon systems. In this emerging nuclear era, the key norms that have underpinned the existing nuclear order—most crucially deterrence, non-use, and nonproliferation—are under stress.** A new norm of disarmament has emerged but it is deeply contested, while other norms, such as arms control, are disappearing altogether. **Most disturbingly, nuclear weapons are being relegitimized in states' security policies.**

The adoption of nuclear weapons postures that permit the first use of nuclear weapons is the result of declining norms, and will increase the risk that nuclear weapons will actually be used.

Tannenwald 18

(Nina, Senior Lecturer of Political Science at Brown University, "The Great Unraveling: The Future of the Nuclear Normative Order," In "Meeting the Challenges of the New Nuclear Age: Emerging Risks and Declining Norms in the Age of Technological Innovation and Changing Nuclear Doctrines" By Nina Tannenwald and James Acton, Academy of Arts and Sciences: Cambridge, MA., 2018. P. 19, This text is available at: https://www.amacad.org/nuclearage, ASH)

The lowered threshold for use is also reflected in the nuclear-armed states' nuclear doctrines. Doctrines are the set of ideas about how nuclear weapons would be used to achieve outcomes. Many of the doctrines today increase the salience of nuclear weapons in security policy, blur the line between nuclear and conventional weapons, and emphasize "early" use. **While the U.S. 2010 Nuclear Posture Review narrowed the conditions under which the United States would use nuclear weapons, even under Obama Pentagon**

planning remained largely mired in outdated Cold War nuclear strategies that emphasize first-strike capabilities. The Trump administration's Nuclear Posture Review, released on February 2, 2018, reverses important progress of the Obama era nuclear policy.49 It increases the role of nuclear weapons in deterring nonnuclear attacks, requests new nuclear warheads that make use seem easier, and seeks to integrate nuclear and conventional forces to facilitate nuclear warfighting. The latter will blur the important "firebreak" between nuclear and conventional weapons that serves as a main barrier to nuclear war. Further, the review advocates with breathless enthusiasm a costly, full-speed-ahead nuclear arms race with Russia and China. While not everything the review calls for will come to pass, the Trump Nuclear Posture Review signals a renewed, dangerous embrace of the risks of nuclear weapons and that the United States has abandoned aspirations for leadership on reducing nuclear dangers.

The second subpoint is significance.

The United States retaining the option to use nuclear weapons first destabilizes crisis management. Although first strike is appealing, the conditions to use nuclear forces first are elusive, and a first strike posture risks misuse of nuclear weapons and a catastrophic nuclear conflict.

Blair 20

(Bruce G., Dr. Bruce G. Blair was a research scholar in the Program on Science and Global Security at Princeton University and co-founder of the Global Zero movement for the elimination of nuclear weapons. "Loose cannons: The president and US nuclear posture," Bulletin of the Atomic Scientists, Vol. 76, No. 1, 2020, https://doi.org/10.1080/00963402.2019.1701279, ASH)

From the standpoint of military expediency, there's an obvious upside to the first-use contingency: With nuclear weapons, going first is far easier to execute than going second. US nuclear forces and command, control, and communications would be intact (though they may suffer considerable damage if a conventional conflict precedes the nuclear strike) and highly capable of co-ordinating an offensive strike that could confer a decisive warfighting edge. By the same token, a first strike could minimize an adversary's potential retribution, limit damage to the US homeland, and position the United States to dominate escalation and thereby terminate war on terms favorable to US interests. But the brief for first use omits myriad downsides. A rational and moral leader would balk at crossing the nuclear Rubicon unless four conditions were satisfied: The threat requiring a nuclear strike rests on ironclad, unassailable intelligence; only nuclear weapons can carry out a successful mission against the threat; predicted civilian casualties would not be so large as to violate humanitarian law and would be otherwise acceptable[10]; and a nuclear strike against a nuclear-armed adversary would not risk escalating to largescale nuclear conflict and devastation of cataclysmic proportions.

In reality, **it is improbable that all these conditions would be simultaneously met. That none would be met is quite possible. History shows repeatedly that intelligence is fallible and often very wrong. (The Iraq WMD threat assessment is Exhibit A.) The need for nuclear firepower is undercut by the US conventional juggernaut; modern precision-guided conventional and cyber weapons can perform almost any mission as well as nuclear weapons, including the destruction of facilities as fortified as missile silos. As for civilian casualties, the carnage and radiation sickness could take a heavy toll** depending on the number and types of targets and the yield of US nuclear weapons employed against them. **And of course, the risk that first use on any scale would trigger catastrophic nuclear escalation cannot be dismissed.**

Plan and Solvency

Thus, we present the plan: The United States Federal Government should adopt a No-First-Use policy for the nuclear forces controlled by the United States.
   The third affirmative contention is solvency.
   This No-First-Use policy would address the harms previously mentioned by forcing changes in doctrinal and operational policies that would limit the risk of accidental or pre-emptive use of nuclear weapons by promoting greater stability in times of crisis.

Tannenwald 18

(Nina, Senior Lecturer of Political Science at Brown University, "The Great Unraveling: The Future of the Nuclear Normative Order," In "Meeting the Challenges of the New Nuclear Age: Emerging Risks and Declining Norms in the Age of Technological Innovation and Changing Nuclear Doctrines" By Nina Tannenwald and James Acton, Academy of Arts and Sciences: Cambridge, MA., 2018. P. 28-29, This text is available at: https://www.amacad.org/nuclearage, ASH)
   The cornerstone of a renewed regime of nuclear restraint would be strengthening the norm of non-use of nuclear weapons through the adoption of a declared no-first-use policy by all the nuclear powers. **There have been increasing numbers of proposals for the United States to adopt a no-first-use policy in recent years,** with compelling analyses. However, the case can be made more strongly for common declared no-first-use policies as the linchpin of a renewed regime of nuclear restraint among the nuclear powers. A no-first-use policy means that nuclear powers would rely on nuclear weapons only to deter nuclear attacks.[87] **Adoption of no-first-use would not simply be "mere words," but rather both doctrinal and operational issues would**

follow from it. ⁸⁸ An operational no-first-use doctrine would eliminate first-strike postures, preemptive capabilities, and other types of destabilizing warfighting strategies. It would induce restraint in targeting, launch-on-warning, alert levels of deployed systems, procurement, and modernization plans. In other words, it would help shape the physical qualities of nuclear forces in a way that renders them unsuitable for missions other than deterrence of nuclear attacks. ⁸⁹ A no-first-use policy also would reduce the risk of accidental, unauthorized, mistaken, or preemptive use. The removal of threats of a nuclear first strike would strengthen strategic and crisis stability. ⁹⁰ It would also make absolute the boundary between nuclear and conventional weapons. Finally, by reducing the overall risk of nuclear dangers, no-first-use policies would move toward addressing humanitarian concerns and reducing the salience of nuclear weapons. ⁹¹

APPENDIX B
Sample Negative Case

Below is a sample negative case which might be read as a response to the affirmative case presented in Appendix A, similarly shortened for demonstration purposes. In compiling this speech, the debater would most likely be drawing from different negative files that correspond to each of the arguments presented. In this case, a disadvantage file was used, a counterplan file, and a case arguments file, parts of which were all combined to produce the speech that you see below. Similar to the affirmative file, headings are used to demarcate the different arguments, and for later speeches, the negative debaters will likely use other arguments from the same file to expand each of these arguments. The reader will note that, other than making different arguments, the structure of the speech as a text is similar to the affirmative and emphasizes finding evidence to support arguments, with more explanation likely coming over the course of the debate.

For the negative, this strategy was designed around both demonstrating that the affirmative plan is dangerous and the status quo should be sustained and proving that the affirmative plan was unnecessary and a counterplan could address the problems raised by the affirmative case. The flexibility in this strategy is helpful for the negative, but by the end of the debate, they will narrow the arguments considerably to either defend the disadvantage and the status quo, or the disadvantage and the counterplan. For a more in-depth explanation of this strategic approach, see Chapter 4.

Disadvantage

The first off-case argument is the deterrence disadvantage.

The first argument is uniqueness. The nuclear posture review conducted by the Biden administration has reaffirmed the commitment to nuclear

forces and their role as a deterrent against foreign adversaries. The emphasis on a flexible response in the NPR is essential for addressing emerging threats like those discussed in the affirmative case.

Payne 23

(Keith B., Dr. Keith B. Payne is a co-founder of the National Institute for Public Policy, professor emeritus at the Graduate School of Defense and Strategic Studies, Missouri State University, a former Deputy Assistant Secretary of Defense, and former Senior Advisor to the Office of the Secretary of Defense. "The 2022 NPR: Commendation and Concerns," National Institute for Public Policy, January 10, 2023. https://nipp.org/information_series/keith-b-payne-the-2022-npr-commendation-and-concerns-no-544-january-10-2023/, ASH)

First, for the most part, **this NPR acknowledges the increasing dangers of the international threat environment and the implications of those dangers for U.S. nuclear deterrence policy.** There is no need to go into detail here about those dangers; they involve the question of how to deter in an unprecedented, uncertain threat environment.[3] The general principles of deterrence are timeless, but the application of deterrence must be adapted to changing circumstances and dangers. **This NPR seems to recognize both the emerging dangers and the need to adapt now.** That recognition is a relief. This point is directly related to **a second background NPR position** that **deserves praise.** That is, **its clear acceptance of the need to "tailor" deterrence to the unique circumstances of opponent, time and place.** The need to tailor deterrence may seem like a no-brainer to those unfamiliar with much of U.S. Cold War policy—which essentially presumed that opponents shared U.S. perspectives on factors key to the functioning of deterrence, i.e., a uniformity of perceptions, values, and modes of calculation. But I assure you, getting to the point where tailoring deterrence to account for the significant differences in these factors is a basic policy principle was decades in the making and is enormously consequential. Why consequential? Because **once the requirement to tailor deterrence to the unique circumstances of opponent, time and place is recognized, so too is the flexibility in deterrence capabilities, planning and strategy needed to be able to tailor deterrence. In short, a spectrum of capabilities, nuclear and conventional, may be required to deter a diversity of opponents at different times and in different contexts.** There is no easy, all-purpose standard of adequacy for deterrence; believing otherwise is the basic dangerous presumption of minimum deterrence policy thinking. This NPR helps to put a nail in that coffin, at least for now. That is no trivial point.

The second argument is the link. **Calculated ambiguity in the U.S. nuclear posture is essential to deterring threats.** Specifically, no-first-use eliminates the possibility of using the threat of nuclear forces to prevent conflicts from escalating; this sharply reduces ambiguity and the ability to respond flexibly.

Costlow 21

(Matthew R., Matthew R. Costlow is a senior analyst at the National Institute for Public Policy. "BELIEVE IT OR NOT: U.S. NUCLEAR DECLARATORY POLICY AND CALCULATED AMBIGUITY," War on The Rocks & Texas National Security Review, August 9, 2021, https://warontherocks.com/2021/08/believe-it-or-not-u-s-nuclear-declaratory-policy-and-calculated-ambiguity/, ASH)

Regrettably, <u>U.S. defense officials have rarely discussed publicly the deterrence and assurance benefits of the U.S. policy of calculated ambiguity</u>. When they have, they mostly frame their thoughts by discussing why they would disagree with a possible shift to an alternative policy like nuclear no first use. However, as I discuss in my latest report, <u>there are a number of benefits to retaining a policy of calculated ambiguity. First, the policy of calculated ambiguity provides a potentially vital deterrent threat before the outbreak of major conflict. By keeping the option open of employing nuclear weapons first, U.S. leaders can make a last-ditch deterrent threat to prevent a major crisis from escalating or a conflict from growing more costly</u>. There is, of course, no guarantee such a threat would work. But <u>alternative policies like</u> sole purpose and <u>nuclear no first use essentially eliminate the possibility of U.S. officials even being able to try in certain dire circumstances. When a crisis or conflict has reached a level of severity where leaders are considering nuclear employment, that is not the time they should be denied what could be their least bad option, threatening nuclear first use to stave off an even worse outcome. U.S. nuclear declaratory policy requires an adversary to gamble twice. First, they gamble that the United States will not respond to an attack with its nuclear forces, and second, that the attack will achieve its goals in the face of a U.S. conventional response. These gambles, enabled by a policy of calculated ambiguity, can aid deterrence by increasing an adversary's uncertainty regarding the type and consequences of a U.S. response.</u>

The third argument is the impact. Nuclear deterrence is essential to prevent the possibility of war between great powers that would cause widespread devastation.

Miller 20

(James N., James N. Miller served as Under Secretary of Defense for Policy in the Obama Administration. He is a senior fellow at Johns Hopkins University's Applied Physics Laboratory and a member of the Defense Science Board. "No to no first use—for now" Bulletin of the Atomic Scientists, January 1, 2020. https://thebulletin.org/premium/2020-01/no-to-no-first-use-for-now/, ASH)

<u>The United States spends more than China, Russia, North Korea, and Iran combined on defense and has by far the most capable military in the</u>

world. None of these nations desires a war with the United States. **It may be tempting, therefore, to suggest that US nuclear weapons are not important to deter conventional aggression.** Before reaching a conclusion on this issue, **it is worth pondering what a non-nuclear war between the United States and China or Russia might entail. It could entail early and extensive attacks on space-based assets, including those critical for nuclear command and control; early and extensive cyberattacks on both military assets and civilian critical infrastructure; and hundreds or thousands of "kinetic" strikes from missiles and aircraft. Of course, it may also involve a combined air, land, and sea invasion of US allies or partners. If so, because of the attacker's advantage of proximity and more secure supply and lines of communication, it is possible that the invasion will initially succeed.** In other words, **it may be possible that the United States may suffer grievous damage to its economy, society, and military, and that its allies or partners may be facing occupation.** Even in this dire scenario, it is by no means clear that an American president would, or should, employ nuclear weapons. US forces were nearly pushed off of the peninsula by Chinese forces in the Korean War, and yet the United States did not use nuclear weapons despite its nuclear superiority. But **if it is plausible that a reasonable future president could make a rational decision to threaten or use nuclear weapons to attempt to end a major power war on acceptable terms, then it certainly would be wise to leave that threat on the table in order to bolster deterrence of armed aggression in the first place.**

Counterplan

The next off-case argument is the "sole purpose" counterplan.

First is the text: The United States Federal Government should declare that the sole purpose of the United States nuclear forces is to deter attacks from adversaries.

Second is the counterplan solvency. The Counterplan solves by avoiding a restriction on the use of nuclear weapons first while minimizing the role of nuclear forces in U.S. policy. This more moderate approach both preserves deterrence and helps address the tensions the affirmative case has described.

Panda and Narang 21

(Ankit Panda & Vipin Narang, Ankit Panda is the Stanton Senior Fellow in the Nuclear Policy Program at the Carnegie Endowment for International Peace. Vipin Narang is an associate professor of political science and a member of the Security Studies Program at the Massachusetts Institute of Technology. "SOLE PURPOSE IS NOT NO FIRST USE: NUCLEAR WEAPONS AND

DECLARATORY POLICY," War on The Rocks & Texas National Security Review, February 22, 2021, https://warontherocks.com/2021/02/sole-purpose-is-not-no-first-use-nuclear-weapons-and-declaratory-policy/, ASH)

But **is sole purpose equivalent to a no-first-use declaration**, as so many have argued? **Not quite**. Even in its most stringent formulation, **a sole purpose declaration is not equivalent to a no-first-use pledge — it comes close, but is not the same thing. No first use is a statement about when the United States would (and would not) use nuclear weapons. It is an explicit employment constraint: It commits a state to not use nuclear weapons except in retaliation for nuclear attacks. Sole purpose, in contrast, is as its name implies a statement about why the United States possesses the nuclear arsenal that it does, not how it will use it. It does not, in extremis, impose employment constraints as a no-first-use policy might**. Rather, **it explicitly de-emphasizes the role of nuclear weapons in overall U.S. national security strategy**. A person can possess a car for what she declares to be the sole purpose of driving to work, but if one day she has to drive to the emergency room, nothing will stop her from using the car for that purpose. A no-first-use pledge, by contrast, explicitly declares ex ante that the car will never be used to drive to the emergency room. Sole purpose stops well short of that. As such, **a meaningful sole purpose declaration can be constructed that is not, in fact, tantamount to a no-first-use declaration — one that simultaneously de-emphasizes the role of nuclear weapons in American security strategy without eroding the robustness of extended deterrence**. The search for an alternative formulation to a no-first-use declaration is itself informative — if the administration wanted to declare a no-first-use policy it could simply attempt to do so. We argue that, instead, an appropriately crafted sole-purpose declaration could help to realize the president's stated vision on nuclear weapons without unduly jeopardizing U.S. alliances. Allies, too, once fully consulted, should be ready to avoid a knee-jerk response to policy shifts — especially if U.S. declaratory policy continues to account for their interests. **Whereas a no-first-use declaration is relatively straightforward, sole purpose maintains some of the traditional ambiguity in U.S. nuclear declaratory policy.** How it does so depends on the precise formulation. The amount of daylight between these various formulations and "we will not use nuclear weapons first" varies from a sliver to a bay window. Despite this, some formulations do come very close to a no-first-use pledge and might understandably cause concern in allied capitals.

On-Case

First, addressing the affirmative harms. The affirmative advantage is predicated on an accidental war; this idea is misguided. War is the product of policy, choosing not to go to war is a better approach than constraining policy choices.

Quackenbush 23

(Dr. Stephen L. Quackenbush is an Associate Professor of Political Science & Director of Defense and Strategic Studies at the University of Missouri, "The Problem with Accidental War," 2023, Conflict Management and Peace Science, vol. 40, no. 6, https://doi.org/10.1177/073889422211496, ASH)

The fact that **war results** here **from leaders' choices** would seem to indicate that **no war is truly accidental or inadvertent, even from accidental war advocates' own perspective**. After all, **if war results from choices, not from chance, then it isn't accidental or inadvertent**, as discussed earlier. Further, **mistaken warning seems to be at the core of many concerns about accidental nuclear war** (Blair, 1993, 1994; Feaver, 1992, 1994; Sagan, 1993, 1994; Thayer, 1994), **but this really seems to be an argument about the danger created by incomplete information**. For example, Utgoff (1985: 126) suggests on-site monitoring as a way "for reducing the probability of accidental nuclear war." The only way for monitoring to affect the likelihood of war is through making the information available to decision makers more complete. **Information revelation can affect the likelihood that leaders will choose to go to war, but it will not affect the probability that a war results from chance rather than choice. Incomplete information is well known as a cause of war** (Fearon, 1995), **and it is already accounted for in** game-theoretic **models of deterrence, including ones that feature accidental war as a mechanism** (e.g. Powell, 1990) and models that do not allow accidental war (e.g. Zagare and Kilgour, 2000). **While incomplete information can certainly make the difference between peace and war, a war that results from deliberate decision-making, even in the face of uncertainty or incomplete information, is not accidental or inadvertent**. Thus, **both logic and evidence contradict the notion of accidental war.**

Second, addressing the affirmative solvency. Their plan would damage the U.S. deterrence capability and risk creating new conflicts. Other approaches to arms control would address the same problems as the affirmative plan, proving that it is unnecessary.

Costlow 21

(Matthew R., Matthew R. Costlow is a senior analyst at the National Institute for Public Policy. "BELIEVE IT OR NOT: U.S. NUCLEAR DECLARATORY POLICY AND CALCULATED AMBIGUITY," War on The Rocks & Texas National Security Review, August 9, 2021, https://warontherocks.com/2021/08/believe-it-or-not-u-s-nuclear-declaratory-policy-and-calculated-ambiguity/, ASH)

Calculated ambiguity is best positioned among all the other alternative policies to provide U.S. and allied leaders the freedom of action necessary

to respond to a growing range of threats. This freedom of action reinforces deterrence against America's adversaries. Nuclear declaratory policy is far too consequential to become a vehicle for merely signaling U.S. good intentions on nonproliferation and disarmament — a job far more appropriate for U.S. arms control proposals and dialogue. Instead, U.S. officials should clearly articulate why U.S. nuclear declaratory policy is important not only for its deterrence and assurance effects, but also for the range of policy options it can provide that have the best chance of achieving U.S. political and military goals. The tension between when to clarify and when to be ambiguous about U.S. intentions will remain, but preemptively removing the ability to make particular deterrent threats continues to be unwise. The policy of calculated ambiguity may remove the "fine distinctions" that Lord Balfour treasured, but for the purposes of deterring nuclear and non-nuclear threats, it is a "high policy" worth keeping.

INDEX

affirmative: burdens 5–7, 40, 42 (*see also* affirmative case, strategy); responses to counterplans 103–7; responses to disadvantages 102–3; responses to kritiks 107–11; responses to topicality 111–3; speeches xvii–xix (*see also* speaker positions)
affirmative case xvii, 34–35; critical affirmative cases 43, 50–3; performance affirmative cases 43, 54–6; policy affirmative cases 40–2, 46–9; research for 15 (*see also* research); sample case 158–63; strategy xviii, 15, 44–5
affirming the consequent 36–7
American Debate Association xiii, 33
American Forensics Association xii
argument strength 95

case arguments 63–7
case list 147
constructive speeches: responsibilities 116 (*see also* speaker positions); sample affirmative constructive 158–63; sample negative constructive 163–70; time limits xvi–xviii; use of evidence in 39–40
counterplan: competition 69 (*see also* permutation); as a part of a negative case 79–80; parts of 68–70; status 70, 100–1; theory 106

COVID 150–1
critical theory 50–1
critique: as an argument 71, 82n1 (*see also* kritik); as negative strategy 61
cross-examination xvii–xviii; drills 144, format 84; question strategy 85–6, 88–9; response strategy 86–7, 89–91; strategic use of 55, 84–5, 114
Cross-Examination Debate Association: history xii–xiv; role in topic selection 3–5

debate resolution 4; resolution for academic year 1954–1955 1–2; resolution for academic year 2001–2002 2; resolution for academic year 2010–2011 2; resolution for academic year 2013–2014 2; resolution for academic year 2023–2024 4–10 (*see also* topic analysis); selection process 3–5
debate theory 106, 108–9, 123, 144
debate topics: analysis of 5–10; selection process 3–5; topic committee 3
debate tournaments: history xi–xii; physical preparation for 146, 153–4; practice for 145; procedure xiv–xvi; tournament preparation 60, 74, 113, 128–9, 134, 145–9
Delta Sigma Rho xi, xxn1
denying the antecedent 37

disadvantage: as affirmative argument 107; parts of 48, 67–68; strategic value 69
disclosure xvii, 113

enthymeme 38, 119
evidence: collection 16, 28–32, 45–6; evaluation of 23–8, 86; peer review 21; roll in debate 38–9, 53–5, 96, 99

fiat 42, 73
file: affirmative file 12–13, 45–6, 49–50; definition of 12–13, 45–6; negative file 63
flex-prep 84
flowing: backflowing 85; drills 143; how to 93–94; in judging debates 130–1; usage of 119, 124
formal logic 35–37
framework: affirmative responses 53, 55; as an off-case argument 77–78; as a part of another argument 73; strategic uses 79

impact: comparison 120–2; framing 120–22, 133–4, 138; impact turn 65–6, 99, 102–3, 110; as part of an argument 67–8, 71–2, 95, 103 *(see also* stock issues, significance)

judging debate xii, xv, xvi, 127–9; decision making 136–8; general principles 135–6 *(see also* paradigm)

kritik 61, 71 *(see also* critique); parts of 71–73; strategy 73, 78–80, 123–4

link: as part of an argument 67, 71–2, 100–3, 109; link turn 66, 80, 98–9, 110

Malthusian theory 65
maverick xvi
modus ponens 35–6
modus tollens 35–6
mutually preferred judging xvi, 147–9

National Debate Development Conference 151
National Debate Tournament xii–xiv, 1, 3, 150–1

negative block xviii, 60, 92, 97, 100, 116, 120
negative case 59–60, 68; construction 79–81; sample negative case 164–170; strategy 60–2
no-first-use 5–7
nuclear arsenal 6–8; size of 95
nuclear triad 4–6
nuclear weapons: policy 46–7; proliferation 47

off-case arguments 67–81

parametrics 41, 132
paradigm 128, 136, 149; critic of argument 134–5; hypothesis testing 132; policy-making 132–4; stock issues 129–130; tabula rasa 130–1
permutation 69, 97, 101 104–6
Plato 8
practicing debate 140–1, 145; individual drills 141–3; team drills 143–5
presumption 62, 136
Pi Kappa Delta xi

rebuttal speeches 94–6, 116–17, 119–22; answering arguments 96–7; answering cases 98–102; answering positions 97–8; strategy 113–14, first affirmative rebuttal role 117–19, first negative rebuttal role 100–2, second affirmative rebuttal role 124–6, second negative rebuttal role 122–4
red-herring fallacy 95
research 12–13; card-cutting 28–32, 39–40; process 16–17, 45; strategy 13–16; where to 17–23

scouting 146–7
signpost 46–7, 49, 96–7
solvency 49, 68, 99, 106–7
Southwest Cross-Examination Debate Association, *see* Cross-Examination Debate Association
speaker positions: first affirmative responsibilities 117–19; first negative responsibilities 100–2; responsibilities xvii–xix, 92–3; second affirmative responsibilities 98–100, 124–26, 113–14; second negative responsibilities 100–1, 122–23
stasis 40–43, 52, 55, 95, 135

status quo 40–1, 57
stock issues 40–3, 46–9, 52, 54–5; as basis for negative arguments 62, 74, 123 (*see also* topicality); desirability 42–3, 51, 61, 65, 71, 73, 97, 105–7, 108–9; harms 40–1, 133; inherency 40, 46–8, 62, 93, 123; in judging 129–31, 133, 136; significance 40–1, 47, 88, 99, 133; solvency as stock issue 40–3, 49, 99, 103 (*see also* solvency); topicality 40–1, 111–3
strategic ambiguity 46–7
strike 148

Tau Kappa Alpha xi
topic analysis 5–8; issue identification 8–10
topicality: parts of 74–6; role in judging 137; strategy 74, 80, 97, 100–1, 123–5
Toulmin model 35, 54; components of 37–9
turn: double-turn 66, 103; impact-turn 64–6, 103, 110–1; link-turn 64–6, 102–3, 110

uniqueness 67, 72, 96, 102, 118–19

verbatim 33n10

For Product Safety Concerns and Information please contact our EU representative GPSR@taylorandfrancis.com
Taylor & Francis Verlag GmbH, Kaufingerstraße 24, 80331 München, Germany